Subalternity, Antagonism, Autonomy

Para Eleni
Para seguir
el dialojo
apenas iniciado
en ma tarde
mexicana

Reading Gramsci

General Editors:
Peter Ives, Professor of Politics, University of Winnipeg
and
Adam Morton, Professor of Political Economy, University of Sydney

Also available:

Gramsci, Culture and Anthropology
An Introductory Text
Kate Crehan

Language and Hegemony in Gramsci
Peter Ives

Unravelling Gramsci:
Hegemony and Passive Revolution in the Global Political Economy
Adam David Morton

Subalternity, Antagonism, Autonomy

Constructing the Political Subject

Massimo Modonesi

Translated by
Adriana V. Rendón Garrido and Philip Roberts

Foreword by
John Holloway

PlutoPress
www.plutobooks.com

First published 2014 by Pluto Press
345 Archway Road, London N6 5AA

www.plutobooks.com

Distributed in the United States of America exclusively by
Palgrave Macmillan, a division of St. Martin's Press LLC,
175 Fifth Avenue, New York, NY 10010

British Library Cataloguing in Publication Data
A catalogue record for this book is available from the British Library

ISBN   978 0 7453 3406 6   Hardback
ISBN   978 0 7453 3405 9   Paperback
ISBN   978 1 8496 4969 8   PDF eBook
ISBN   978 1 8496 4971 1   Kindle eBook
ISBN   978 1 8496 4970 4   EPUB eBook

Library of Congress Cataloging in Publication Data applied for

10 9 8 7 6 5 4 3 2 1

Typeset from disk by Stanford DTP Services, Northampton, England
Simultaneously printed digitally by CPI Antony Rowe, Chippenham, UK and
Edwards Bros in the United States of America

Contents

Series Preface

Antonio Gramsci (1891–1937) is one of the most frequently referenced political theorists and cultural critics of the twentieth century. His pre-disciplinary ideas and especially his articulation of hegemony are commonly referred to in international relations, social and political theory, political economy, historical sociology, critical geography, postcolonial studies, cultural studies, literary criticism, feminism, new social movements, critical anthropology, education studies, media studies and a host of other fields. And yet, his actual writings are steeped not only in the complex details of history, politics, philosophy and culture that shaped Italy's formation as a nation-state as well as the wider turmoil of twentieth-century world history.

Gramsci began his practical and intellectual odyssey when he moved to Turin University (1911). This move to mainland industrial Italy raised cultural and political contradictions for the young Sardinian whose identity was deeply formed by the conditions of uneven development in the 'south'. These issues were pursued by Gramsci whilst devoting his energy to journalism (1914–18) in the newspapers *Il Grido del Popolo*, *Avanti!* and *La Cittá Futura*. His activity centred on the Factory Council movement in Turin – a radical labour mobilization – and editorship of the journal *L'Ordine Nuovo* (1919–20). Exasperated by the Italian Socialist Party's lack of leadership and effective action during the *Biennio Rosso*, Gramsci turned his attention to the founding and eventual leadership of the Italian Communist Party (PCd'I) as well as the organization of the workers' newspaper *L'Unitá* up to 1926. Gramsci spent from May 1922 to December 1923 in the Soviet Union actively involved in organizational issues within the Communist International (Comintern). This included functioning on the Executive Committee of the Comintern in Moscow as the representative of the PCd'I and as a member of various Commissions examining organizational, political and procedural problems that linked the various national communist parties. During this period, Gramsci had direct contact with Leon Trotsky and led discussions on the 'Italian Question' including the united front tactics to tackle Fascism, the trade union relationship, and the limits of party centralism. These issues were developed by Gramsci through the work of ideological hegemony carried out by the PCd'I and, following his Moscow period, as a central author and architect of 'The Lyon Theses' – a collection of positional statements on the tactics and strategies needed in response to Fascism. The theses are regarded as a major survey of the conditions of uneven development confronting social forces within Italy and the European states-system at the time.

By 1926, after drafting his famous essay, 'Some Aspects of the Southern Question', Gramsci was arrested as a Communist Party deputy by the Fascist authorities and was incarcerated until a few days before his death in 1937. Gramsci wrote almost 500 letters in prison, over half were to his sister-in-law, Tatiana Schucht who was living in Rome and became his key supporter and his most frequent visitor. She also conveyed Gramsci's ideas to another significant patron, Piero Sraffa, the Italian economist then at Cambridge. These letters constitute a rich mixture of intellectual, cultural, and political analysis as well as representing the daily struggle of prison life including increasingly severe health problems. But the most enduring and influential component of Gramsci's legacy is the 33 notebooks that he penned between 1929 and 1936 that together constitute the *Quaderni del carcere* [*Prison Notebooks*]. Tatiana Schucht hid these notebooks in a vault at the Banca Commerciale Italiana while she arranged for their transportation to Moscow. Publication of the *Prison Notebooks* then ensued from the late 1940s onwards in Italian and has continued in various languages ever since.

The breadth of the above political and intellectual journey is perhaps matched by the depth of detail and coverage contained within Gramsci's pre-prison and prison writings. The study of intellectuals in Italy, their origins and grouping according to cultural currents; his engagement with, and critique of, Italy's most important intellectual of the time, Benedetto Croce; the study of comparative linguistics and the Italian language question; analysis of the Sicilian writer Luigi Pirandello and the potential his plays offered for transforming Italian culture and society; and discussion of the role of the serialized novel and popular taste in literature would be later expanded into a wider plan. This chiefly focused on Italian history in the nineteenth century with special attention directed to Italy's faltering entrance into capitalist modernity under conditions of 'passive revolution' including the imposition of a 'standard' Italian language; the theory of history and historiography; and the expansion of the capitalist labour process through assembly plant production techniques beyond the United States under the rubric of 'Americanism and Fordism'. In summary, issues of hegemony, consciousness and the revolutionary process are at the centre of Gramsci's attention. It is for such reasons that Antonio Gramsci can be regarded as one of the most significant Marxists of the twentieth century who merits inclusion in any register of classical social theorists.

Reading Gramsci, however, is no easy task. He plunges into the complexities of debates of his time that are now obscure to many readers and engages in an enormous range of topics that at first seem unrelated. Moreover, the prison conditions and his own method yield a set of open-ended, fragmented, and intricately layered *Prison Notebooks* whose connections and argumentation do not lead linearly from one note to the next, but seem to ripple and weave in many directions. This has sometimes led to aggravation on the part of Gramsci scholars when they see how often his name is invoked by those with quite partial or superficial understanding of these complexities. It has also generated frustration on the part of those who want to use Gramsci's ideas to illuminate their own studies, analyses, and political acumen. After all, while Gramsci himself was a meticulous researcher with a rigorous philological method, he was deeply committed to people understanding their own political and cultural contexts in order to engage and change them. These points, about the necessity of deploying an openness of reading Gramsci to capture the branching out of his thought *and* the necessity of deploying a practical interest in understanding the here and now of contemporary events, were central to Joseph Buttigieg's original idea for initiating this 'Reading Gramsci' series. Buttigieg's contributions to Gramscian scholarship extend also to his monumental and superbly edited and translated English critical edition of the *Prison Notebooks* (Columbia University Press), the final volumes of which are still in process. In keeping with Buttigieg's initial goals, this series aims to provide expert guides to key features and themes in Gramsci's writings in combination with the pressing political, social and cultural struggles of our time. Rather than 'applying' Gramsci, the point of the series is to provide monographs that think through and internalize Gramsci's method of thinking about alternative historical and contemporary social conditions. Given that no single study can encapsulate the above political and intellectual depth and breadth, each volume in the 'Reading Gramsci' series is focused in such a way as to open readers to specific aspects of his work as well as raise new questions about our contemporary history.

Peter Ives
Adam Morton

Abbreviations and Acronyms

APPO Asamblea Popular de los Pueblos de Oaxaca [Popular Assembly of the Peoples of Oaxaca]

BR Brigate Rosse [Red Brigades]

CERES Centre d'études, de recherches et d'éducation socialiste [Centre for Socialist Studies, Research and Education]

CFDT French Democratic Confederation of Labour

CGI Confederazione Generale Italiana de Lavoro [General Italian Confederation of Labour]

CGT General Confederation of Work

FIOM Federazione Impiegati Operai Metalmeccanici [Trade Union for Metallurgical Workers]

GP Gauche Prolétarienne [Proletarian Left]

ICO Informations et Correspondances Ouvrières [Worker Information and Correspondence]

IGC International Gramsci Society

ILO Informations et Liaisons Ouvrières [Worker Information and Liaisons]

IMF International Monetary Fund

JCR Revolutionary Communist Youths

LC Communist League

LCR Ligue Communiste Révolutionnaire [Revolutionary Communist League]

LO Worker Struggle

OCI Internationalist Communist Organization

PCF French Communist Party

PCI Italian Communist Party

PO *Potere Operaio*

PS Socialist Party

PSI Italian Socialist Party

PSU Unified Socialist Party

PSUV United Socialist Party of Venezuela

SoB Socialisme ou Barbarie [Socialism or Barbarism]

SS Subaltern Studies

SSG Subaltern Studies Group

UEC Union d'Étudiants Communistes [Union of Communist Students]

Acknowledgements

This book, like any intellectual effort, is an individual production that synthesizes and interprets aspects of a collective reflection, even more so insofar as it is an exercise in militant thought. At the same time, I want to emphasize, recognize and acknowledge concrete contributions from friends and colleagues, who helped shape this text one way or another. Without a doubt, in the first place, the loving critical readings of my life partner, Teresa Rodríguez de la Vega, whose contribution has been invaluable. I also appreciate the support of Guillermo Almeyra – example and master of militant commitment; Horacio Tarcus, Emir Sader and Pablo Gentili – promoters of this publication. I would also like to thank Maristella Svampa unreservedly for reading the entire manuscript and making acute observations which guided my final corrections, as well as the timely contributions from Benjamín Arditi, Elvira Concheiro, Horacio Crespo, José Gandarilla, Jaime Massardo, Fernando Munguía, Roberto Oseguera, Matari Pierre, Raquel Sosa and Hugo José Suárez.

Regarding the English edition, I would like to acknowledge the further proofreading work and secondary translation undertaken by Philip Roberts and supported financially by a research grant application initiated by Adam Morton at the University of Nottingham. I would also like to thank María Vignau for her support in the development of the English version of this book and her participation and collaboration on the further steps taken towards the progress of this line of research.

Foreword

Sounds in the Undergrowth

John Holloway[1]

We hear sounds in the undergrowth. A confusion of sounds. Cries of pain, screams of defiance, the confident voices of those who explain how they are building a different way of living. It is the noise of a world in labour, the sound of a new world being born. Perhaps.

We hear other sounds too, louder. The roar of the machines of the mining companies tearing the earth apart, the explosions of the tear gas bombs of police repression, the raucous whirr of the chainsaws of the drug gangs as they decapitate their victims. It is the sound of a world in its final agony, the closure of all hope. Perhaps.

Massimo Modonesi and I, both born in Europe, both having chosen to live in Mexico, cannot fail to be deafened by the din of hope and despair. We are surrounded by it. We hear of the shining, brilliant experience of the Zapatista *escuelita* (possibly their most profoundly revolutionary initiative to date) on the same day as we listen to reports of the finding of yet another mass grave of tortured victims of the drug wars.

It is not just Mexico, of course. The bloody slaughter of hope is ubiquitous, truly globalized. The unctuous words of politicians spread death throughout the world. Everywhere the sliminess of money finds its support in brutal repression. The sound of domination is loud, broadcast on radio and television. It is the sounds of rebellion that are sometimes hard to hear. And yet they are there all the time, and growing. Massimo in his introduction mentions Chiapas and Bolivia and Argentina, and it has become common over the last 20 years, and with good reason, to think of Latin America as the land of hope. But it is not just Latin America. In recent months rebellion has been leaping around the world like a drunken grasshopper: one week Stockholm,

---

1   My thanks to Eric Meyer for his assistance in the preparation of this Foreword.

the next Istanbul and Ankara, the next Rio de Janeiro and Sao Paulo, then it is the turn of Sofia, and on and on.

We try to hear, we try to understand. The old classifications do not necessarily work. There is a change in the patterns of rebellion, and with it comes a change in the ways of thinking about rebellion. Or rather, not just a change but changes. New theories emerge, new ways of thinking about the possibility of radical change. Each theory seeks to present a coherent picture of what is happening but, when taken together, the effect may be to increase confusion.

This is where the present book comes in. Massimo seeks to give coherence to recent discussions by focusing on three key concepts: subalternity, antagonism and autonomy, and he suggests that these three concepts can be seen not just as competing but also complementary. I do not agree with all of Massimo's arguments, but I am struck by the relation between the three concepts that he singles out and what I see as the three aspects of our relation with capital: we exist in-against-and-beyond capital.

We exist in capital simply by being born into and living in a capitalist society. We are, in Massimo's words, subalterns; we are subordinate to capital. We may choose to call ourselves anticapitalist revolutionaries, but that does not alter the fact that we live in capital, that our conditions of acting and of thinking are shaped by the society within which we live. Our concepts of time, space, language, thinghood, possibility, institutionality, all have their feet in this society. Our subalternity is part of our daily experience and cannot, unfortunately, be simply wished out of existence.

If we simply existed *in* capital, if our lives were characterized solely by domination, by conformity, we might just as well sink into a slough of despond, yawn and weep and give up. But to exist *in* capital is inevitably to exist *against* capital. This is not a matter of choice, not a matter of conscious decision. It is simply the expression of the fact that capital is not still, but rather a dynamic of aggression. The very existence of capital is an attack against us, a constant attack against the way that we live, the way we think, the way we love, the way we get up in the morning and go to bed at night, the way we are born and the way we die. We are born into an antagonistic relation, not just into a world of domination. That is why, for me, the second category singled out by Massimo, antagonism, is central, and must be the starting point of reflection. If we read or write a book like this, we are already stating that our relation to the world around us is an antagonistic one, that it is not simply a relation of domination. The concept of subalternity or domination encloses us, tells us that we are victims, that we are dead. The idea of antagonism brings us to life, treats us as subjects, opens perspectives of hope. By 'antagonism' I do not refer necessarily to conscious struggle, but rather to the dynamic of attack and counter-attack into which we are projected on birth (or perhaps conception). Capital attacks and we cannot fail to resist. We resist by yawning at work, by throwing the proverbial alarm clock against the wall when it is time to get up, by loving and falling in love, by the fact that we still do not accept, despite all the inducements offered to us, that we should become robots. And often our non-subordination becomes open insubordination and even rebellion. Rebellion against the form of social organization that attacks us, and rebellion against our own subordination.

Inevitably too, we exist *beyond* capital, the element that is highlighted in Massimo's third category, autonomy. Again, this is not a matter of choice or a privilege of the chosen few. The very fact of being constrained by a form of social organization that we do not control pushes us beyond those constraints, in our dreams, our thoughts, our fantasies, our actions. The fact of living in a society that is producing its own annihilation pushes us to find, in thought and increasingly in action, other ways of organising our activity and our relations with other people. This grows out of the *against*, but takes us a step farther: to fight against capital, we shall live the world we want to create, we shall organize and act in a manner that corresponds to that world. Our struggle then is prefigurative: not just against capital but already creating the bases of another world. We live that which is not yet. Clearly this is not a real autonomy: autonomy (or self-determination) remains a dream, but living that dream becomes central to the struggle for its realization.

In, against, beyond, or rather in-against-and-beyond, for the three should not be separated, for they are three aspects of our daily existence. The three aspects are moments of a unity-in-separation, but inevitably they drift apart in our perceptions, and in our theorizing. In this sense, Massimo Modonesi is surely right both to focus on the three concepts (subalternity, antagonism, autonomy) and then to explore their complementarity. There is always a danger in drawing lines too clearly, in transforming the different faces of our experience into rigid identities: reform against revolution, antagonism against autonomy. In fact, reform (in-ness) and revolution (against-ness) and creation of a different society (beyond-ness) are part of the experience of all of us, although the balance between them will be affected by our particular social experience, by our personality, our age, whether we are hungry or have just had a good meal, by our understanding of society, and so on. To transform these experiential tones into differences of identity (you are a reformist, I am a revolutionary) is to promote the deepest penetration of capital into anticapitalist thought: to promote identitarian thinking, in other words. In fact, the sentence 'I am a revolutionary' is blatantly self-contradictory: at the same time as it would negate capital, it reproduces capital in its most insidious form, as identification.

Not that we should all play happy families and pretend that our theoretical differences do not matter. They matter deeply and should be fought out with passion. But it should be done on the basis of understanding that they reflect different moments of a common experience and that we are all inevitably self-contradictory. Revolutionary purity and theoretical correctness have no part in anticapitalist struggle, no place in building the different world that we so desperately need. That is why we must listen to the sounds coming from the undergrowth, look for the figures emerging though the haze of urban pollution.

Puebla, 28 August 2013

Introduction

The concepts of *subalternity*, *antagonism* and *autonomy* are developed within Marxist reflection on the subject and political action, which forms a constant that, based on Karl Marx's thought, spans the great debates on contemporary Marxism in search of clues for interpretation that allow us to understand how 'men make their own history but do not do it of their own free will, under conditions chosen for them, but under directly existing, given and inherited conditions' (Marx, 2003: 33).

Within this wide field of sociological inquiry, these concepts of Marxist origin stood out both for their dissemination in academic language and political discourse as well as the central position they occupy in theoretical perspectives oriented towards the characterization of processes of *political subjectivation*, that is, the ways and dynamics of formation of political subjectivities around a group or series of collective experiences born out of *relations of domination, conflict and emancipation*.[1]

I

The first objective of this work will be to study the theoretical efforts built around the concepts of *subalternity*, *antagonism* and *autonomy*, evaluating their scope as well as their explanatory limits in order to rescue, emphasize and define them as Marxist analytical instruments for the analysis of processes of *political subjectivation*.

The first three chapters deal with the analysis of the genesis and theoretical development of these three categories, reviewing the work of the authors that adopted them and the historical moments which gave rise to their reflections. Given that these are Marxist intellectuals and communist leaders, we assume their work is not only closely linked to social reality but also strategically oriented to maintain a series of practices and lines of political action.

Before we address the analysis of theorizations on the three concepts, it will be necessary to situate their origins and previous usage in classic and contemporary Marxist thought, for every concept, in order to disclose the political and theoretical problems to which these categories refer, as well as to outline the perimeter of the theoretical fields in which they appeared. Beyond the use of these categories, the issues they refer to appear and occupy a fundamental place within the Marxist tradition and refer to the subjective implications of the relations of domination, conflict and emancipation, and, particularly, to the juxtaposition, the overlap and passage between *spontaneity* and *conscience*.

This book will highlight and analyse the most complete efforts towards categorical synthesis, that is, the theorizations aimed at building a perspective of observation, analysis and interpretation of the processes of political subjectivation around a concept *–subalternity*, *antagonism* or *autonomy*. In this sense, we showcase the few authors who took up the challenge to develop these concepts theoretically as specific approximations to the general problematic of the formation of subjectivities in the context of relations and processes of domination, conflict and liberation in their desire to recognize, emphasize and analyse *the experiences of subordination, insubordination and emancipation* that characterize them.

While I do not rule out reflections that deal with the same problematic without using these categories, I will insist on the need to configure specific conceptual referents in line with a rigorous social theory vocabulary and grammar. In this sense, I focus my attention on the categorical crystallization these authors encourage assuming it corresponds to a theoretical densification that strengthens its explanatory capacity. Consequently, I do not intend to synthesize the history of Marxist thought on the theme of the subject, but rather to look for prints of the three concepts that I find particularly useful as analytical instruments.

In the first chapter, I discuss how the notion of *subalternity* in the work of Antonio Gramsci throughout the 1920s and 1930s acquires a theoretical density that configures a specific focus for the study of processes of political subjectivation linked to relations of domination and, specifically, to the condition and *experience of subordination*. Similarly, in the second chapter I analyse the way in which the notion of antagonism in Antonio Negri's work in the 1970s articulates a perspective that connects the political formation of subjectivity in conflict, and particularly, to the *experience of insubordination*. In the third chapter, I consider how the idea of *autonomy*, developed in the Marxist sense by Cornelius Castoriadis and Claude Lefort, framed by the proposals of the group Socialism or Barbarism in France – followed by the slogan of autogestion at the heart of the French movements of the late 1960s and throughout the 1970s – makes up a perspective defined by observation of the dynamics of political subjectivization related to the processes and *experience of emancipation*.

In each case, for every concept, I proceed in the same manner within the first three chapters. After addressing in general terms the place of each and the problems each present within Marxist debates, I will do an in-depth study of the authors, currents, groups and schools that, in light of the processes of mobilization and subjective emergence of their time, have put forward a theory based on those concepts, developing their explanatory scope and consolidating their theoretical consistency. I wish to make clear that I do not defend nor commit to the comprehensive oeuvre of the authors I write about, nor do I intend to establish a debate or dialogue among them. Rather, I seek to rescue their contributions looking to consolidate a wealth of Marxist concepts guided towards the understanding of the processes of political subjectivation.

II

In the diversity of trajectories and approaches I have studied I find a guiding thread around which we intend to weave an eminently theoretical proposal that will be synthesized in the fourth and last chapter. Its purpose is complementary to the rescue of the concepts as Marxist tools of analysis of the dynamics of formation of political subjectivities. This sociological proposal proceeds from the conclusions obtained from the review of the work of these authors. On one hand, it recuperates their contributions insofar as they created original perspectives and advanced in the direction of the categorical solidification and consolidation of the notions of *subalternity*, *antagonism* and *autonomy*. On the other, it tries to overcome the analytical limits that appeared in the heart of these perspectives, and which I identify at three interconnected levels: the *explanatory hypertrophy* of the concepts, the *essentialism* and the *overpoliticization* of the theory. These limits caused a disaggregation and even a contest between three concepts susceptible to complementarity and, therefore, reduced the scope for observing and understanding the formation and configuration of sociopolitical subjectivities.

I maintain the possibility of articulating them, recognizing a level of theoretical homology between them that, along with the specificity of each one, allows for the configuration of a categorical triad or a tripartite focus where *subalternity*, *antagonism* and *autonomy* are *complementary* to the extent that they shine a light as much on a simultaneous aspect and dimension – synchronic – as on a significant passage that allows a process-based reading – diachronic.

Thus, I conclude that *it is possible and pertinent to analyse the processes of political subjectivation at the synchronic level, starting from the recognition of uneven combinations of subalternity, antagonism and autonomy – respectively understood as experiences of subordination, insubordination and emancipation born from the relations of domination, conflict and liberation – and, simultaneously, at the diachronic level, according to an organizing principle that structures and characterizes the shape of the dynamics of formation and configuration of concrete political subjectivities at a historical moment.*

This is only a synthesis of the conclusion that will be developed throughout the text and whose theoretical-methodological culmination is found in the last chapter.

Before delving into the argumentative sequence that leads to this conclusion, it is pertinent to refer to some of E.P. Thompson's theoretical intuitions that frame, inspire and sustain the axis of reasoning to be developed in the chapters.

III

Even though Thompson (1981) denounced the poverty of theory versus the richness of history,[2] he did make a series of sporadic yet profound theoretical and methodological statements of great scope. For the purposes of this work, Thompson offers at least two reference points that guide it.

In the first place, as a historiographical exercise he formulated a notion of *experience* as key to the analysis of the processes of subjective formation.[3] For Thompson (1981), experience appears from 'the dialogue between the being and social conscience', it is 'the print that is left by the social being in the social conscience'.[4]

> With this expression men and women return as subjects: not as autonomous subjects or 'free individuals', but as persons who experiment the productive situations and the given relations in which they find themselves as needs and interests and as antagonisms, elaborating their experience within the coordinates of their conscience and their culture (two other terms excluded by theoretical practice) by the most complex avenues (avenues, yes, 'relatively autonomous'), and later acting on their own situation (often but not always, through the class structures imposed upon them). (ibid.: 253)

Situated as a 'middle term' between *being* and *consciousness* (ibid.: 160), between structure and process, the *experience* operates as a mediation and interlocution mechanism between the subjective assimilation of the productive relations –that is, the material determination relative to a social formation and a mode of production[5] – and their social, political and cultural projection in the 'disposition to behave as a class'[6] (Thompson, 1965).

> This means that historical change takes place not because a 'base' must give way to a corresponding 'superstructure', but because changes in the productive relations are *experimented* in the social and cultural life, refracted in the ideas of men and their values and reasoned through their actions, their choices and their beliefs. (Thompson, 2000: 43)

Thompson assumes that the relationship between base and superstructure goes through and is synthesized in experimentation and is 'refracted' in consciousness.[7] *Experience* is presented as a process – experimentation – as a relationship between social being and social consciousness and as a turning point for the appearance and formation of subjectivities. In this sense, taking Thompson's formulation as a starting point, we assume that *experience* designates the incorporation or subjective assimilation of a material or real condition[8] which already includes a principle or embryo of consciousness – 'the disposition to behave as a class' and not consciousness as full identification – built on the accumulation and processing of collective life experiences, knowledges and practices.[9] Said differently, every process of subjectivation goes through a series of *experiences* that – in the intersection between spontaneity and consciousness – confer upon it shape and specificity.

In the second place, starting from the relational character of *experience*, Thompson insists on noting the superimposition of processes and the articulation of dimensions. First, when he affirms that 'class did not appear like the sun, at a specific hour. It was present in its own formation' (Thompson, 1989), he is plainly assuming the Hamletian dilemma that accompanies the debate on the working class, assuring the complementarity of both hypotheses – the subject *is* and *is not* – to the extent in which they fuse in the process: *the class is becoming*. Following the English historian, class – the political subject – does not only struggle because it exists, rather, it exists because it struggles; it is forged through the processes it activates.[10] In this dialectical circularity, class cannot be conceived of as a thing or a given identity but as a relation and a process marked by fire and by the seal of conflict. To take it as a fact or a given subject of action can only be a metaphorical recourse, says Thompson.[11] From this view, distanced from all essentialism, this Marxist historian deployed the analysis of the subjectivation processes of the English working class, assuming that subjective formation – the *making* of a subject – is a 'structured process' that combines diverse dimensions, contradictory in appearance and, therefore, we add, concretely articulated and theoretically distinguishable:

> By class I understand a historical phenomenon that unifies a series of disparate and apparently disconnected events regarding the prime matter of experience as well as consciousness. (Thompson, 1989)

In line with what we are interested in developing and assuming as backdrop, the socioeconomic matrix of classist conditioning and putting the sociopolitical dimension to the fore – tied to the relations of domination and power – we assume that the processes of political subjectivation are configured starting from 'disparate and apparently disconnected' *experiences* of subordination, insubordination and emancipation, that is, of *subalternity*, *antagonism* and *autonomy*.[12]

IV

The last clarifying introductory note necessarily concerns the spatial-temporal location of the intellectual and political concerns and preoccupations that underlie, move and give practical sense to the theoretical exercise I propose.

The last decade of social and political struggles in Latin America make up the historical context – the horizon of visibility as René Zavaleta (1989) would say – from which this investigation was born. Regionally, the neoliberal loss of hegemony since the antagonistic emergence of popular movements opened up gaps that seemed inconceivable 20 or 30 years ago. In the midst of crisis, anti-neoliberal ruptures and conservative revolutions, an era born of the defeat of the 1970s and the hegemonic normalization of the 1980s, ended and a transition began that forces us to think with new conceptual tools, or by renewing and recuperating classical ones.

The Bolivian experience has been the reference that most directly motivated this research. The heterogeneous ways of the movements that, from the historical subalternity of the indigenous, peasant and working world, led an antagonistic cycle between 2000 and 2005, forged autonomous fields and ended up in the current contradictory situation, between the crystallized power of the popular government headed by Evo Morales, the mobilizations that accompany and defy it, the inexorable return of forms of subalternity, the persistence of horizons of autonomy and the latency of antagonism. This historical tangle questions critical thought and – from my perspective – evokes the concepts I choose to try to understand the processes of emergence and formation of political subjectivities. On the other hand, another Latin American experience arose in my reflections and investigations: the 2001 crisis and its sequels. The popular irruption of 19–20 December 2001 was not only a forceful antagonistic manifestation, but it resulted in the dazzling proliferation of autonomous practices: *piqueteros*, neighbourhood assemblies and occupied factories. Argentina thus became the headquarters for an autonomist narrative that, even in the midst of its successes, failed to see and break – and still tends to ignore – the persistence of subalternity, from which we can understand the rearrangement that, starting in 2002 but more clearly with the Kirchner governments from 2003 until today, deactivated a great deal of the antagonistic and autonomous potential of the subjectivities forged or strengthened in 2001. Finally, it is impossible not to mention the Mexican 2006 election in which apparently contradictory diverse political forms like the emergence of the Andrés Manuel López Obrador (AMLO) movement, *la Otra campaña* (the Other Campaign) of the Zapatistas, and the Asamblea Popular de los Pueblos de Oaxaca (APPO: Popular Assembly of the Peoples of Oaxaca) were combined. The need, even the urgency, to read and interpret the combinations, the superimpositions and the impurities that characterize the processes of political subjectivation lead to the conceptual triad that occupies this work. The categories of *subalternity, antagonism* and *autonomy* are ways of naming, making explicit and defining a number of problems that circulate inside popular movements and critical Latin American thought.

In this sense, the theoretical effort I present in these pages is indebted to the social and political reality of Latin America. It is an exercise in categorical definition destined to return – in my future work – to the study of concrete processes, the history of struggles, in order to decipher its codes, look for keys of articulation and participate, within the limits of my potential, in thinking of another possible world.

In light of this historically Latin American moment, the recuperation of Marxist approaches centred in conflict, crisis and the formation of anticapitalist subjectivities makes sense. After the defeat and the tendencial retraction of critical thought, a change of era and a new political climate favour the intellectual opening and reactivation of concepts that, under a different denomination, blossom from the practice of the struggles. In this sense, a selective journey into the history of Marxist ideas on the formation of political subjectivities acquires relevance in the field of political sociology, not only as a defense of tradition but as a way to understand and explain reality.

In our contemporary Latin America, in the intersection between past and future, through the concepts of *subalternity, antagonism* and *autonomy*, Marxism offers us keys for interpretation and theoretical tools to understand the processes of uneven and combined formation of the subjects and the sociopolitical movements that are born of the cracks of capitalist domination and that defy it, opening uncertain yet luminous roads to emancipation.

1

Subalternity

The concept of *subaltern*, a formidable analytical instrument, has turned into a *passepartout* in academic and intellectual language and an elegant verbal resource of the progressive or erudite radical political discourse. As a synonym of *oppressed* or *dominated*, the word *subaltern* avoids the economic or ideologizing connotations of the notion of the *exploited* while it amplifies and pluralizes the notion of the *working*, *labour* or *proletarian* class by including other *popular* forms and modalities.

This common usage of the concept seeks the categorical opening that Antonio Gramsci sought in his creative itinerary of Marxist thought. Nonetheless, its instrumental naturalization dilutes the explanatory impact of the notion of *subalternity* and dissolves the articulations that Gramsci himself established around him, which might result in the formulation of approximated and slippery political analyses and theories. Particularly in academia, a tension between the concept of *subaltern*, a theory of *subalternity* and a *subaltern* focus can be observed.

To exemplify this problem and rescue the theoretical density of the concept as a perspective of analysis of the processes of political subjectivation, after locating its origins and background in Marxist thought, we will review its development from its inception in the work of Gramsci until its application on behalf of the School of Subaltern Studies in India, the movement that recuperated and used this notion more systematically.

Subalternity, Domination and Subordination

The notion of *subalternity* was created to speak of the subjective condition of subordination in the context of capitalist domination. Nevertheless, Marx never used the word *subaltern*, while Engels,

Lenin and Trotsky – to name a few representative examples – used it frequently in its conventional sense, referring to a subordination derived from a hierarchical stratification, mainly in relation to army officers and, eventually, to officials in public administration. As we will later expose, in an explicit attempt to enrich the categorical heritage of Marxism, the notion of *subalternity* acquires, for the first time, a theoretical density by Antonio Gramsci's initiative in relation to his reflections on hegemony in his *Prison Notebooks*, with the aim of finding a conceptual correlation of alienation in the superstructural terrain, the sociopolitical equivalent on the plane of domination of what this indicates in the socioeconomic plain: the relative deprivation of the subjective quality by subordination.

This Gramscian initiative departs from the assumption that, not proposing a specific context, Marx left at the core of the Marxist problematic the need to characterize subordination as a relationship, experience, social condition and subjective politics. Marx's constant effort is evident in his political and historical work to understand the clues that explain and maximize the emergence and formation of a transformative sociopolitical subject, from its subordinated condition and the restrictions that prevent, delay and sidetrack it.

In this sense, there exists in Marx's thought an *ante litteram* preoccupation for subalternity – without a name or specific context – that opens the field of analysis. No subsequent Marxist reading of reality could and can do without the study of social relations that, in the historical context of capitalism, lay down forms and rules of a social and political domination of a class to which corresponds the subordinated condition of another class. In the frame of this theoretical and methodological assumption shared by all Marxisms, the specific interest in the understanding of forms of production and reproduction of subordination has been deployed, from which studies and analyses were carried out that developed and tuned the analytical and explanatory capacity of Marxism in this fundamental, even genealogically primary, aspect for every theory of social process.

Within this vast theoretical field – whose revision does not make up the objective of this work – the theoretical contribution of Antonio Gramsci is emphasized and, within it, the genesis and theoretical elaboration of the concept of *subalternity* is particularly relevant.

Subaltern Subjectivation in the Thought of Antonio Gramsci

In order to understand the concept of *subalternity* in his *Prison Notebooks*, it is fundamental to show that Gramsci wrote his notes in prison according to an evaluation of his previous political experiences: the impact of the Bolshevik Revolution, the councils and occupations of factories between 1919 and 1920, the foundation of the Communist Party in Italy (PCd'I) in the historical Congress of Livorno in 1921, the debates within the Third International and the rise of fascism. The purpose of the *Notebooks* is to review and develop the group of ideas that were forged due to these events. It is debatable whether the process of reflection in prison forced Gramsci to strengthen his thought concerning continuity, rupture and renovation. Beyond these three possible interpretations, their nuances and implications, at the very least a change in emphasis and thematic hierarchy has to be acknowledged.

Prior to his reflections on subalternity, Gramsci focused his attention on antagonism and autonomy, that is, on the subjective emergence built from the experiences of insubordination and gestation of areas of independence and emancipation for the working class. The wave of occupations of factories and the workers' councils between 1919 and 1920 led by communist groups under the auspices of the Bolshevik Revolution encouraged an enthusiasm that turned towards the exaltation of the autonomous formation of the worker and communist subject, its capacity to struggle, and the construction of a new society. Gramsci's thoughts and the political and intellectual effort set in *L'Ordine Nuovo* headed in this direction in those years. The first stage of the newspaper directed by Gramsci himself (65 volumes between 1 May 1919 and 24 December 1920) is an unequivocal showcase of this emphasis.[1] The revolutionary subjectivism inspired by Bolshevism was built around the idea of autonomy even when it was not made nominally explicit and did not constitute the centre of the theoretical reflection,[2] which instead spans the classic themes of Third International Bolshevism, *en primis* the topic of the *soviets*, and announces what will be known later, inside the communist movement, as *councilism*.

Therefore, even though this set of reflections does not belong to the topic of subalternity we want to highlight in this chapter, it is very important to note the existence of a Gramsci who, in his Leninism, exalts the dimension of political struggle as rupture –antagonism – and aims for the realization of a soviet revolution, based on workers' councils and, thus, maintains the tendency towards autonomous reflections.[3]

The following passage from an editorial in *L'Ordine Nuovo* was written by Gramsci as editor of the paper:

> The Factory Council, as autonomous form of the producer in the industrial field and as base of the communist economic organization, is the instrument of a mortal fight for the capitalist regime as it creates the conditions in which the society divided in classes is suppressed and a new division of class becomes 'materially' impossible. (Gramsci, 1921: 2)

The autonomy of work acquires political shape in the Council: the producer becomes a political subject. However, after the defeat of the Factory Councils' movement in northern Italy, Gramsci takes up the idea of autonomy in an exclusively classical manner, as synonym of the political independence of class rather than as process and experience of emancipation; as a line that traces the process of political subjectivation, from the relative autonomy of work towards the self-determination of the worker by means of the control of the productive process. He writes, for example, already in the fascist period in 1926:

> Our party ended up being the sole mechanism that the working class has at its disposal to select new leading cadres of class, that is to regain their independence and political autonomy. (Gramsci, 1926)

An in-depth analysis of the diverse meanings of the concept of *autonomy* and its theoretical implications occurs in the third chapter, so this mention of Gramsci's work in the 1920s is essential in order to understand his later theories on hegemony and to locate the origin of the concept of *subalternity* as counterpart or as correlation of previous autonomist positions.

Gramsci's *Notebooks* are a complex work due to their elaboration throughout years of incarceration during which notes on different lines of thought, some of which eventually led the author to reproduce and rewrite entire paragraphs in the so-called 'special notebooks' where he attempted to arrange them by theme, accrued over time. The philological approaches have permitted the reconstruction of various passages of an arborescent work. In particular, after the thematic compilations made by Palmiro Togliatti in the 1950s, the thorough work by Valentino Gerratana allowed the publication of the *Notebooks* in 1975 in the order in which they were written, accompanied by an entire volume of references by Gerratana.

The interpretation of Gramsci's thought branched out and at times polarized due to the heterogeneous character and the dispersion of the notes that make up the *Notebooks*. Thus, within *Gramscian studies* several guiding ideas have been emphasized in the *Notebooks*, among which one stands out for its centrality: that which has to do with hegemony. Gramsci weaved a web of reflections around this problematic and it developed into noteworthy theorizations such as the *organic intellectual*, *passive revolution*, *integral State*, *organic crisis* and *Americanism and Fordism*, as well as a conceptualization of *civil society*, and so on. The notion of the *subaltern* stands centrally among them.

It should be noted that the selection of the noun and adjective *subaltern* in the *Prison Notebooks* is not circumstantial or a simple way to avoid fascist censorship, as Gramsci did not stop using the notion of *working class* and *labourers* in other notes. Therefore, the use of the concept provides a perspective or a theoretical insight that corresponds to the core of a creative thinking within Marxist debate. This reflection emerged from a historical juncture – the defeat of the workers' council movement and the rise of fascism in Italy at the beginning of the 1920s – and Gramsci's polemical will: the historicist positioning in defence of the centrality of the *praxis* that translates into a critique of economism and voluntarism. This polemical locus results in complex thinking that, to my knowledge, will be overinterpreted in the subsequent dispute about Gramsci's place within theoretical and political Marxist debates.[4]

Beyond the full, partial or differentiated recuperation of his thinking, he provides a conceptual tool to Marxist theory, the *subaltern* as expression of the experience and subjective condition of the subordinated, determined by a relation of domination – in Gramscian terms, of hegemony – and a sketch of a theory of subalternity. However, Gramsci did not use the noun (*subalternity*) – which tends to fix a relationship or a property – always preferring the qualifying adjective (*subaltern*), by which we infer he did not intend to formulate a theory of *subalternity*, instead, he opted for a theoretical insight linked to historical observation. Gramsci established a concept as a theoretical base for concrete analysis. After Gramsci, no reflection on conflict and emancipation can diminish the importance of *subalternity* as expression and counterpart of the domination incorporated in oppressed subjects, base, and thus inescapable starting point of all processes of conflict and emancipation.

We will review some fundamental passages of the creation of the concept in the *Prison Notebooks* and their main characteristics. Before jail, Gramsci did not use the adjective *subaltern* to refer to the dominated classes even though the reflections in 'Some Aspects of the Southern Question' (1926) pointed in that direction. (See, for example, Green, 2007: 199–32.) In fact, this adjective appears in the *Notebooks* for the first time in relation to the hierarchical structure in the army in reference to subaltern officials (Gramsci, 1975, Q1, Vol. 43: 37; Vol. 48: 60 and Vol. 54: 67). This conventional use still sets the origin of the concept in the context of the analysis of the power of *direction*, of the hierarchical relationship of command and obedience and the condition of subordination. In the first notebook, the notion of *subaltern* is used to refer to the subordination of an individual or an institution – for example, the Catholic Church (ibid.: Q1, Vol. 116: 105 and Vol. 139: 127).

In the third notebook, written in 1930, the concept moves to the terrain of social and political relations, when Gramsci places subalternity as a fundamental characteristic of the dominated classes and thus titles note 14 *History of the Dominant Class and History of the Subaltern Classes*, a programmatic title that inaugurates a line of reflection in the *Notebooks*. The concept is born in this note and one of the fundamental nodes of Gramscian theoretical thinking is presented and a horizon of investigation is opened, as demonstrated by the fact that this theme will be the object of a special notebook – Notebook 25 – in which the notes on the history of the subaltern classes are compiled.

14 History of the Dominant Class and History of the Subaltern Classes. The history of the subaltern classes is necessarily disaggregated and episodic: there exists a tendency towards unification even if only in provisional levels, but that is the less visible part and demonstrable only after consummated. The subaltern classes suffer the initiative of the dominant class, including when they rebel; they are in an alarmed state of defence. Thus, any outbreak of autonomous initiative is of invaluable wealth. (ibid.: Q3, Vol. 14, 299–300)[5]

According to the notion of *hegemony*, the 'initiative of the dominant class' refers to the use of power as consensus and not primarily as coercion. Gramsci sets *domination* (hegemony) against *subalternity*, creating an equation that accompanies his theoretical work and seals the specificity of his thought within Marxism. This emphasis on the relationship of domination marks the preoccupation of the author with the superstructure –methodologically differentiating dimensions in its interior (political society and civil society) – and its relationship with the economic base. The meaning of the notion of *civil society* that – along with *hegemony* – was taken as Gramsci's great contribution to both Marxist theory and political theory in general, is a logical derivation of the problem of domination as a superstructural counterpart to exploitation. Gramsci understands domination as a relation of forces in permanent conflict and defines the dominated as subalterns, proposing a new concept and outlining their characterization. This characterization will be systematically called *subaltern classes* (or *subaltern groups*), and it starts to take shape from the following distinctive elements: plurality, disaggregation, episodic character of their action, and a weak tendency towards unification 'at a provisional level'.

In the 1934 transcription of this note, Gramsci substitutes the noun *class* for *group*, which opens up two possible interpretations: that Gramsci wanted to be more precise in his use of the notion of class and to not subject it to the multiplicity of forms of subalternity – to identify its political density or its productive and strictly labour feature – nor abandon the strictly Marxist frame to analyse the diversity of political and sociocultural phenomena. They might just be two levels of analysis and abstraction, although both could be articulated.

Giorgio Baratta, an eminent student of Gramsci's work, advances the idea of an internal double nature in the category of subaltern, which would comprise both the *proletarian-subalterns* ('instrumental classes') and the *subproletarian-subalterns* (the marginalized, in the 'margins of history'). Baratta wonders who Gramsci was thinking of when he created the category. To answer, he refers to a formulation by Gramsci in Notebook 27 in which he defines the people as 'a set of subaltern and instrumental classes'. Based on this definition, Baratta proposes two hypotheses of interpretation: in the first, the subalterns distinguish themselves from the productive classes; in the second, he assumes that the concept of *subaltern* is more ample and includes the 'instrumental classes'. To understand this dilemma he refers to the passage in Notebook 3, in which Gramsci mentions the 'more marginal elements and peripheral of these classes, who haven't attained class consciousness for themselves ...' For Baratta (2007: 120–2), the concept of subalterns encompasses both proletarians as well as the *subproletarians*. On the other hand, he maintains that peasants occupy an intermediate step in the internal stratification of subalterns (ibid.: 123).

Nevertheless, the fact that he was reading between the lines demonstrates that Gramsci thought, assuming a certain degree of diversity among groups, in terms of convergence and subjective unification according to the place of the subaltern in relations of domination as well as those at the margins that by manoeuvring become detached from it. The concept of *subalternity* is thus constructed in the attempt to understand a specific subjectivity as well as its potential transformation through consciousness and political action. Gramsci believes that, once they have gradually conquered their autonomy, the political trajectory of the subaltern sectors cuts through civil society, disputes hegemony and, potentially, directs itself toward the State to definitively 'break' the domination.

There are two more relevant corrections of Notebook 25 which correspond to the strengthening of the idea of *subalternity* and the incorporation of the idea of 'break'.

2. *Methodical Criteria.* The history of the subaltern *groups* is necessarily disaggregated and episodic. It is unquestionable that, in the historic activity of these *groups*, there is a tendency towards unification even though it is in provisional plans, *but this tendency is continuously broken by the initiative of the dominant groups and can therefore only be demonstrated once the historical cycle is finished, if it concludes with a success.* The subaltern groups always suffer the initiative of the dominant groups, even when they rebel *and rise: only*

the 'permanent' victory breaks, and not immediately, the subordination. In reality, including when they appear triumphant, the subaltern groups are only in an alarmed state of defence. (Gramsci, 'Criteri metodici', 1975: Q25, Vol. 5: 2289; emphasis added)[6]

The modifications presented in the transcription introduce the idea of a *break*, which refers to the relations of 'military' forces that Gramsci distinguishes in another passage of the *Notebooks*, that is, defeat and victory as the last and definitive moments of conflict understood as progress. This shows that, contrary to certain social-democratic and liberal-democratic readings (see Liguori, 1997), Gramsci considered the revolution as a political event and not just a sociocultural one, and the 'military' confrontation as a moment and a specific and determining form of conflict. On the other hand, the corrections reinforce the weight of subalternity to the extent that Gramsci makes absolute ('continuously', 'always', 'including when they appear triumphant') the bindings of subordination that he had established in 1930.

In effect, one phrase can be considered foundational: 'the subaltern classes always suffer the initiative of the dominant class, even when they rebel'. The solidity of the subaltern experience is thus established: the non-violent imposition and the assimilation of subordination, that is, the internalization of the values proposed by those who dominate or morally and intellectually *lead* the historical process. Gramsci reinforces this by pointing out that this relational device operates including in rebellion, with which he implicitly rejects any Manichaean dualism that intends to divide the real subjects by the separation of rebelliousness and submission as separate moments. In the same manner he will later reject the spontaneity-conscious direction dualism. At the same time, once the limits are established, the enigma of why and how they rebel is opened.

Eppur si muove. Even though Gramsci points out that real subjects are subalterns even in rebellion, in the same passage he recognizes his dialectical counterpart: the tendency towards autonomy against and within the borders of domination and of its State hegemonic expression. Gramsci foreshadows in subalternity the existence of 'features of autonomous initiative', features that make up the red line of Gramscian search.

Next we will have a look *in extenso* at the note in which the concept of subalternity is presented and a core of Gramscian thought is configured.

5. *Methodical criteria.* The historical unity of the ruling classes happens in the State and their history is essentially the history of States and groups of States. *We should not believe that such unity is strictly juridical or political even though this form of unity has an importance that goes beyond the formal:* the fundamental unity, by its concretion, is the result of the organic relationships between State or political society and 'civil society'. The subaltern classes, *by definition, are not unified and cannot unify unless they can become the State:* their history, therefore, is interlinked with that of civil society, it is a disaggregated and *discontinuous* function of the history of civil society and, *thus, of the history of States or groups of States.* Therefore, it is necessary to study: (1) the process of objective formation of subaltern social groups through the development and transformations that take place in the world of economic production, its quantitative diffusion and origin in pre-existing social groups, *whose mentality, ideology and ends they maintain for some time*; (2) their active or passive adhesion to dominant political formations, the attempts to influence the programmes of these formations in order to impose their own claims and *the consequences that such attempts have in the determination of decomposition and renewal or newly formed processes*; (3) the appearance of new parties from the dominant groups to maintain *consensus* and control of subaltern groups; (4) the formations from subaltern groups *for claims* of restrained and partial character; (5) the new formations that affirm the autonomy of subaltern groups albeit in the old quadrants; (6) the formations that affirm the integral autonomy, and so on. The list of these phases can be made more precise with intermediate phases or with combinations of various phases. The historian must note and justify the line of development towards integral autonomy, starting from the most primitive phases he must identify each manifestation of the Sorelian 'spirit of division'. But the history of the parties of subaltern groups is very complex in that it must include all repercussions of the party's activities, for the entire area of the subaltern *groups* in its totality, *and for the attitudes of the dominant groups and must*

include the repercussions of the more efficient activities because they are maintained by the State, of the dominant groups over the subaltern and their parties. Among the subaltern *groups* one will exercise or *tend to exercise a certain hegemony through a party* and this must be fixed by studying the development of the other parties insofar as they include elements of the hegemonic *group* or of the other subaltern *groups* that suffer this hegemony …

The study of the development of these innovative forces of subaltern groups to *leader and dominant* groups must investigate and identify the phases through which they have acquired autonomy from enemies that needed to be abated and the adherence of the groups that actively or passively helped them, when this whole process was historically necessary for them to be unified as a State. The degree of *historical-political* consciousness that these innovative forces through the various phases had progressively achieved is measure by these two parameters and not just by their separation from the previously dominant forces. (Gramsci, 1975: Q3, Vol. 90: 182–3 and 1975: Q25; 2287, 2288, 2289; emphasis added)[7]

In this note from 1930, one of Gramsci's main contributions is formulated and presented for the first time: the 'organic' relationship between State and civil society as realization of the hegemony of the dominant classes, which will lead him to elaborate the notion of the extended State, 'political society + civil society'. At the same time, in opposition to liberal conceptions, Gramsci hierarchically locates the subaltern classes in the periphery of civil society that is, as *integrating* parts yet not completely *integrated*, of the relation of domination that is created there: integrating but subordinated and disaggregated. On the other hand, Gramsci established the stages and forms of action as a process of separation – of excision, after George Sorel's image – that, within the hegemonic frame tends to trace the possible exits towards forms of autonomy through a series of interrelations of influence that open the possibility of a subaltern group to develop the hegemonic capacity to articulate a *historical bloc* in its surroundings. The methodological sequence reproduces a process-based typology that starts at the material existence of subalterns and goes through different possibilities and modalities of affirmation of consciousness through advances in their autonomy. Giorgio Baratta (2007: 130–2) points out that the 'and so on' that follows point 6 opens up other phases and levels, where autonomy becomes the intermediate passage between subalternity and a new hegemony-domination, which is tantamount to saying that autonomy (for Gramsci, the *Modern Prince*, the Communist Party) is a necessary condition of the struggle for hegemony.

In the paragraph entitled 'Spontaneity and Conscious Direction', he introduces other fundamental elements for the characterization of the subaltern classes:

> In the 'most spontaneous' movement, the elements of 'conscious direction' are simply uncontrollable, they have not left any verifiable document. One might say that the element of spontaneity is therefore characteristic of the 'history of the subaltern classes' and even of the more marginal and peripheral elements of these classes, who have not reached the consciousness of class 'for itself' and because of this do not suspect their history might have any importance and that it might be valuable to leave documentary traces of it. There exist a 'multiplicity' of elements of 'conscious direction' in these movements, but none of them is predominant, or outweighs the level of the 'popular science' of a determined social stratum, of 'common sense', that is the conception of the world (traditional) of that determined stratum. (Gramsci, 'Passato e presente. Spontaneità e direzione consapevole', 1975: Q3, Vol. 48: 328–9)[8]

In this passage, Gramsci proceeds following the same methodological sequence stated a few pages back. On one hand, he establishes spontaneity as a characteristic of how the subaltern classes proceed as a correlation of the absence of a full class consciousness for themselves. On the other, he recognizes embryonic elements of a conscious direction that he describes as 'popular science' or 'common sense', as a popular traditional idea of the world, opening a branch that will lead him to study popular culture, language, and *folklore*,[9] in an attempt to 'translate the elements of historic life into theoretical language and not the other way around, to present reality according to an abstract scheme' (ibid.: Q3, Vol. 48: 332). In this sense, the concept of subaltern is located between social being and social consciousness. It alludes to an *experience from subordination*, a combination of spontaneity and consciousness that manifests itself progressively using Thompson's formula, as a 'disposition to act as a class'. At the same time, the uneven combinations between spontaneity and consciousness tend to be modified in favour of the second to the extent in which one advances from subalternity to autonomy.

With these elements, in the third notebook in 1930 – before writing the famous notes on Machiavelli in which he develops the notion of *hegemony* – the central core of Gramsci's thought is constituted and one of the most fertile categories of contemporary Marxism is configured around the concept of *subalternity*.

The value of this contribution is widely recognized in three fundamental aspects: as historiographical proposal, as base for historical political interpretations, and as outline for a project of emancipation.[10] The concept of *subaltern* allows attention to be focused on the subjective aspects of subordination in a context of hegemony: the subaltern experience, that is, on the incorporation and relative acceptance of the relationship of command and obedience and, at the same time, its counterpart in resistance and permanent negotiation. This concept is so central to Gramscian thought we can talk of an outline of the theory of subalternity, that is, a theorization that develops along the theory of hegemony, like its subjective correlation: the study of the corresponding process of political subjectivation. The political conclusion of this approach is that the webs of hegemony cannot be dismantled by a simple and sudden voluntary act but rather must be recognized and unwoven gradually in the same manner they were woven, in the same subjective ground they covered. In this sense, the elements of characterization of subalternity that Gramsci proposed do not show the bindings of subalternity but also, simultaneously, outline a theory of political configuration of the subject in a context of domination and hegemony, emphasizing the process of autonomization through which the subalterns stop being so.

The focus of subalternity configures a synchronic and diachronic relationship between subordination and resistance, avoiding the rigidity of the dualist schemes that appeared in the Marxist tradition: consciousness/false consciousness, rationality/irrationality, spontaneity/conscious direction, and class in itself/class for itself. On the contrary, it opens up the analysis of combinations and superimpositions that historically characterize the processes of politicization of the collective action of subalterns. The field of analysis of these processes includes areas of subjectivation whose political character was previously denied, for example, popular culture, myths, *folklore*, and all popular expressions liable to be the object of dispute between conservative and transformative projects. The subaltern field, furthermore, appears configured by an ensemble of groups, which establishes the classist dimension as a result of social and political processes of convergence, and not as a starting point in keeping with Marx's original approach; class as a process and a relationship and not as a statistical fact.

This approach makes it possible to do subtle historiographical and sociological analyses able to trace the *movements* of the subalterns, the internal process of political subjectivation in the relationship of domination, built on the experience of domination and the dynamics of awareness-raising that correspond to them. In this sense, the concept includes the ambiguities and contradictory aspects of this process, the oscillations and combinations between the relative acceptance of domination – as a result of hegemony – and an equally relative rejection through resistance, just like between the combined experience of spontaneity and consciousness.

At the same time, precisely because the concept of subalternity has this plasticity in the historiographical, historical and political fields, it still contains a certain degree of imprecision at the theoretical level. When do subalterns stop being subalterns? At what point in their journey of autonomization? Gayatri Spivak affirms that if subalterns are allowed to speak, this act means they have a minimum of organization and, thus, they stop being subalterns and are on the long road to hegemony (Spivak, 2003: 297–364). On the opposite, Gramsci maintains they 'always' are, even when they rebel, which would indicate that only a definitive 'break' – becoming the State through revolution, becoming the leading class, that is, hegemonic and dominant – would end subalternity. In Gramsci, there is a *continuum* of subalternity between two poles – acceptance and the questioning of domination –characterized by an uncertain relationship of forces between the hegemonic colonization driven by the dominant classes and the autonomization maintained by the subaltern classes. Nevertheless, even when they remain subalterns, insofar as their original characteristic remains present, would such a comprehensive category keep us from clearly visualizing its differentiation-progressive autonomization (albeit oscillating) and not distinguish the forms and moments of a process in the midst of which they are transforming?

Before we provide an answer that values the scope and limits of this conceptual delimitation, we will look at the use of this category by *Subaltern Studies*, the School of Subaltern Studies in India.

From Subalternity to Subalternism: Subaltern Studies

In the midst of the proliferation of the use of the word *subaltern* in both academic and political speech, a relatively systematic use and a simultaneous effort to develop the concept can be found in the research carried out by the so-called Subaltern Studies Group (SSG or Subaltern Studies),[11] founded by Indian historians educated in the UK in the 1980s in parallel to the *Cultural Studies* or Birmingham School (see Stuart, 2008; Mattelart and Neveau, 2008; Bowman, 2007), but recognized globally since the 1990s, when their main works were translated into different languages and became the source of inspiration and interlocution with other related currents like *postcolonial studies*.[12]

The Subaltern School has as its primary objective to liberate and reveal the point of view of the subalterns, the *voices* denied by the statisms that dominated both colonial culture as well as what was promoted by Hindu nationalism and Marxism, in their political positions and the historiographies they housed.

In this sense, Ranajit Guha writes:

> Nevertheless there is a statism that manifests itself in the nationalist and Marxist discourses. The referent in both cases is a state that differs in one significant aspect from that in colonialist literature. The difference is that which exists between an already realized power in a formed and stable regime, rooted for many years, and a power that has not yet been realized; a dream of power. (Guha, 2002: 24)

This critique of the view from above, from State-power as established regime or as objective, encouraged a reading of the history of peasant rebellions in India contrary to the dominant thesis and the formulation of an innovative historiographical perspective.

The historiographical originality of subaltern studies is an object of discussion. At the national level it allowed a deepening of historical knowledge and problematization of existing literature. At the regional level – the regions with a colonial past – it offered an alternative framework of interpretation to the modernist and modernizing approach of colonizers and the decolonized, whose adoption and application is currently in place, particularly in postcolonial studies. At the general theoretic level, while it undoubtedly is an interesting conceptual elaboration and problematic, and it recognizes the specificity of colonial societies, it does not propose an approach that varies substantially from historical studies that were produced by historicist Marxism under Gramsci's influence nor fundamentally, from British social history since the 1960s and, particularly, the work of E.P. Thompson and Eric Hobsbawm.[13] At the same time, it is a call for attention to the epistemological limits of an academic knowledge determined by the sociopolitical denial of the subalterns, particularly in postcolonial societies (Beverley, 2004: 13–32).

Let us have a look at the main postulates of the SSG. From the founding manifesto, Guha directly and explicitly recognizes the link with Gramsci's work and in particular with the quoted methodological note that establishes the concept of *subalternity*. Another textual reference to the Notebooks that guides Subaltern Studies refers to the already mentioned note on 'spontaneity and conscious direction' from which Guha critiques the mechanical association between statism, organization and politics, and widens the notion of politics including phenomena that, according to traditional historiographies, were not considered *political*:

There was nothing here in the militant movements of their rural masses that was not political. It could not have been any other way in the conditions they worked in, viewed and conceived the world…

The element of coercion was so explicit and was so present in all their dealings with the peasant that they necessarily had to consider such a relationship as political. For the same reason, by undertaking the destruction of this relationship they committed to what was essentially a political job, a job in which the existing nexus of power had to be overthrown as a necessary condition to repair any particular offense. There was no way the peasant was going to throw himself into such a project unconsciously. (Guha, 1997a: 101, 104)[14]

While its extension may imply a loss of specificity, this amplified notion of *politics* clearly refers to historical materialism, even though it is formulated in a polemic with disdain towards the peasantry that characterizes various currents of Marxist thought and finds its foundation in parts of Marx's own work. In line with historicist Marxism and leaning directly on Gramsci, Guha proposes an approach to the theme of consciousness that rejects its reduction to reason and logic:

> In any of the cases, the insurgency is considered as something external to the peasant consciousness and the Cause is erected as a substitute ghost of Reason, the logic of this consciousness. (Guha. 2002: 45)

The open use of the notions of *politics* and *consciousness* – and their gradual superimposition – to acknowledge the action of subaltern classes constitutes the polemical core of the SSG proposal, which emphasizes, in peasant mobilizations, the decisive appeal of a non-*rational* yet *reflexive* consciousness resulting from experience and collective deliberation:

> There was nothing spontaneous in this, in the sense of being thoughtless and non-deliberated. The peasant knew what he was doing when he revolted. The fact that his action was directed above all at destroying the authority of the elite that was above him and did not imply a detailed plan to replace it does not put him outside the sphere of politics. On the contrary, the insurgency affirmed its political character precisely by this negative procedure that attempted to invert the situation. By trying to force the mutual substitution of the dominant and the dominated in the power structure, it did not leave any doubt about its identity as a project of power. (Guha, 1997a: 104)

The rejection of the idea of a strictly rational consciousness embodied in India by both colonial and nationalist discourses, led the Subaltern

School to rescue premodern traditions – recuperating Gramsci's thoughts on *folklore* – as areas of collective action and politics. This assessment allows the recognition of a line of separation of Western thought from the practices of resistance and rebellion of Indian peasants. At the same time, this perspective of separation is liable to slips like the one presented by Bolivian historian Silvia Rivera when she says:

> The proper notion of subalternity is built as something different, outside of and preexisting the Western world – reason as history – while acknowledging that it is this same world which has bequeathed this concept from the Gramscian branch. (Rivera Cusicanqui and Barragán, 1997: 11)

This affirmation contains possible excesses – verbal more than analytical – of a postcolonialism, Latin American in this case, that in the exaltation of the *premodern* as contrary to dominant visions, establishes its irreducible separation and its purity before Western modernity. This dualism without dialectic blurs the outlines of the relationship that – throughout history – kept modifying one and the other pole: the *premodern/traditional* developed in and against modernity and the other way around.

The fact is nothing is built – unless we confine ourselves to prehispanic origins – as 'distinct, alien and pre-existing' the Western world, much less subaltern forms that, by their own nature, refer to a relationship of domination. In effect, beyond the verbal extremisms, the investigations undertaken in the frame of subaltern and postcolonial studies reveal the variegated character of indigenous subjective construction, which implies knowing its interiority with respect to the Western world to recognize levels of permanence and the reproduction of a relative exteriority.[15]

In effect, the definition of *subalternity* derived from the relationship of domination and defined in terms of the devices of subordination clearly appears in the works produced within the frame of the SSG. Nevertheless, attempting to anchor the insurgency to subalternity, one of its most distinguished members, Partha Chatterjee, writes:

> The insurgent consciousness was, first of all, a negative consciousness in the sense that its identity was only expressed through an

opposition that consecrated at the same time its difference and its antagonism in terms of the dominant ones. It was an identity whose limits were marked by the same conditions of subordination under which the peasantry worked and lived; but the relationships were inverted. (Chatterjee, 1997b: 199)

It is worth asking if the five elements of the insurgent consciousness that appear in this formulation – denial, opposition, difference, antagonism and inversion – correspond to the scope of the definition of *subalternity* used by this current and to what extent they elude or minimize the subordinated matrix that frames the concept and corresponds to its genesis in Gramsci's thought to emphasize one dimension – insurgency – which, while it emerges from the frame of subalternity, strains or surpasses it.

On the other hand, the notion of *subalternity* that Guha uses in the founding manifesto of the School, beyond Gramsci's quote, contains a slippery confusion when he says:

The terms peoples and subaltern classes have been used as synonyms throughout this note. The groups and social elements included in this category represent the demographic difference between the entire Indian population and all those we have described as elite. (Guha, 1997b (1981): 32)[16]

Outside of the ambiguous reference to the notion of a *people* and conceding that later developments in subaltern studies focus on the qualitative and not quantitative analysis of subalternity, this confusion is notable given that one of the uses of *subaltern classes* in common public discourse is exactly that: a definition derived from defect and excess, all the social sectors that are not dominant classes and that exceed the working class.

While obvious, Guha admits that the problem of subalternity is not determined demographically or quantitatively, and he synthetically and precisely defines what he considers to be its four constitutive pillars (property, law, religion and tradition):

Their subalternity was materialized by the structure of the property, institutionalized by the law, sanctified through religion and made tolerable – even desirable – by tradition. (Guha, 2002: 43)

Guha and Chatterjee acknowledge, referring again to Gramsci, a certain degree of contradiction between the insurgency seen as an incorporation of domination and its rejection.

For Guha:

The insurgency was, in effect, the meeting place in which the two mutually contradictory tendencies of this still imperfect, almost embryonic, theoretical consciousness – that is, a conservative tendency constituted by the inherited material of the dominant culture, absorbed without criticism, and another radical one, looking towards the practical transformation of the conditions of rebel existence – came together to undertake a decisive test of strength. (Guha, 1997a: 106)

For Chatterjee:

The peasant consciousness is thus a contradictory unit of two aspects: in one, the peasant is subordinated, accepts the immediate reality of the power relations that dominate and exploit him; in the other, rejects these conditions of subordination and affirms his autonomy. (Chatterjee, 1997b: 205)

In these passages, the authors present the unstable equilibrium of a consciousness composed and tensioned by opposite tendencies of conservative and transformative character. This unstable equilibrium and the consequent tensions correspond to the notion of subalternity forged by Gramsci and open up the understanding of the experience of subordination as a process of political subjectivation. At the same time, and this seems to me the main defect of the theoretical approach of the SSG, this contradiction is diluted when Guha (1997c: 28) associates subalternity with an 'autonomous sphere': 'This is an autonomous sphere since it did not originate in the politics of the elite, nor did its existence depend on it'.[17]

The dialectical relationship, turned into a dualism, in polarity, disappears and with it is eliminated – even if only temporarily – the dependent and subordinated side of subalternity, the relative autonomy – autonomization as process – becomes integral, absolute, without the mediation of the uneven and combined process that Gramsci broke down in six points. If *subalternity* is *autonomous* and *spontaneity* is *conscious*, why then so many words?

According to Guha, autonomy detaches from the origin and capacity for survival of this sphere at the margin of the elites. It could be true but irrelevant if we consider the political character of any community before colonization. It is contradictory when Guha himself acknowledges – and even the concept of subalternity implies it – a relational character that excludes the possibility of full autonomy, beyond the interdependence of the relations of domination. The principle of the relational character of domination is so unquestionable that the SSG clearly assumes that elites do not have full autonomy either; rather, they constantly negotiate and renegotiate domination. If we assume its relational relativity, the theme of the origin and development of all autonomy refers us to witness that not everything is unilaterally imposed, that there are shielded fields, knowledges and communitarian resources that are not born from subordination as imposition and become instruments of struggle. Nevertheless, beyond their origin, these resources acquire meaning and materiality in their context of domination and, thus, cannot isolate themselves from the corresponding relationship between command-obedience/resistance. In this sense, it is fundamental to analyse how and why certain knowledges and practices become resources for self-determination and others do not, how the communitarian construction of resistance and rebellion in terms of relative autonomies is oriented, never completely outside the reality of domination, in the oscillation between the logic of obedience and the possibility of conflict.

In this sense, Chatterjee's following argument is unsustainable:

An opposition of relational power necessarily meant that the dominated should be awarded their own field of subjectivity, in which they were autonomous and not dominated. If that was not the case, the dominators would consume and completely obliterate the dominated in the exercise of their domination. Domination would then stop being part of a social relation of power with its own conditions of reproduction. Therefore, in this specific case, an autonomous sphere or dominion should be awarded to the peasantry. (Chatterjee, 1997b: 198)

According to Chatterjee's reasoning, if there is a relationship of power, there are subjects, if there are subjects, there is self-dominion (autonomy). His counterargument proceeds as proof *ad absurdum* suggesting it could not be any other way and concluding that this quality must be awarded. Beyond the use of the verb 'to award', which refers to an intellectual operation more than a derivation from empirical observation, the result is less than satisfactory insofar as it ends in a contradictory essentialization: the subaltern is, by definition, autonomous.

Aside from the unfortunate and paradoxical formulations, there is evidence of a substantial theoretical problem that goes beyond the use of the notion of *subalternity*. Before we delve deeper into this aspect, let us have a look at some other problematic passages from the most important authors of the Subaltern School.

Even when the SSG clearly recognizes a contradictory tension within the subaltern consciousness – between acceptance and denial of domination and their parameters – at other times during the analysis it places dualism and contradiction outside the subaltern classes in their confrontation with elites:

As a measure of the difference between two mutually contradictory perceptions, it tells us a lot, not only about the mentality of the elite, but also about what opposes it, that is, about the subaltern mentality. The antagonism is, in effect, so complex and so firmly structured that, from the terms declared by one, it should be possible, inverting their values, to derive the implicit terms of the other. (Guha, 1997a: 111)

Inversion – which had previously appeared in a quote by Chatterjee – operates as a device of separation, of opposition without mediations or superimpositions. The contradiction within subalternity, which seems compact before its dominant opposite, disappears. *Subalternity* is thus confused – that is, the political subjectivation arising from the relationship of domination and the experience of subordination – with the subjectivation forged in conflict, in the experience of insubordination, that is, as we will see further on, in *antagonism*.

This confusion will be acknowledged *a posteriori* by members of the SSG. Chatterjee mentions a shift within the School as a way to rebalance the initial approach:

It is between 1987 and 1989, starting with the fifth and sixth volumes of *Subaltern Studies*, that a new orientation appears. We started admitting more seriously than before, that the histories of subalternity were fragmentary, unarticulated and incomplete, that the subaltern consciousness was fissured, made up of elements appearing from the experiences of the dominant classes as well as from the dominated. To the same degree as the signs of autonomy manifested by ordinary people in the time of rebellion, the forms of subaltern consciousness subjected to the daily regime of subordination became an object of study (Chatterjee, 2006a).

On the other hand, Saurabh Dube acknowledges the theoretical origin of the problem in Guha's work:

That Guha resorted to sets of binary oppositions led him to see a clear separation between passivity and resistance and to trace an abrupt distinction between the elite and the subordinated groups in colonial India; separation and distinction that ignored the alchemy of approval and apathy (and the levels and forms of subordination) between subaltern groups. (Dube, 2001: 70)

Nevertheless, beyond the self-critique and readjustment – which can lead to the extreme opposite, to the absolutism of the acceptance of subordination – the initial approaches by the SSG inspired the proliferation of a slippery concept of *subalternity*.

An illustrative example of the landslide led by the SSG perspective appears in a book written by Rhina Roux, inspired by Guha's work, on subalternity in Mexico. In several passages, taking up James Scott,[18] Roux locates with precision the base of subordination and it's still minimal margins of operation:

What the political character gives the action by the subalterns is not its reference to state institutions or its peaceful or violent nature, but its orientation towards a redefinition of social bonds and its capacity to question the normative order in which a form of domination rests...

If subalternity does not indicate a material shortage but a relational location (sub/alter: the other below), then domination is an eminently conflictive process that passes through the recognition, on behalf of the dominant, of the will of the subordinated and through the attempt, on behalf of the oppressed, to put conditions and walls to the domination...

The political character of the subaltern classes is historically configured from their own experience, in relation to those dominating and from a cultural framework common to both that includes myths, religiosity and collective representations. (Roux, 2005: 42–3, 157)

After having focused the analysis on negotiation by way of questioning, conditions and barriers, Roux makes the same leap as Guha and his colleagues:

Because it is a social process that rests on domination, the nationalization of social life is always pierced by conflict and overwhelmed by the autonomous politics of the subaltern classes, which are always attempting to get included in the state relationship. (ibid.: 45)

Suddenly, without mediations, conflict, overgrowth, and autonomy appear. Antagonism and autonomy are subsumed as parts of subalternity, when – following Gramsci – conflict is a resource and autonomy a progressive conquest and not a state of things. It is not a question of denying the relationship between subalternity, antagonism and autonomy but about not subsuming the latter two to the first, diminishing the specificity of the three fundamental concepts for understanding the processes of resistance and rebellion.

Another direct reference by the SSG to Gramsci's thought is the notion of *passive revolution*, which for the Italian author is a process-based correlate of subalternity: the possibility of a transformation proposed and guided from above, directed at restructuring the relation of domination by offering the 'transforming' illusion of change at a superficial level looking to guarantee underlying continuity. The use of this concept appears in the works of Partha Chatterjee as the analytical instrument that allows him to interpret the constitution of the nation-State after independence in terms of the elements of continuity with the colonial past (Chatterjee, 1997a: 211–33). However, it is surprising to find in this study that Chatterjee visualizes the process from above, from the manipulation of the authors that drive the *passive revolution* and not from the masses that embody it, that incorporate the process. The approach of subaltern studies is paradoxically inverted insofar as it analyses the imposition and its mechanisms instead of the assimilation. At the same time, the surprise fades when we find in this interpretation an effect of deformation derived from the previous scheme: if the subalterns are autonomous, they can only be subordinated from an external imposition. There is no hegemony, only naked domination.

As a reflection of the Gramscian openness of the concept of *subalternity*, the SSG seems to get confused in the dismantled oscillation between two interpretative strands. On one hand, subalternity as an *autonomous politics* that exalts rebellions and its partial outcomes, still circumscribed within the cultural consolidation of communities in resistance. On the other hand, subalternity as an expression of the effectiveness of domination that encourages a history of the impossibility of success and of the permanent failure of the projects and wishes embodied in peasant movements.

Beyond the theoretical reshuffling within the SSG, the underlying problem is not solved insofar as the concept of *subalternity* is used as the philosopher's stone of an investigative alchemy that mistakes the shine for the gold.

It is possible that this oscillatory frame is a voluntary choice with a view to encourage the opening of the analysis and to surpass the difficulties of conceptual precision, from the rejection of theory that Thompson tried to theorize about versus the Althusserian scientism and in defence of historicist Marxism (Thompson, 1981). At the same time, another explanation is that this focus derives from an involuntarily skewed reading of Gramsci's work. Guha read a selection of Gramsci's Notebooks, a British compilation that – like Palmiro Togliatti's classic – is based on a thematic order that does not respect the sequential logic of Gramsci's development of thought in prison. The critical edition coordinated by Valentino Gerratana, published by the Gramsci Institute in 1975, was a response to this philological gap and encouraged a shift in Gramscian studies. The reading of the work of the Italian Marxist by the members of the Subaltern School apparently does not take into consideration the totality of his work.

A renowned expert, Joseph Buttigieg, affirms they missed a systematic study of the work (Buttigieg, 1999: 196). The concepts elaborated by Gramsci are appropriated by the authors and used, building on their openness and the suggestions they contain, because the fragmentary character of the drafting of the Notebooks encourages it and because it can be considered a field of inspiration and a frame of reference.[19] This creative practice constitutes an engine for the development of thought, particularly Marxist; at the same time, in this case, it seems to have been counterproductive. In the notion of *subalternity* used and developed in the research by the SSG, problematic dimensions and articulations proposed by Gramsci in his work disappear, including: classes, power, the link between social subject and political subject (the Party), social relations that include but surpass the dominant-subaltern relationship in a strict sense (civil society), the form of domination in an ample sense (hegemony), and the role of intellectuals.

Thus, the SSG contributed to the diffusion but not to the strengthening of the focus of subalternity and got confused in the attempt to square a *subalternism,* that is, an essentialism that was able to reconcile the experience of subordination as matrix of the processes of political subjectivation with the practices and experiences of resistance, rebellion and autonomy. The nominal assimilation of differentiated phenomena caused a theoretical ambiguity that, while it allowed the advancement in historical studies, it obstructed the theoretical reflection. However, we should not forget that Gramsci's own conceptual legacy was confusing, even when he never made autonomy an absolute nor separated the moments of subalternity, being careful to maintain the different expressions or moments of the subaltern linked within the frame of a historical process branched with possibilities and potentialities, thus avoiding any essentialist, defining and definitive temptation.

Beyond the valorization of undisputable historiographical and epistemological successes, as well as the possible theoretical missteps by the SSG, there is still the question about the analytical limits and scope of such a comprehensive concept.

Conclusion

The concept of *subaltern* elaborated by Antonio Gramsci in the frame of his theoretical political thinking generated a perspective that allowed the frame of analysis of the processes of political subjectivation to open. In the terms of E.P. Thompson, Gramsci conceptualized subalternity as an *experience of subordination*, expressed by the tension between *acceptance/incorporation* and the *rejection/autonomization* of the relations of domination and materialized in a 'disposition to act as a class' that combines spontaneity and consciousness.

On an eminently academic plane, the School of Subaltern Studies of India, founded by Ranajit Guha recuperated the concept and throughout a series of applications in historical studies, advanced in making theory that, intending to fix the elements of subalternity, formulated an uncertain notion of subalternism at first centred in the exaltation of the phenomena of autonomy and rebellion and later oscillating between the two aspects noted by Gramsci. The SSG became confused at the step that Gramsci did not want or could not take: to attempt to fix the essence of the subjects, to establish a finite definition of its characteristics, to offer a finished synthesis of the dialectical relationship between the dimensions that configure it. This attempt to develop the concept of subalternity, beyond the historiographical advances it allowed, was trapped in an essentialism, a theorization based on a reductionist focus on subalternity from an all-encompassing pretension that proposes the assimilation of a subjective dimension with the totality of the composition of the subject, a one-dimensional resolution of the dialectic between acceptance and rejection of domination, between spontaneity and consciousness. In contrast to Spivak's critique which contests Gramsci's and the SSG's notion of subaltern in the name of Foucauldian micrology (Spivak, 2004: 283–4), I consider the solution does not lie in minimizing the analytical scope of the concept but in the acknowledgment that subalternity is a fundamental component but not unique nor essential.

The horizon traced by Gramsci constitutes a theoretical starting point crucial to the study of political subjectivation processes and not, as follows from the Subaltern Studies Group, a point of arrival. If at the historiographical level it is possible – and fruitful – to frame a determined set of processes under the seal of subalternity, at the theoretical level the temptation to operate the same synthesis leads to a conceptual confusion.

Starting from Gramsci's reflections we can understand subalternity as a condition and as a process of subjective development – of political subjectivation centred in the experience of subordination – that includes combinations of relative acceptance and resistance, of spontaneity and consciousness. This implies distinguishing levels and dimensions as situations and moments, recognizing different forms and passages, diverse manifestations of subalternity that would be necessary to qualify. At the same time, widening the perspective regarding processes and dynamics of political subjectivation that surpass resistance – as a defensive posture – implies the incorporation of other dimensions and concepts.

To advance in this direction, we will see in the following chapters how the concepts of *antagonism* and *autonomy*, along with that of *subalternity*, were placed at the centre of analytical perspectives on the processes of political subjectivation, what their scope was, their limits, and, finally, the extent to which they can articulate and complement each other to open the horizon and strengthen Marxist analysis of the processes of political subjectivation.

2

Antagonism

Unlike the category of *subalternity*, *antagonism* is not commonly used in political discourse. This concept occupies an important place in Marx's work and thus maintained a significant presence in later Marxist language, in which it appears frequently, generally as a synonym of conflict, contradiction, opposition, confrontation, and struggle.

The concept of *antagonism* was the object of theoretical development on only one occasion – in the work of Antonio Negri in the 1970s – where he specified its meaning, attempted to locate it in the centre of a Marxist perspective of analysis of subjective processes corresponding to the practice and *experience of insubordination*, of the forms and dynamics of political subjectivation derived from situations of conflict and struggle.

In this chapter we will study the origins and uses of the notion of *antagonism* in the work of Marx as a precedent that justifies and frames the later effort by Negri to emphasize its subjective implications. Later we will analyse the scope and limits of Negri's theorization influenced by the theory and practice of workerism and the intense mobilizations of the 1960s and 1970s in Italy. Finally, in an *excursus*, we will review the trajectory of Negri's thought from the 1980s onwards to account for the later development of the concept.

Antagonism, Struggle and Insubordination

In contrast with the concept of *subalternity*, *antagonism* appears regularly and frequently in Marx's work. Its use can be unpacked, on an initial level, into a particular and a general meaning. The general meaning refers to a wide or extensive use as synonym of contradiction or contraposition and, therefore, susceptible to application to diverse situations. The particular meaning – qualitatively more relevant –

focuses its use on the relationship with conflict between capital and labour and class confrontation, which implies another unfolding.

Let us take a look at some significant moments of this definition in Marx's works. Since the *Manifesto of the Communist Party*, the concept of *antagonism* appears on several occasions and is situated at the centre of discourse and history as synonym of class struggle: 'All prior societies, as we have seen, have rested on the antagonism between the oppressed classes and the oppressors'[1] (Marx, 1985c: 122). Further on, in this same text, it reappears – on one sole occasion – to characterize the capitalist moment and its structural form of 'antagonism of capital and wage labour' (ibid.). In this manner, it is located discursively as synonym of class struggle or conflict between capital and work, according to the more subjective or structural emphasis of discourse.[2] Clearly, when it comes to struggle, the concept highlights the connotation that, in linguistic terms (from the Greek *agon*: struggle and *antagonizomai*: struggle against) it is proper to the word, which emphasizes the subjective human character of confrontation.

Antagonism is linked to the problem of consciousness in other passages of the *Manifesto*:

> It is not strange, then, that the social consciousness of all eras abides, despite all the variety and all the divergences, by certain common forms, forms of consciousness until the class antagonism that informs them does not disappear radically ...
>
> But all this without stopping work for a single instant among the workers, until it is affirmed in them with the utmost clarity possible the consciousness of the hostile antagonism that separates the bourgeoisie from the proletariat. (ibid.: 127, 140)[3]

To speak strictly of antagonism as a melting pot of 'forms of consciousness' or of the 'consciousness of antagonism' would reinforce the connotation of antagonism as structural conflict, objective, of which one acquires consciousness in the subjective plane. However, the formula 'consciousness of antagonism' could easily become *antagonistic consciousness* and open a series of subjective dilemmas linked to struggle and insubordination as experiences. What impact does conflict have on consciousness? What consciousness appears from the experience of antagonism? What subjective constitution corresponds to this antagonistic consciousness? These questions pass through Marx's political and theoretical preoccupations and will remain present in later Marxist debate.

Another passage in the *Manifesto* is particularly suggestive to the extent that it links the idea of antagonism to that of autonomy. Referring to the utopian socialists, Marx and Engels write:

> The authors of these systems penetrate the class *antagonism* and the action of dissolving elements that germinate in the core of the governing society. But they fail to see yet a historical independent action in the proletariat, a proper and peculiar political movement. (ibid.: 136)

In addition to establishing a close relationship between autonomy and antagonism as complementary elements, Marx – by using 'yet' – leaves a margin to understand that the utopian socialists did not see autonomy as being the level following antagonism, which would derive from the assumption that independence is constructed from conflict, that is, that autonomy is forged in antagonism.

In the 'Preface' to *A Contribution to the Critique of Political Economy*, with a clearly different connotation, antagonism appears in a lone paragraph that sets a formal, structural definition of the concept, which will be recurring in *Capital*.

> The bourgeois relations of production are the last antagonistic form of the social process of production, antagonistic, not in the sense of an individual antagonism, but that of an antagonism that appears from the social conditions of life of individuals, but the productive forces that develop in the heart of bourgeois society create, at the same time, the material conditions to solve this antagonism. (Marx, 1982: 67)

In *Capital*, the concept appears in multiple occasions with a structural emphasis and, as such, reinforces this connotation[4] (Marx, 1999). In the midst of its systematic use at a structural level as synonym of contradiction – as *moment* and *shape* of the contradiction –a single passage in *Capital* states directly the subjective dimension of antagonism:

It is the ensemble of the means of production monopolized by a certain part of society, the products and conditions of exercise of the living labour force opposite this force of labour that this antagonism personifies as capital. (ibid.: (3) Ch. 48)

The idea of the personification of living labour in opposition to capital opens the possibility of a meaning of antagonism as counterposition between subjects and as field of constitution of subjectivities in the struggle of an objective conflict.

However, this branch is kept on a second plane on the basis of the main aims of *Capital* that translate into an analysis of how capitalism works. This does not mean that *Capital* has no aim in terms of the subjectivation of labour, but that this follows the structural analysis which is the main argument of this work. Thus, in the same chapter where the aforementioned appears, Marx centres the concept on the structural terrain in another paragraph:

The arrival of the moment of crisis is announced when the contradiction and antagonism between the means of distribution are presented and gain strength and profundity and, thus, the concrete historical form of the corresponding relations of production, on the one hand, and on the other, the forces of production, the capacity of production and the development of its agents. A conflict then blows up between the material development of production and its social form. (ibid.: (1) Ch. 51)

The structural meaning of antagonism in *Capital* does not correspond to an equivalent development of a subjective meaning in the historical and political works of Marx.

In *The Eighteenth Brumaire of Louis Bonaparte*, the notion of *antagonism* appears several times in reference to diverse situations. In Chapter 3, it is used throughout a long paragraph on 'the most motley mixture of manifested contradictions' in the Constitutional Assembly, between la Montaigne, the realists, the Executive Power and the Republic.[5] Later, it appears as the 'old antagonism between the city and the country, the rivalry between the capital and the property of soil', as 'antagonism of classes in general' (ibid.: (3) 35, 41). In Chapter 4, it figures again as class antagonism but also between Louis Bonaparte and the National Constitutional Assembly.[6] In Chapter 6 it appears as antagonism between 'the supremacy of the territorial property or that of money', between fractions of the party of order (ibid.: (3) 77).

In *The Civil War in France*, a passage with strong theoretical implications reaffirms the general idea of class antagonism:

> While the progresses of the modern industry developed, widened and deepened the class antagonism between capital and work, the state Power was acquiring more every time the character of national power of the capital over work, of public force organized for the social enslavement, of machine of class despotism. (Marx 1985b: 214)

Later, Marx points out the antagonism between 'the rival fractions and factions of the appropriating class, in its antagonism, now openly declared, against the producing classes', but also 'between the Commune and the state Power', or he ironizes on innocent visions that assume 'antagonisms still in the bud' (ibid.: 214, 218, 220).

In synthesis, outside a wide use as simple synonym of conflict or contradiction, the concept of *antagonism* in Marx acquires density in the oscillation between a more systematic structural definition (capital conflict/labour) and a more uncertain subjective meaning (class struggle), which is perfectly coherent with the purposes and scope of the sequence established in the research programme that underlies his work: the material relations are created in the economic base and on which the superstructures are configured, the combination and the passage from social being to social consciousness as process of subjective construction. The culmination in *Capital* of the maturation of Marx's thought seals the most complete definition of antagonism as synonym of conflict and contradiction over struggle. Nevertheless, considering the unfinished nature of this work as well as Marx's research programme, particularly what refers to the studies on the structure of classes that he could not carry out, and the use of the concept since the *Manifesto*, the existence of a theoretical pitch is evident and leads to a subjective definition of antagonism which, without being systematic and precise, remains the inseparable counterpart of the structural definition of the social being in the frame of the capital/labour contradiction.

It is possible that because it is a concept that acquires specificity in Marx's work, antagonism stayed – with the exception of Antonio Negri's work, which we will examine later – relatively frozen in the structural use of *Capital,* even when the subjective sense of the *Manifesto* continued to offer the possibility of a semantic variation and of another analytical scope.

At the same time, beyond denomination, the inquietude of the theme of conflict impact (struggle) in the formation of the subject and the consciousness of oneself have been such a constant in Marxist thought it would be absurd to try and isolate it as a specific line. We could even also affirm that all Marxist political reflection has approached this problem that constitutes – more than subalternity and autonomy – the crux of Marxist political thought, the characteristic trait. In this case the list of references include, to name some significant examples, V.I. Lenin, Rosa Luxemburg, Mao Zedong, and Ernesto Che Guevara, who, from the analysis of subordination, spread their intellectual efforts towards understanding the subjective emergences related to the experiences of conflict, struggle, insubordination, and rebellion. This vast trajectory of Marxist reflections frames the theoretical problem that we are interested in emphasizing, but its timely following undoubtedly transcends the treatment we are suggesting both for its breadth as well as for the strictly theoretical ends we are pursuing. We will limit ourselves to the observation that, outside its conceptual formulation, the problem of the subjectivities forged in the struggles has occupied a strategic place which, besides the obvious political implications, is an indicator of the theoretical centrality we will defend in the last chapter.

In conclusion, beyond the nominal use of the category of *antagonism,* the persistence in Marxism in the search for interpretive keys of the subjective conformation born of conflict and struggle – or, said another way, of the experience of insubordination – is a constant that passes decades and centuries. However, it is relevant to point out that, with the exception of Negri, no other Marxist defined or called the processes *antagonistic* as forms of political subjectivation. Paradoxically, there is a non-Marxist (or *post-Marxist*) recovery of the concept from strictly academic perspectives in authors like Alberto Melucci and Ernesto Laclau (see Melucci, 1999; Laclau and Mouffe, 2004).

The relevance of Negri's work in the 1970s lies in the fact that we find in it the most systematic attempt – perhaps even the only one – within the Marxist tradition to develop a theory of the subject focused on the concept of *antagonism*. In addition to putting forward a specific notion of *autonomy*, Negri's main contribution during these years resides in the use and theoretical development of the concept of *antagonism* in a subjective sense of agency, not just as synonym for conflict but fundamentally as a characteristic of class struggle, as process of political subjectivation, as interiorization of the experience of conflict, struggle, and insubordination.

In the following paragraphs we will demonstrate the development of this perspective in Negri's trajectory, as well as the movements and oscillations in the use of the concept of *antagonism* from its first appearance in the texts in the 1970s until its blurring in his most recent work, which had a greater diffusion and acknowledgment than the previous ones. Without the pretence of rescuing the totality of the thought of a particularly creative author, in some respects hermetic and contradictory and in constant evolution, we will focus on tracing a conceptual pillar of his body of work. This exercise will offer an approach to the categorical construction of the notions of *antagonism* and *autonomy*, a monographic view of his work.

Before we examine the sequence of the texts, we must situate the origin of Negri's thought in the context of the political struggles of the 1960s and 1970s in Italy and the appearance of the workerist movement, of which Negri is not only an outstanding intellectual expression but a particularly lasting and significant one. A brief historical tour will serve to temporarily and politically locate Negri's ideas as well as to demonstrate that the origin of his thought, unlike Gramsci's, is directly linked with and influenced by a moment of intense mobilization, by potential political crisis and, thus, by revolutionary optimism.

In this sense, to review the trajectory of the workerist movement in Italy – little known in Latin America – will allow us to show the relation between the perspective of antagonistic subjectivation advanced by Negri within a theoretical strand of thought and a socio-political movement.

The Workerist Movement in Italy: Antagonistic Theory and Praxis

The 1960s and 1970s were the years of the so-called *new left*, of the diffusion – in the torrent of social struggles – of debates and Marxist and socialist heterodoxies (Teodori, 1978). In these 20 years of light and shadow, victories and defeats, a theoretical and political experience stood out in Italy: *workerism*.[7]

Workerism was the most original movement of the wave of struggles that characterized the history of Italy from the beginning of the 1960s until the end of the 1970s; a political movement that participated in a great social movement and internally branched into diverse experiences and different organizations.[8] *Workerism,* as a set of theoretical perspectives and as a political movement, shook the hegemony of the Italian Communist Party (PCI) – the largest in the West – during two decades and defined the history of the communist movement and Marxism in Italy.[9]

In an interpretative balance of the history of republican Italy, Enzo Santarelli thus synthesizes the political scope of *workerism*, by referring to his thesis:

> … have a disruptive value: something similar to the revolutionary syndicalism in other times, they reinstate the debate and stimulate action. There is not only a sure intuition – the potential awakening of the working class – but also a method – the social survey – and a perspective – worker democracy.[10] (Santarelli, 1997: 145)

Workerism is born with the magazine *Quaderni rossi*, whose first number came out in 1961 from the initiative of diverse political groups established in various industrial Italian cities. The main figure of this first experience was Raniero Panzieri, who militated in the left wing of the Italian Socialist Party (PSI), defending the idea of worker democracy and maintaining a critique of the party-form with Luxemburgian echoes, denouncing their degeneration into an instrument of elite reproduction and of conservation of the organization as an end in itself. Panzieri founded *Quaderni rossi* after the PSI had veered definitely to the right in the 1959 Congress, which inaugurated the era of the centre-left governments, headed by Christian Democracy, within which the socialists said they sought 'structural reforms' that would transform Italian capitalism.[11]

In effect, the emergence of *workerism* is tightly linked with the rapid process of modernization of Italian capitalism since the second postwar, which Claudio Albertani describes:

The exodus of the country, the industrial take-off, the increase of the tertiary sector, and the diffusion of mass consumption, profoundly modified the social structure of the country. Even though there had always existed strata of unqualified workers, the industries of the north began to require increasing amounts of cheap labour to boost the development of the automotive and petrochemical sectors. The production fragmented and, with the diffusion of the assembly chain, there appeared a new generation of young immigrants from the South who had no political culture, nor the 'resistential' values of their elders. They lived a particularly difficult situation because local society did not accept them and the union did not trust them. Soon, however, they would be protagonists of important protest movements. (Albertani, 2003: 172)

In this context, in its birth as an original proposal, workerism formulated a radical critique of the traditional Italian left – communist and socialist parties and unions – accused of focusing their vision on the development of the productive forces. This stance, according to workerists, led to the acceptance of an idea of progress that led to a favourable attitude towards capitalist development, a logic of negotiation with redistributive ends that translated into an opening with regard to the industrial bourgeoisie of the 'golden era' of capitalism, the Fordist-Keynesian era of capitalist planning (see Tronti, 1963: 44–73). The political pact that had allowed the elaboration of the Constitution of 1948, after the tensions of the first stage of the Cold War, moved to the socioeconomic arena in the context of the growth during the 50s and 60s, ending in policies of class collaboration that, implicitly or explicitly, were respectively supported by the PCI and the PSI.

The workerists, by denouncing the dominant reformism of the left, pointed out the inherent contradictions of this apparent balance and intended to sustain – objectively and subjectively – a revolutionary stance.

The main contradictions revealed by the workerists were found in the relationship between technology and power, and in the emergence of a new worker figure that was potentially subversive. In the first *workerism* – in the 1960s – the positive reading of technological development, which was proper to the traditional left, was critiqued.

On the contrary, technology was the base of a reconfiguration of the system of domination, and they concluded that the incorporation of scientific innovations into the productive process was a fundamental operation in the re-articulation of the power structures of capital (see Panzieri, 1961: 53–72). This reading extended to society to the extent that:

> At the highest level of capitalist development, the social relation becomes a *moment* of the relation of production, the entire society becomes an articulation of production, that is, the entire society lives according to the factory, and the factory extends its exclusive domination over society as a whole. (Tronti, 1962: 20)

This reading of the *factory-society* derived from the observation of the emergence, in the framework of accelerated industrialization, of *company towns*, the interweaving between factories, cities and working class neighbourhoods in the industrialized north, headquarters of the studies and of the actions of the workerist groups. The transition of the logic of the factory to society was measured by the existence of a State (Toni Negri defined it as 'planning-State') that, under the guise of the mediation between capital and labour, organized exploitation at a social scale.

Aside from exposing the contradictions of a process that intertwined capitalist development, elements of redistribution and extension of control on behalf of capital, the workerists were the first to recognize, during the capitalist expansion of the 1950s and 1960s, in the new composition of the class, the emergence of a subject with a tendency towards insubordination: the so-called *mass worker*. By analysing the mutations in the composition of class, the workerists marked the transition of the centrality of the figure of the professional worker – a worker that maintained certain margins of interference in the productive process insofar as it dealt with a certain technical expertise and abilities – to the emergence of the *mass worker*, the unqualified worker, a simple cog in the assembly line. This analysis was confirmed by the characteristics of the labour struggles that started to appear in the beginning of the 1970s and that were generalized later, led by young workers, immigrants in their majority, recently hired, weakly integrated in the unions and located in the lower echelons of worker hierarchy. Members of a generation whose studies and expectations distanced them from their parents but that still ended up as workers or employees just like them, generating frustrations and rejection towards the valid rules of social integration. These struggles – that appeared for the first time in the confrontations of Piazza Statuto in 1962 – were opposed to the conciliatory attitude of the unions, of the 'worker aristocracy' and proposed a radical rejection of the domination in the factory in which the workers read an anticapitalist revolutionary potential.

These theoretical preoccupations translated into empirical investigation, in the effort to get to know in detail the new worker condition in which this new actor was gestating, whose subversive and antagonistic character called the attention of workerists and refreshed the revolutionary hypotheses. To maintain this effort of investigation and to articulate it with political work, a methodological proposal was made called *conricerca* – a model of participative investigation primarily developed by Romano Alquati – that implied a relationship between the researchers and the workers that allowed a precise and profound knowledge of class and fostered, at the same time, the awareness by the latter.[12]

From the first intuitions and the empirical support that the event offered, workerism set the foundations for a daring proposal of methodological inversion, a 'Copernican revolution' (Turchetto, 2001: 296). In the words of Mario Tronti, one of the most brilliant and contradictory intellectuals of workerism:

We have also seen before the development of capitalism and the labour struggles afterwards. It is a mistake. We must invert the problem, change its bias, and start again at the beginning: and the beginning is the struggle of the working class. (Tronti, 1964a: 1)

He proposed a methodological inversion that opened up an innovative theoretical perspective. In synthesis, for the workerists, understanding capital implied starting at the class struggle and, in particular, from the construction of the antagonistic class, the working class. Capital appeared as the dependent variable: the development of capitalism could be read as a process of permanent adjustment directed at containing labour, the workers that were always a step ahead, liberating themselves at the margins discovered in the system of domination, defying capital, forcing it to change. In this sense, workerism re-established a dialectical reading before the causal logic proper of the Marxism of a great part of the traditional labour movement: not only do the transformations of capitalism determine the constitution of the class *in itself* and *for itself,* but this composition directly impacts upon capital, as form and relation of power. Instead of being a circular vision, the workerist approach enriched the theoretical debate and opened a line of reflection that allowed the understanding of a series of ongoing processes.

This vision bifurcates in the reading of concrete processes. On one hand, objective processes that led to the study of the transformations of capitalism in the second process of the post-World War I – the glorious 1930s – technological development and the Fordist-Taylorist modes of production and their crisis later on. On the other, the accent lay firmly on the subjective dimension, on the worker subjectivity and its closest expression: the conflict in the factory. The workerist idea of *class composition* as correlate of the *composition of capital* enabled the formulation of an articulated reading of the technical and productive processes of transformation in parallel with the political subjective dimension, without subordinating the second to the first. In this sense, the political centrality of the labour class was emphasized from the perspective of struggle; the factory turned into the main space of conflict, a space of domination but also of gestation and deployment of antagonism.

Based on these claims, *workerism* formulated political theses that stood in opposition to those of the PCI and PSI, which already fulfilled the role of the left wing of the Christian Democrat regime.

In the programmatic field, the revolution was radicalizing, transitioning from social struggle to political struggle. In this sequence, the classic theme of wage claims was conceived as an area of rupture, not of negotiation. In the first instance, wage increases needed to be detached from the increases in productivity to break the logic of capital; second, they should lead to guaranteed wages, at the margins of production, outside the rules of the game; third, they should promote wage egalitarianism that would break with the hierarchies and divisions within the factory. On the other hand, the labour struggle should transcend the topics of salary and work conditions to extend to the reappropriation of social wealth in terms of use value: housing, transportation, commodities, etc. Finally, for the workerists, the labour condition implied an ulterior rupture in terms of the work, the so-called *rejection of labour*, the rejection of being a commodity, an absolute estrangement of the worker with respect to the means of production that results in sabotage, absenteeism, and other forms of struggle that looked to give a political way out of alienation. The workerists maintained that worker intelligence should not be dedicated to production but should instead be invested in militancy. The idea of the rejection of labour was in the antipodes of the culture of work that the historic labour movement encouraged, the first aimed at the radicalization of confrontation in terms of the violent overcoming of the capitalist system, the second to a gradual appropriation within the frame of the existing rules in light of an indefinite transition to socialism. Once again, reform and revolution were an antinomy in the grammar of the left.

When the *composition* of the emerging subject was recognized, the lines of conflict demarcated and the political project established, the picture needed to be completed by determining the forms of organization. The workerists were opposed to the Italian traditional left armed with a critique of bureaucratization and the moderation of parties and unions, putting the struggle, class and the movement to the fore. The initial approach was: class determines the strategy, the party deals with the tactics. However, many different interpretations were built on this general formulation and important divisions were produced. In fact, the same experience of the *Quaderni rossi* ended in 1964 with the separation of a majority group headed by Mario Tronti, Toni Negri and Alberto Asor Rosa, who, with other intellectuals and militants, founded *Classe Operaia,* a workerist magazine with a more activist profile that intended to link itself to the more combative labour groups. *Classe Operaia* would end its run in 1967, following another rupture over the same problem of political organization (see Milana and Trotta, 2008).

In synthesis, as will be evident in the diaspora of the 1970s, the debate saw the confrontation of more spontaneist stances – that rejected rigid organizational crystallizations – and more Leninist postures that assumed that the movement necessarily had to imply the existence of a vanguard and, within them, those who preached the transformation of the PCI from within and those who thought of the construction of an *ex novo* revolutionary party. This produced different branches of *workerism*: an important part after the first stage returned to the traditional parties, preaching *entryism* in mass organizations; another component resulted in movementism and merged into *Lotta Continua*; another group chose a vanguard stance giving life to *Potere Operaio* (PO) (see Gramsci, 2003; Balestrini and Moroni, 1997, particularly chapter 7); a small core returned to the source, the micro work in some factories, others dispersed in local experiences.[13] In the 1970s, fragments inherited from *workerism* would be identified as an 'area of autonomy' (see Bianchi and Caminiti, 2007; Wright, 2007). The tension between organization and diffusion of the movement was maintained as an unresolved contradiction.

While this was happening, the country was simmering. Since 1968, the radicalization of the student movement had reinforced *workerism* thanks to the affluence of young militants with intellectual training, and because of the opening of a panorama of struggles that extended from the factories to society. In this opening, the category of *social worker* appeared, proposed by Toni Negri, which substituted the *mass worker*, pointing out the new class composition and the subjective transformations that accompanied the Fordist-Keynesianist crisis and allowed a reading of outsourcing as an extension of wage labour and a process of proletarianization. This transition signals a leap in terms of continuity and rupture between *traditional workerism* and *worker autonomism*.

Since 1969, the *hot autumn* of strikes and factory occupations had shown the force of spontaneous labour struggles. The original constitution of the *Factory Councils* in a first instance surpassed the unions and seemed to constitute the base for the revolutionary organization, the Italian soviets. However, the ebb of the strike movement, linked to the sensitivity and political capacity of the communist unions – particularly the Federazione Impiegati Operai Metalmeccanici (FIOM) and Confederazione Generale Italiana del Lavoro (CGIL) – managed to channel the Councils into the framework of a partially renovated traditional unionism (see Balestrini and Moroni, 1997, particularly chapter 6).

At the end of 1969, with the State attack in Piazza Fontana, the epoch of the *strategy of tension*, a counterrevolutionary project promoted by reactionary political sectors, national and American secret services and neo-fascist groups, whose end was to create a climate of violence and fear that justified repression and fostered the move to the right. Like the massacre of Tlatelolco in Mexico, the 'strategy of tension' and the hardening of the repression led important bands of the movement towards direct confrontation and armed struggle, the critique of arms. Several armed groups made their appearance, among which the *Brigate Rosse* (BR) stood out, some of them directly associated with workerist organizations like *Potere Operaio* whose service of semiclandestine nature would partially converge in the BR at the time of their dissolution in 1973 (see Gramsci, 2003; Galli, 2004).

Since 1973 – emblematic year of the economic crisis, but also of the coup in Chile and the beginning of the communist politics of historical commitment made by Berlinguer – the groups of labour autonomy were growing and taking the streets of the main Italian cities.

In this stream of struggles, autonomism was born. The notion of *autonomy*, according to Franco 'Bifo' Berardi, did not refer only to the independence of the main unions and the political parties but to the rejection of mediation in general, the rejection of the rules that governed all kinds of means of discipline, starting with work. For Bifo, autonomy was configured as an alternative to the traditional concept of revolution, combining the negative idea of abolition of the existing order with the positive creation of spaces of self-determination. In autonomism, precariousness was assumed as a form of freedom, existential claims contained the political, and spontaneity was frontally opposed to Leninism. In this sense, the author himself acknowledges the existence of two axes of the autonomous and pro-autonomy movement, a 'desiring' creative wing – others would call it *diffuse* autonomy – and a political wing organized in struggle against the State (Berardi, (2007: 40–54).

The movement's turning point came in 1977. The new wave of mobilization fed on the multiple facets of a complex and articulated movement that rested on the accumulated experiences and spread in territory and social fabric. With the quantitative growth, spatial extension and the broadening of the organs of diffusion and cultural influence, the slogan of autonomy was fully expressed, not only as autonomy of movement in relation to parties and unions, but as the manifestation of the autonomy of the organized subjects, their capacity to create free spaces, autonomous in relation to the rules of the system. The initiatives of self-management flourished: diaries, radios, magazines, sit-ins, demonstrations, etc. The experience of the struggles had triggered a process of conflictive politicization that left important balances in the constitution of political subjectivities.

At the same time, with radicalization and as a response to the repression, confrontations, attacks, imprisonments, and deaths increased. In this kaleidoscope in which the pieces were diversely interconnected, the strategy of tension achieved its objective and the violence functioned as a turning point: the State used all its legal and extra-legal power, the PCI backed the hard line and ended up supporting the Christian Democrat governments and, finally, the movement broke up, victim of the repression and its own contradictions. (See Balestrini and Moroni, 1997, particularly chapter 10.) The reflux of the social struggles in Italy was announced in 1977 and marked the end of *workerism-autonomism* as a political movement of the masses. In 1978, the kidnapping and execution of Aldo Moro by the BR closed the political cycle definitively.

With polarization in sight, the movement passed to the defensive by taking up the denunciation of the repression as the axis of all political activity. On the other hand, the armed struggle acquired a centrality that displaced mass mobilizations. If the autonomous groups – *in primis Potere Operaio* – had always maintained the need for an armed struggle as condition for revolutionary victory, the strategy and the role of the vanguard remained anchored to the mass movement. With relative demobilization, the armed struggle filled the void but, as Guido Borio points out, it contributed to its increase, giving the sensation of an increase in force that proved to be an illusion while it subtracted forces and elements of a vanguard from the movement itself. The growth of the armed wing facing the emptying of the movement ended up in a separation based on the vanguard delegation, exactly what autonomy had questioned. On the other hand, the armed illusion emerged out of a false assessment: the accumulation of forces in mobilization was irreversible (Borio, 2007). The passage from the 'illegality of the masses' that characterized the street actions to the armed vanguards was lethal for the movement.

Beyond the historicity of the political experience and its antagonistic features, *workerism* would survive as a theoretical school. The first workerist groups of the 1960s were made up of young intellectuals and later – in the 1970s – the spread of workerist thought attracted and formed another generation in the same theoretical vein. Within a context of political formation, workerist thought developed and branched out as a specific theoretical proposal.

Within the wide intellectual universe of workerism, two intellectuals stand out whose participation goes back to the *Quaderni rossi* experience and whose journey goes through the history of the 1960s and 1970s until today. Mario Tronti was undoubtedly – from Panzieri's intuitions – the ideologue of the first stage insofar as his texts – compiled in the classic book *Workers and Capital* (Tronti, 2001) – set down the fundamental principles and constituted the workerist gospel.[14] However, Tronti's trajectory remained within the PCI[15] and, by the 1970s, was oriented towards a theoretical review that partially discarded the original seed of his own thought. His later work in particular – *The Autonomy of the Political* (Tronti, 1977) – was submitted to harsh critiques on behalf of the workerists-autonomists that – loyal to the traditional line – rejected any concession to institutional mediations, including the traditional leftist parties.

The other emblematic intellectual of workerism is Antonio 'Toni' Negri – who since the 1960s had managed to articulate a solid political core in the northeast, with a relevant labour base in the petrochemical industry of Porto Marghera – would become the main ideologue of worker autonomism in the 1960s. In fact, in this decade, the main slogan – autonomy – would come from his work and would be adopted as the denomination of the movement: Worker Autonomy.

If creation of the foundations is owed to Tronti, the most audacious and most finished developments of workerist thought in its autonomist translation must be attributed to Negri. It would be Toni Negri who would adopt and develop the concept of *antagonism* as the fundamental piece of a theoretical body oriented towards understanding the subjective anticapitalist configuration. In a way, in keeping with the experiences of politicization, mobilization and radicalization – the processes of antagonistic subjectivation derived from the experiences of insubordination during these years – he was an intellectual of the time, symptomatic and synthetic, the theoretical spokesman of a political expression of the crisis of these years.

At the same time, as we will see, the scope and meaning of the concept of *antagonism* was modified throughout the intense intellectual trajectory of this prolific author.

In effect, even when Antonio Negri is known globally in terms of the *autonomist* movement and thought, we will see in the following pages how the concept of *antagonism* constitutes the fundamental element of his theoretical reflection in the 1960s, while the notion of *autonomy*, undoubtedly relevant and complementary in these years, will grow until it becomes the axial concept of the new course of his thought beginning in the 1980s.

Antagonistic Subjectivation in the Work of Antonio Negri in the 1970s

Since the 1960s, Antonio Negri wrote diverse texts on the philosophy of law besides the numerous theoretical-political articles in *Quaderni rossi* and *Classe Operaia*. However, it would be in the 1970s – which coincided with the attainment of a chair at Padua University – when he would systematically develop a political thought and original theoretical proposal, anchored in the workerist matrix but extended towards an autonomist perspective.

In the writings of the 1970s in full deployment of the movement, in his role as ideologue and political leader first of *Potere Operaio* and later of other workerist and autonomist groups, Negri advances a set of ideas within which the concepts of *antagonism* and *autonomy* are highlighted as pillars of a Marxist reflection on the revolutionary subject. Let us follow the development of this reflection with a chronological itinerary of the texts of this decade.

Since 1971, in *Crisis of the Planner-State* – a text in which Negri characterizes the Keynesian State and glimpses its crisis – he starts using the concept of *antagonism* to designate the form and the main characteristic of the emergence of the *social worker*, successor of the Fordist *mass worker*, while still using it as synonym of structural conflict, of an objective dynamic. Following the typically workerist preoccupation with the *political composition and recomposition of class*, Negri calls the subject that is configured in conflict *antagonistic*:

The acceptance of the polarity of the tendency, of its capacity for contradiction and the possibility to turn it into antagonism, in revolutionary process and in insurrectional initiative, does not constitute any hypostatic procedure in terms of the analysed reality, but it is the presupposition of any meaningful analysis. Objective truth does not exist in principle: it must be built in the struggle, for the struggle, for the transformation of praxis. (Negri, 2004a: 50–1)

In this passage, Negri establishes a difference between the notion of *polarity* – as objective, structural meaning – and *antagonism* – as initiative and praxis – a distinction that is formulated as a passage from 'contradiction to antagonism'. A subjective use of the concept that will be developed throughout later texts is outlined in it.

In 1975 in *Proletarians and the State*, within the critical analysis of the politics of 'historical commitment' promoted by the Secretary General of the PCI, Enrico Berlinguer, and the theses on 'the autonomy of the political' developed by Mario Tronti, the concept of *antagonism* – even in its classic use – reappears as an analytical instrument oriented towards the definition of the sociopolitical subject:

The system of needs is substituted by the system of struggles: an alternative system of struggles that knows how to be the antagonistic reappropriation of the productive forces for the proletarian subject, as living social work ...

To destroy the collective negotiation of the agreement is to destroy the last plane of the capitalist manipulation of needs and, thus, from that moment on, to face the discovery of the struggle against the system as such, the discovery of that field of revolutionary appropriation, antagonistic, which is currently the existence of the proletariat and its hope. (Negri, 2004e: 207, 210)

The association between the concept of *antagonism* and the idea of *appropriation* that, in Negri's thought is synonymous with *self-valorization* – the retention of the use value and the productive capacity on behalf of the workers – is particularly relevant in these passages. It is understood as the positive counterpart to the *rejection of work*, the antagonistic activity *par excellence* insofar as it breaks the domination of capital and, with it, expresses worker autonomy.

In this text, autonomy is presented as a material (as self-valorization) and structural result of stages of confrontation with institutions (State and factory) in which contradictions become *antagonism*, qualitative aspects of conflict, a specific form of worker subjectivity, experience of insubordination.

In a text inspired by Lenin, the extension to the subjective plane of the notion of *antagonism* becomes more explicit, as is demonstrated in the following text:

> Nevertheless, if the constitution of the capitalist State changes materially, it is due to the fact that, imminently, the State must assume a similar process: the constitution of the insubordinate proletarian subject. If up until now the analysis has made us understand the formal possibility of antagonism in completely objective terms and, thus, has helped us to understand the need for the constitutional mutation of the capital, from now on we are interested in analysing another aspect, that is, how the subversive subject is constituted, continually remodelling itself in this process. The formal possibilities of antagonism in the reproduction-circulation of capital refer us to the effective consideration of the expression of worker antagonism within and against the reproduction of capital. From the anatomy of reproduction to the physiology of the worker struggle. (Negri, 2004b: 252)

From this view, Negri investigates and emphasizes the 'antagonistic character' and the 'antagonistic potentialities' of the masses, taking antagonism as a qualitative substantial element of worker subjectivity, whose existence and dimensions is related to the experience of the transforming potential of which it is a carrier and the real impact it causes on exploitation and the relationship of domination. The sequence between *proletarian independence, self-valorization* and *counterpower* allows him to argue the formation of a new composition of working class (*recomposition*) in these years and the formation and affirmation of a subversive and insubordinate subjectivity: the *social worker*.

However, in spite of the clarity of the displacement of the concept towards the subjective, by understanding antagonism as valorization and liberation of living labour, the concept tends to get confused with that of *autonomy*. Antagonism and autonomy appear simultaneously as starting point, process and purpose. They designate the same argumentative texts and the same concrete referents with a specific emphasis. At the same time, beyond the explanation of the subjective emphasis, the concept of *antagonism* starts to get used with such frequency that it becomes an omnipresent element in discourse – a *passé-partout* – that is still variously used as a simple synonym of conflict and struggle or as contradiction. Thus it appears as: 'class antagonism', 'between capital and work', as 'antagonistic relations', 'antagonistic form of the entire process', 'antagonistic mechanisms', 'antagonistic contents', 'antagonism between economic forms and institutional forms' or 'fundamental antagonistic contradiction: that which is determined between the organization and power of command, between the process of work and the process of valuation' (ibid.: 256–63).

In 1977, while the Italian movement was in boom, Negri published a set of lectures on Lenin's thought – *The Factory of Strategy* – in which he significantly advanced on his subjectivist interpretation of Marxism:

> For each historical stage of the class struggle we must elaborate a definition of the composition of the working class that includes not only its general situation within the mode of production, but also the set of experiences of struggle, behaviours and the way in which fundamental, vital, needs are renovated and defined each time in a new way. Marxist thought is confronted with this object as its real referent: the object of Marxism is the constitution, modification and recomposition of this subject because – and we must always have this present – the true relationships of force can only be measured within this subject. (Negri, 2004d: 22)

The selective recovery of Lenin's thought on behalf of Negri focuses on some issues that fertilize his own intellectual political project. He insists on the continuity between economic struggle and political struggle to uphold the subversive potential of factory conflicts, he underlines the idea of 'leap' as acceleration of historical processes to underpin a revolutionary perspective and the possibility of insurrection. In another item, he freely recovers the idea of *organization* as a condition for strategic action, Leninist preoccupation *par excellence*, opposing – with

Lenin – the ideas of *organization-process*, *struggle-process* and *direction-process* to highlight the party as mediation between spontaneity and direction and as instrument of management of workers' power. On the other hand, Negri emphasizes and exalts a double Leninist sequence: class composition-organization-insurrection and vice versa. Obviously, underpinning the theses elaborated in *Potere Operaio*, Negri takes up the insistence in the abolition of the State from Lenin, he even rejects the hypothesis of the 'transition to socialism' in favor of the immediate establishment of communism. Lastly, a methodological aspect that Negri recovers from Lenin for his own ends is the 'determined social formation' and 'determined abstraction' that allows him to retake the Marxist idea of *tendency* – that implies recognizing the dynamic and potentially dominant element of a social formation as an overdetermining form that characterizes the process qualitatively, orienting its course and glimpsing its outcome. The use of this methodological device – already present in prior works – will be a constant throughout his work.

In terms of the categories that interest us, the concepts retain a traditional use: *autonomy* appears as synonym of *class independence* and *antagonism* as synonym of *conflict* or *contradiction* between capital and work. At the same time, there are two relevant emphases. In the first place, Negri insists on the need for proletarian autonomy (independence) that excludes alliances with the related popular classes, recovering an issue laid out in a polemical editorial in *Classe Operaia*, 'Operai senza alleati', workers without allies (Negri, 1964: 1, 18). In the second place, he differentiates mere antagonistic activity from 'communist creation', which could be read as a characterization of antagonism as a negative form or force, eminently destructive and a possible distinction from autonomy, self-valorization as emancipatory process.

In 1978 Negri's thought experiences an important moment of development and explanation in an essay entitled *Dominion and Sabotage*. Says Negri (2004c: 290]: 'I am being called upon again to admit the preponderance of the subjective hypothesis that we have proposed at the beginning when explaining the current dialectic of capital.'[16]

Throughout its pages, the subjective meaning of the concept of *antagonism* appears repeatedly: 'the antagonistic components of the proletariat', 'the antagonistic meaning, though not the reality, of the worker movement' (ibid.: 283), 'the antagonistic content of the struggles' (ibid.: 308), 'The radically antagonistic potential of the processes of worker self-valorization' (ibid.: 306). In other texts, he exalts the 'antagonistic independence', 'the antagonistic project' (ibid.: 326), 'the antagonistic characteristics of the workers' power' (ibid.: 307), and 'the antagonistic, subversive force of the project of worker self-valorization', with which he establishes a circular relationship, ontological and genealogical between the terms by saying that autonomy is antagonistic – antagonistic independence (ibid.: 319) – and assuming that antagonism produces autonomy and vice versa, in an uninterrupted coming and going.

The subjective establishment of the concept is unequivocal even when it simply appears as mere synonym of 'revolutionary potential', which expresses the incorporation of conflict, the experience of struggle and insubordination as the constituent form of the subject and the countervailing power as its expression or direct manifestation.

On the other hand, the idea of *autonomy* is expressed in this text not just in terms of *independence* but of *separation*:

The process of the constitution of independence of class is today, before anything else, a process of separation …

The constitution of the independence of class develops, before anything, in its separation. But separation means, in this case, rupture with the capital relation. It also means that, by reaching the maximum point of socialization, the working class breaks the laws of the social mediation of capital. (ibid.: 287, 290)

The autonomous rupture is marked by the process of *self-valorization* of live work that implies the exit of the exchange value and the recovery of the use value with which 'the mechanisms of reproduction of capital and the mechanisms of reproduction of the working class stop working synchronically' (ibid.: 298). If the 'separation' outlines the territory of autonomy, the process of 'separation', that is, the construction of autonomy appears as the specific arena of antagonism.

The other fundamental idea that appears in this text is that of *sabotage* as a concrete manifestation of worker self-valorization: 'Self-valorization is sabotage' (ibid.: 309). It is defined as 'continuous activity as sniper, as saboteur, as absentee, as deviant, as criminal' (ibid.: 311), which operates the separation and its positive counterpart, class solidarity. The reduction of the work schedule appears as key for self-valorization insofar as it liberates spaces for the emancipation processes. In this sense, autonomy is a destructive force and is superimposed on the notion of *antagonism* as *insubordination*.

Another slippery affirmation appears here that will remain at the center of Negri's thought, who maintains that the 'logic of separation' produces a confronted double autonomy: that of the capitalist power and that of worker power. The hypotheses of exteriority and interiority in the relation of domination are superimposed; the relation itself is affirmed and denied.

In *Dominion and Sabotage* another fundamental piece of Negri's thought is developed: the rejection of work. This is done under the guise of sabotage, strike, direct action:

> The rejection of work as content of the process of self-valorization. Beware: content does not mean objective. The objective, the finality of the process of self-valorization is the total liberation of live work, in production and in reproduction; it is the total use of the wealth at the service of collective freedom. It is, therefore, something more than rejection of work that, anyway, covers the fundamental space of the transition, characterizes its dialectic and establishes its rules. Rejection of work, then, is still a moment of the process of self-valorization in its destructive relation with the law of value, with its crisis, with the enforceability of productive work for all society. That everybody has to work, in the society based on self-valoriza-tion, in the transition phase, is a rule that concerns the rejection of work exactly as it concerns the programme of the reduction of the work schedule, of the work obligatory to reproduction and transformation. (ibid.: 322)

Thus, self-valorization is the vector of emancipation and manifests itself as antagonism. This approach credits a notion of *relative* and *non-absolute* autonomy. At the same time it advances the idea of the 'destructive relationship' as the synthesis of antagonism and autonomy, of interiority and exteriority, as negative dialectic.

Even though he insists on the negative, destructive dimension of antagonism and self-valorization (autonomy), Negri adds a constructive counterpart, 'a positive measure of non-work', that he calls *invention*, 'the qualitative determination of a mode of production not dominated anymore by the categories of capital' (ibid.: 322–3). On the other hand, throughout the approach there is confusion when autonomy appears as an ontological quality in itself and not as the product of antagonism but as its producer, and thus pre-existing. We shall see more of this inclination in Negri's later work.

In effect, while Negri does not plainly make clear the relationship it is possible to assume that, beyond the superimposition, antagonism refers to the relational character of the process of subjectivation that derives from the experience of insubordination while autonomy refers to the relatively free condition that makes struggle possible, the assumption of the irreducible freedom of living labour and the process of emancipation that this, in its self-valorization, keeps maintaining. In this sense, autonomy would be positioned at the beginning of a sequence; it would be the data from which antagonism is generated even if it leads to the deepening of autonomy by reiterating the sequence *ad infinitum*. At heart, this is the base of all workerist and autonomist thought: the principle of worker autonomy as platform of all antagonist and emancipatory process.

In terms of the party, Negri maintains its necessity as expression of the consolidation of separation, as instrument and not as end, as antagonistic tool:

> The answer must necessarily be situated within the logic of separation: the party is a function of the proletarian force to guarantee the process of self-valorization. The party is the army that defends the borders of proletarian independence. And naturally should not, cannot get involved in the internal management of self-valorization. The party is not a direct counterpower, radical, implanted in the materialness of self-valorization. It is a function of power, but separate, at times contradictory with the process of self-valorization. The party, if you will, is a religious combative order, but not the ecclesial totality of the process. (ibid.: 328)

The difference with Gramsci here is clear, for whom the party was the most finished expression of autonomy understood as class independence, whereas for Negri it is an instrument of the process of emancipation that is conducted through antagonism and self-valorization. It is an instrument of defence and promotion of antagonism and self-valorization, which refer in the last instance to subjectivity, to class in its real composition above its transitory political forms.

On the other hand, in *Dominion and Sabotage* Negri approaches the theme of violence as antagonistic rupture and the production of autonomy:

> For us, violence is presented always as synthesis: of form and content. Above all, as expression of the proletarian counterpower, as manifestation of the process of self-valorization. Later, to the exterior, as a destructuring and destabilizing force. Therefore, as productive force and as anti-institutional force. (ibid.: 333)

This passage textually exemplifies the ambiguity. It is not clear whether Negri assumes the identity, the distinction or what type of articulation there is between self-valorization (autonomy) and antagonism (counterpower), between the inside of production and the outside of the political struggle. This oscillating tension between interiority and exteriority crosses his thoughts.

Finally, Negri concludes this essay with a page on sabotage that seems to clear up the relationship:

> Sabotage is, therefore, the fundamental key to rationality that we possess at this level of class composition. A key that allows us to reveal the processes through which the crisis of the law of value has progressively impregnated the entire structure of capitalist power, depriving it of all internal rationality and forcing it to turn into an efficient spectacle of dominion and destruction. A key that allows us, on the other hand, to identify the rhythm of capitalist disintegration (though not in a homologous way), the capacity of the proletarian struggle to become independent, to proceed to the process of its own self-valorization, in order to transform the rejection of work according to the process of liberation. (ibid.: 336)

In this formulation, antagonism (proletarian struggle, rejection of work) precedes autonomy (self-valorization, liberation). However, as we have seen, this logical sequence is inverted in other moments of Negri's thoughts.

In 1978, Negri strengthens the ideas presented in *Dominion and Sabotage* in the Marxian field with an eminently theoretical text on the *Grundrisse* – *Marx Beyond Marx* (Negri, 2001) – the product of a seminary he taught at the École Normale Supérieure de Rue d'Ulm in Paris, an academic sanctuary for Althusserians and a great part of French Maoism.

Negri finds in the *Grundrisse* the bases of *antagonistic subjectivity* that he promotes insofar as labour does not appear in them as a 'simple antagonistic pole but rather as a revolutionary class'. From this angle, according to Negri, Marx traces the appearance of the subject-class at the heart of the capitalist process. In this direction, Negri puts forward a reading of Marx that allows him to emphasize the separation and the conflict that the working class achieves by the rejection of work – as denial of the power of command of capital – liberating time inside and outside the labour process, self-valorizing itself in the struggle, understood directly as 'affirmation of communism'. In this sense, Negri ends up defining Marxism as the science of crisis and subversion, a science where contradiction becomes antagonism and in which subjectivity cannot be reduced to exploitation.

However, despite his claim to theoretically establish this proposal, the use of the notion of antagonism expands to the point of hypertrophy. Throughout the pages, it appears incessantly to name a wide series of phenomena – objective and subjective – and turn them into the signifier of the totality, the movement and engine of history. Let us look at a significant passage of this categorical hypertrophy:

> You just need to stop here to understand that the categories of the Marxist method are, at this happy moment of the foundation of the system, at their most mature: mature, above all, in the sense of an antagonistic and dynamized foundation, where antagonism is the motor of the development of the system, the foundation of a continuous resurgence of antagonism each time the project, the history of capital, progresses. All materialist objectivism also disappears: the relationship is open insofar as it is founded in

antagonism. One can, justifiably, object that here, nevertheless, the development of contradiction – and the deepening of its antagonism – stays at the level of capital, at the level of the categories of capital and development, and that – consequently – the subjective component of the process is underestimated. (ibid.: 69)

However, beyond the exhaustive use and the subsequent lack of precision and conceptual specificity, Negri again shows labour as activity rather than commodity, as source of value rather than value, and he presents use value as a subjective force. In this sense, he still thinks of antagonism as a subjective dimension, as the central aspect of the subjectivation of work. We will look at two revealing texts dealing with the tension between autonomist rupture and the antagonistic relation:

This antagonism has its origin in the relationship of schism between the use value and the exchange value – a relationship of schism in which two tendencies are liberated from the forced unity to which they have been submitted: on the one hand, exchange value is autonomized in money and capital, and on the other, use value is autonomized as working class...

We must see in these two spaces the formation of opposing subjectivities, opposing wills and intellects, opposed valorization processes: in sum, an antagonistic dynamic required for the development of those conditions we have considered until now. A theory of the subjectivity of the working class and the proletariat constitutes, then, a presupposition and a task vis-à-vis the theory of profit, opposing the reality of this robbed surplus labour, objectified, socialized, with which capital has simultaneously reached its own unification as class and the control of exploitation. The Grundrisse show a theory of subjectivity of the working class confronted by the beneficial theory of capitalist subjectivity. (ibid.: 88–9, 111)

By stating the idea of an antagonism between two autonomous entities – capital and working class – there exists a possible conceptual confusion, which raises the question: are they interdependent insofar as they antagonistically interact or are they independent? At least it is not clear that autonomy is an unfinished process and not a given quality. What would the relationship between autonomic rupture and antagonistic relationship be? The notion of 'relationship of schism' does not appear sufficient to solve the enigma of the superimposition of antagonism and autonomy and to establish the terms of their articulation. The fact that it assumes that 'the trajectory of subjectivity is totally internal to the capital relation, does not deceive itself thinking it has alternatives, but in the development of its separation it can destroy the relationship' (ibid.: 169), confirms that Negri navigates with two interpretative hypotheses – separation and relationship. Besides acknowledging the antagonistic interiority, which is the same as the autonomic exteriority, two qualitative moments within the *continuum* of the process are distinguished – separation and destruction – implicitly admitting that throughout the process of autonomic rupture the antagonist relationship is maintained.

In *Marx Beyond Marx*, while Negri reaffirms the workerist principle that the class struggle drives capital, he maintains that the constituent process of worker subjectivity and its transformative scope is irreversible – even though it can be hindered and temporarily blocked. Once more, in his argument, Negri resorts to the method of tendency:

All this demonstrates, to me, that communism – the communist reality of class composition – anticipates and conditions the forms that capitalist development will acquire. Communism appears, in its role of dynamic and constituent element, as the engine and force that destroy capitalist development. All the dynamics indicated by Marx – that we have seen in the last movements of the Grundrisse and that represent the initial articulation of the process in development – all these dynamics find here their conclusion. The contradiction is no longer indicated but it is current: its terms are antagonistic and, furthermore, their separation, their difference and development, contrary. The conditioning that self-valorization imposes upon capitalist development is no longer an effect of the dialectic resolved within capitalist relations; on the contrary, it is a true conditioning, a logic imposed on the adversary through positions of force – separate positions that are self-determined. We can advance 'beyond Marx' on this road that Marx indicates since the first pebbles. But once we have leapt, the image of the fulfilment of communism, its dynamic, has such strong connotations we have to repeat ourselves despite our incredulity: yes, we have come beyond Marx.

This point of view is that of antagonism, where overcoming the obstacle does not tend to create new limits but to develop the use value and the force of live work more fully. In this passage, with this method, the worker subjectivity transforms into the revolutionary class, the universal class. In this passage the constituent process of communism finds its total development. We must immediately underline that in this light, the antagonistic logic stops having a binary rhythm, stops accepting the fantastic reality of the adversary on its horizon. It rejects any binary formula. The antagonistic process tends here towards hegemony, tends to destroy and suppress its adversary. (ibid.: 207, 210)

This shows a synthesis of Negri's theoretical trajectory in the 1970s. Communist anticipation as a dynamic factor, the subjectivized contradiction in antagonism, the denial of dialectic, the tendency towards the constituent separation of the autonomy of live work, by which it is imposed upon capital, creating the conditions for the revolution. At the same time, with them, the backdrop of conceptual ambiguity becomes evident: worker autonomy is arbitrarily imposed and antagonism stops being a relational frame but a unilateral process. On the other hand, the hypothesis is confirmed that, in logical terms, autonomy is the condition for the emergence of antagonism, even though this later becomes the vector of autonomization.

Conclusion

In Negri's intellectual trajectory during the 1970s, beyond the validity of his conclusions and the rigour in the use of the categories throughout his texts, we must recognize and emphasize an original theoretical reflection and the development of the concept of *antagonism* in a subjective sense that allows us to recognize, identify and name the process of construction of subjectivities in conflict, interiorization or incorporation of the struggle and insubordination as experiences and as factors of subjectivation, of dialogue between social being and social consciousness, of formation of a 'disposition to act as a class'. In this sense, antagonism would be the characteristic trait of conflictive subjectivity, that is, the matrix of configuration of the subjective aspects forged in the heat of the struggle and through the experience of insubordination, at the crossroads between spontaneity and consciousness. Thus, Negri theoretically deploys the subjective connotations of the concept of *antagonism* according to the implications present in Marx and Engel's *Manifesto* and counter to the relative structural anchoring in which it had been maintained, in line with the use in *Capital*, in the lexicon of contemporary Marxists. With Negri, the notion of *antagonistic subjectivity* or *antagonism* as subjectivation acquires density and positions itself theoretically, assuming a specific connotation. From this perspective, it is possible to use the concept as a tool of analysis of the processes of political subjectivation.

The implied limit in Negri's approach – besides the problems already pointed out and in particular the superimposition and oscillation of the concepts – derives from his comprehensive zeal, from the intention of reducing to antagonistic subjectivation the ensemble of the process of formation of subjectivity, the hypertrophy of the concept and the *essentialism* that synthesizes in the struggle the moment and shape of the sociopolitical subject without considering that, besides the conflict, domination does not disappear in the moments of struggle; it reappears at every pause between them and, in its core and through it, subjectivities are configured from the relationship of subalternity. While it is true that Negri contemplates, by the notion of *autonomy*, the subjective dynamics derived from experiences and practices of emancipation, we have seen how the emphasis, the aim and the heart of the theoretical perspective he elaborates focus on conflict, struggle and the corresponding subjectivation processes. Put differently, autonomy does not acquire the specificity of designating the subjectivation of the experience of emancipation, instead it presents itself as data or process, as an assumption that feeds, stirs up the conflict, the struggle, antagonism, which appears as the data or subjective process *par excellence*. Deep down for Negri, autonomy – theoretically and politically – is the condition that permits and justifies antagonism, more than the opposite. Formulated in other terms, the (relatively) free condition of work spills into its capacity for insubordination, in which it expresses its subjective experience. The exteriority derived from the separation is tends to be imposed on the interiority of the relationship. Thus, there is no place for the notion of *subalternity* or an equivalent, insofar as it fully expresses the interiority of the subjective construction of the relation of domination. As we shall see when we review Negri's later work, antagonism, by subordinating to autonomy, tends to get fixed, losing its process-based character, turning into a property, a quality, an intrinsic datum of the subject instead of designating the incorporation of practices and experiences in the frame of the process of subjectivation.

However, beyond these limits and the subsequent vicissitudes of the concepts of *antagonism* and *autonomy* throughout Negri's later work, it is unquestionable that his development in the works of the 1970s configures a significant contribution to Marxist thought: the perspective of antagonistic subjectivation. In this meaning, the category is situated at the level of *subalternity* and *autonomy* and potentially configures an analytical triad able to apprehend the different dimensions that, synchronically and diachronically, constitute the political subjectivities in the process of permanent formation.

In addition to this sense and the corresponding perspective, one must register that the concept of *antagonism* is far from being an object of consensus and its theoretical status appears questionable. In effect, it has a fluctuating meaning even among the few authors that adopt it as a central piece of their theoretical reflection. On one hand, the persistence of its frequent use within Marxist studies is notable, as synonym of *conflict, contradiction* on a structural or objective plane. On the other, the rare attempts at displacement of the field of analysis of the conformation of subjectivities tend to go beyond the Marxist theoretical framework.

In the following section we will review other perspectives of the development and use of the concept of *antagonism,* not so much for the ends of categorical configuration we are interested in but rather for two parallel objectives: to broaden the study of the later categorical development advanced by Negri and, with that, to emphasize the specificity of the previous definition.

Excursus: Antagonism in Negri's Work from the 1980s until the Present

In this section, following Negri's work from the 1980s up to now, we will follow the displacement that the concept antagonism goes through in itself and in relation to that of *autonomy*, corroborating, along the way, some hypotheses that were previously outlined.

In the 1980s, coinciding with the ebb of the social struggles, Negri starts a cycle of reflections that, between continuity and discontinuity, move the sense of the notions of *antagonism* and *autonomy* towards new theoretical horizons. In particular, we will demonstrate how the perspective of autonomy absorbs that of antagonism, which results in an autonomist essentialism.

Since 1982, in *Máquina tiempo* (Negri, 2006c), the central theme becomes the (new) 'context of antagonism', the passage from *formal subsumption* to the *real subsumption* of labour to capital, understood as the framework of a puzzle that requires a new paradigm. Stating the need to overcome the 'old categories', Negri defined the antagonistic subject as a 'multiple collective complexity' (ibid.: 118). However, even in this opening to diversity, the concept of *antagonism* is still formulated in relation to the theme of class. Referring to Thompson, Negri opens the concept of class by basing it on 'the complexity, ... the differences, and the multiplicity of the struggles and of the antagonistic behaviours we truly verified'.[17] The opposition between *unity* and *multiplicity* starts to cause tension with the concept of *antagonism*.

On the other hand, the passage to real subsumption leads Negri to speak of the 'coextensiveness of the subjects', of the end of antagonism (counterpowers) in the State-form.

> ... given the real subsumption of labour on behalf of capital, the logic of antagonism proposed the absolute separation, the definition of two totalities that lacked relation. On one hand the totality of the State, as a whole one can only describe with criteria of systematic inference; on the other, the proletarian totality, that can only be described as process of self-valorization, as ontologically stabilized and concluded separation. To the system of power is opposed the genealogy of prowess. (ibid.: 42)

The end of antagonism in the State-form exalts the logic of separation above the logic of the relationship. Autonomy prevails over antagonism and it, by being subordinated, loses its own explanatory scope even though it does not disappear as an analytical referent. It does not disappear because the antagonistic relationship and its weight in the subjective configuration come back through the window after being thrown out the door. They return, for example, in the disputes between the time of capital and the time of liberation as distinct and countervailing temporal practices.[18] The constitution of time is assumed as a collective essence, as a constituent machine of the subject:

> At this point, antagonism explodes. The time of cooperation is constituted as subject against capital. It is use value. It is the beginning of crisis, latent or effective, but always the beginning of crisis. In Marxian literature use value is frequently interpreted as a naturalist foundation or a mere function of exchange value. These conceptions were still possible, alternatively or ambiguously, before the step to real subsumption. In the phase of subsumption, time is presented as collective substance of value and as antagonistic subject. (ibid.: 122)

The concept of *antagonism* blows up and starts the dissolution of the antagonistic subject even though Negri continues to link, in the last instance, by ontological vocation, time to the class struggle, that is, 'the negative work of the proletarian self-valorization' within the frame of real subsumption, of the fusion between production and reproduction, where the working day corresponds to the vital workday and the quality of life is juxtaposed against the quantity of work.

> Here, then, more than work, we insist on its negative worth but we direct attention to one issue: to highlight, in the independence of the negative, in the antagonistic autonomy of cooperation, that specifically economic moment, that is, of compensation of the human search for material wealth and of intellectual perfection that transforms the negative work into work of self-valorization. (ibid.: 148)

Cooperation appears as a pillar of self-valorization instead of the rejection of work: *antagonistic autonomy displaces autonomic antagonism*. The separation consumes the relationship, exteriority kills interiority. The enigma of the superimposition is solved clearly in favour of the primacy of autonomy.

We must point out that in Negri's thought of the 1980s there is the influence of Spinoza (see Negri, 1981), and antagonism is linked – or subordinated – to the idea of *potency*, which credits the theoretical priority of autonomy versus antagonism, insofar as the mediation of counterpower does not appear between *protests* and *potency*. In fact, taking potency as a counterpower denies the specificity of the counterpower, that is, it confuses it with and superimposes it upon the *power to do*.

> The real is a context of countervailing powers. The subject is configured as a counterpower. But it would be better to say as potency, as counterpotency, to define the inherency of antagonism to the definition of potency itself. (Negri, 2006b: 285)

This is confirmed to the extent in which the works of the 1980s, antagonism – always oscillating between dualism and monism – stops being an object of analysis in itself or a central problem, but an assumption that crosses and constitutes a frame of analysis, a principle of conflict that moves the process but is no longer the constituent element, the matrix of conformation of subjectivity.

In the 1990s, Negri will make another leap in continuity. In 1991, along with Maurizio Lazzarato he will launch the concept of *immaterial work* that recovers, develops and exceeds the category of *social worker*, which had already substituted for the *mass worker* in the mid 1970s in order to capture the transformations introduced by the new forms of production, particularly the loss of centrality of the Fordist factory (Lazzarato and Negri, 2001[19]). Using once again the method of *tendency*, Negri maintains the emergence since the 1970s of the centrality and the tendential hegemony of the immaterial, cognitive and qualitative worker, dedicated to jobs of 'control, management of information, of capacities of decision that asks for the investiture of subjectivity' (ibid.). Subjectivity becomes force and source of production and capital attempts to control, to command. However, for Negri, immaterial work gives rise to an autonomous subject – 'able to organize its own work and relationships with the company' (ibid.).

Starting from the Marxian notion of *general intellect* that appears in the *Grundrisse*, Negri maintains the emergence of a new force:

Work is integrally transformed into immaterial work and the labour force into 'mass intellectuality' (the two aspects that Marx calls *General Intellect*). Mass intellectuality can transform into a politically hegemonic social subject. (ibid.)

A paragraph reveals the paradigmatic leap already present in previous texts:

When we say that this new force cannot be defined within a dialectic relation, we mean that the relationship this has with capital is not just antagonistic, but it is beyond antagonism, it is alternative, constituent of a different social reality. Antagonism is presented as the form of a constituent power that is revealed as alternative to the existing forms of power. The alternative is the product of two independent subjects, that is, it is formed in the plane of potency, and not just power. Antagonism cannot be solved by staying in the field of contradiction, but when it manages to end up in an independent, autonomous constitution. The old antagonism of societies established a continuous relationship, even in opposition, between the antagonistic subjects and, as a consequence, imagined the passage of a situation of power, given that victory of antagonistic forces, as a 'transition'. In postindustrial societies, where the *General Intellect* is hegemonic, there is no place for the concept of 'transition', but there is for the concept of 'constituent power' as a radical expression of the new. The antagonistic constitution is thus no longer determined from the data of the capitalist relation because it breaks with it, not from wage labour but from its dissolution, not on the basis of work figures, but from those of non- work. (ibid.)

The rupture of the relation that was, *in nuce*, in previous thought, becomes reality. Autonomy goes beyond antagonism not just as process but it skips the moment of antagonism and no longer dwells there: the subject is not constructed in conflict, does not base its autonomy in struggle. Autonomy is given, independence is an originating genetic feature that develops over time and shapes the subject.

In this sense, Negri reorients the analysis assuming that in the postindustrial society contradictions between workers and capitalists are no longer relevant, but 'the autonomous processes of constitution of alternative subjectivity, of independent organization of workers' are (ibid.). This exteriority leads to a modification of the concept of *revolution* that is based on the *ontological potency* of the subjects, and is self-sufficient to transform reality. The change of paradigm modifies the essence of power that becomes a 'politics of communication', a 'struggle for the control or liberation of the subject of communication.' Thus, transformation, liberation lies in the autonomous and constituent potency of the subjects that reappropriates the 'machine of communication' and, from it, develops the subjects themselves.

In 1992, in *Constituent Power*, Negri continues his reflection on the State and the law – which subsequently will give life to *Empire* – critiquing the idea of sovereignty and of the sovereign to maintain the idea of a constituent subject opposing the constituted (see Negri, 2002). The constituent subject is seen as the head of the *potency*, understood as revolution, rebellion, resistance, and transformation. The axis of reasoning is woven around the displacement from the structure to the subject (this is how the sequence Empire-Multitude will be justified). The constituent power is, for Negri, a synonym of communism to the extent it embodies Marx's definition of 'the real movement that voids the existing state of things'. The extended and uninterrupted character of the transformation it involves makes Negri define it as a 'permanent revolution', although it is legitimate to ask if it does not blur the principle of rupture and the temporal condensation that characterizes the idea of revolution in Marxist thought.

Old and new Negrian categories appear surrounding *constituent power*. Constituent power is living labour, cooperation, creativity, potency, autonomy, a multitude of subjectivities. It is, ontologically, subject to the margin of the process, of all antagonistic configurations, which will eventually appear in a second moment as an epiphenomenon, as a derivation of the autonomy and function of its establishment and development. The political is defined as ontological potency of a 'multitude of cooperating singularities' and the constituent sabotage of the crowd proclaimed as a horizon of transformation (ibid.: 411). Displaced from the centre of the analysis, removed from the heart of subjective configuration, the notion of antagonism appears simply as a synonym of conflict, of juxtaposition (see, for example, ibid.: 246, 274).

In 1995, in *The Labour of Dionysus*, written with Michael Hardt (Hardt and Negri, 2003[20]), Negri takes up once more the set of more recent conceptual tools and, in the first part,[21] he addresses again the classic themes of self-valorization and antagonism in an attempt to articulate – without much success – new and old problems, new and old categorical devices, and shows that these have been clearly displaced in analysis by the more recent approaches and categories. The most relevant passages for the purposes of this genealogy refer to the considerations on the displacement of 'social antagonisms' in the State by civil society – proper to the previous stage – to the extinction of civil society to the extent that 'the State is not interested in mediation but separation', which marks the passage of disciplinary societies into control societies.

On the other hand, there are some previous theses that reappear in a radicalized manner. For example, the liberation of work in post Fordism is assumed when there are no factories or capitalist power. New forms of the exploitation of immaterial work are mentioned, controlled from the exterior by the capitalist power; yet Negri does not stop assuming – as a tendency – the potency of cooperation and subjectivities outside the machinations of capital and by 'completely autonomous processes of self-valorization'. The *exodus* is exalted as a process that tends to the configuration of 'constituent power' and enacts the 'definitive separation of the two subjects', work and capital (ibid.: 107).

Thus, the appearance of a 'new political subject: the social proletariat organized in immaterial and productive work thanks to cooperation' is endorsed – 'free and victorious' – and the production of the 'autonomy of the masses' is celebrated, showing that both capital and the State are now irrelevant to the flows of production (ibid.: 109–10). In this analysis the theme of antagonism remains a simple descriptive referent. The triumph of autonomism is unqualified.

At the end of the 1990s, in 'Kairos, Alma Venus, Multitudo' (1999) (Negri, 2006b), Negri introduces a series of concepts that will form part of his current conceptual body of work. The theme of poverty, love and *the common* appears as a base for the resistance versus *biopolitics*, a concept taken up from Michel Foucault (Revel, 2008: 24–7). The *multitude* is glimpsed as the central subject of the resistance: a multitude constituted of 'multiple singularities', of the brain as vital instrument and cooperation as a productive force. Starting with the centrality of immaterial and intellectual work, the multitude is presented as a 'set of productive constellations of subjectivity' (Negri, 2006b: 403). The *exodus* – the flight from the relations of domination – turns into a strategic option.

Thus, the concept of *antagonism* appears repeatedly in *Empire* as a verbal resource rather than as a theoretical tool (Hardt and Negri, 2000).[22] The notion of *multitude* becomes the new philosopher's stone of Negri's thought:

> In the same manner that the Empire with the spectacle of its force continually determines systemic recompositions, new figures of resistance are composed in the sequences of the events of struggle. This is another fundamental characteristic of the existence of the multitude, today, within the Empire and against the Empire. New figures of struggle and new subjectivities are produced in the juncture of events, in the universal nomadism, in the mixing and crossbreeding of individuals and peoples and in the technological metamorphosis of the imperial biopolitical machine. These new figures and subjectivities are produced because, even though the struggles are truly antisystemic, they do not simply rise against the imperial system, they are not simple negative forces. They also express, feed, and positively develop their own constituent projects; they work for the liberation of living labour, creating constellations of powerful singularities. This constituent aspect of the movement of the multitude, in its infinite aspects, is really the positive arena for the historical construction of the Empire. This is not historicist positivism but, rather, a positivity of the *res gestae* of the multitude, a creative, antagonist positivity. The deterritorializing power of the multitude is the productive force that maintains the Empire and, at the same time, the force that makes necessary and calls for its destruction. (ibid.: 71)

The multitude exists – autonomously – within the Empire, it is immanent, it manifests against it but goes beyond. Resistance and constituent power are the two faces of the coin, negation and creation that arise from the antagonism between multitude and empire. Once again, Negri's dilemma of the exterior interiority or the interior exteriority appears.

However, in this new conceptual configuration, antagonism becomes an adjective, a more descriptive than analytical instrument, many times synonym of conflict, in tendency between multitude and empire and capital and work but also in relation to a series of other situations (among the workers themselves, cultural blocks, tribal antagonisms, first and third world).

In the context of the empire and in the heart of the multitude, exploitation does not disappear according to Negri, but is instead translated into the dimensions of communication and cooperation as 'expropriation of the cooperation and the nullification of the senses of the linguistic production'. Antagonisms appear from the resistance to this intention to control, based on a subjectivity 'wholly submerged in language and exchange'.

> The technological development based on the generalization of the communicative relations of production is an engine of the crisis, and the general productive intellect is a cradle of antagonisms. (ibid.: 350)

By becoming plural and descriptive, antagonism stops representing an explanatory axis and loses its categorical strength.

The term *autonomy*, as synonym of independence, still occupies an important place to the extent that it indicates the distinctive quality of the multitude: its autonomous power.[23] According to Negri, the multitude emerges within the Empire but outside of capital as a relation, based on its autonomy – its acknowledgment of its 'own use value' – and is characterized by the 'mobility, flexibility and perpetual differentiation'.

However, once again, the antagonistic relation with the Empire reappears constantly in parallel to the exaltation of the autonomy of the *multitude* as separation and as subject in itself and for itself:

> However, in its autonomy without territory, this biopolitical existence of the multitude has the potential to transform into an autonomous mass of intelligent productivity, into an absolute democratic power, as Spinoza would say. If that were to happen, the capitalist

domination of production, exchange and communication would be overthrown. To prevent this is the first objective of the imperial government. But we should not forget that the constitution of the Empire depends for its own existence on the forces that represent this threat, the autonomous forces of productive cooperation. Its powers must be controlled but not destroyed. (ibid.: 315)

In his subsequent work, *Multitude*, Negri – again with Hardt – takes up once more and develops the ideas contained in the last part of *Empire* (Hardt and Negri, 2004). The idea of *multitude* is amplified and reinforced from the same elements that originated it: immaterial work as the real and qualitatively hegemonic base, *biopower* and *biopolitics* as forms of domination and resistance, communication and cooperation as lymph of the multitude, poverty as subjective condition, democracy as horizon, and love as a transforming act.

The *multitude-form* is based on the web form that both the production processes and their political counterparts assume – the Empire and the resistances.

Loyal to the workerist principle of inversion, Negri states the primacy of the resistance before power and, at the same time, states the simultaneity of the resistance, the exodus and the construction of a new society (ibid.: 96). The singularities of the multitude cannot be reduced; only articulated around *the common*, forming a movement of non-identity based movements founded in cooperation and struggle, with which Negri and Hardt defend – at the theoretical level – that the notion of *multitude* is a class concept.

By applying the Marxian and Leninist idea of *tendency*, Negri and Hardt project the multitude as a transforming agent, based on mobilization and resistance. Having incorporated the critiques of their previous work, here they do not underestimate the problem of process and assume that immaterial work 'is not paradise' but that it continues being exploited by capital.

Based on this consideration, the concept of *antagonism* reappears in the analysis, in permanent theoretical oscillation:

And it is here where antagonism intervenes, the third element of the Marxian method we are following. Today, as always, the word exploitation names the constant experience of the antagonism of the workers. The theory of exploitation must reveal the daily structural violence of capital against the workers, which is what generates this antagonism and, at the same time, is the base for the workers to organize and reject capitalist control. (ibid.: 181)

When Negri affirms that 'the subjectivity of the workers is also created in the antagonism of the experience of exploitation', *also* is the confession of a fundamental theoretical displacement. The notion has not only lost centrality but also slides and gets confused when Negri states that deprivation generates 'rage, indignation and antagonism but the revolt is only generated from wealth, as a result of an excess of intelligence, experience, knowledge and desire', an excess that cannot be expropriated (ibid.: 249). In these affirmations, the distinction between *antagonism* and *revolt* goes against the previous Negrian staging. The concept of *antagonism* is, in a way, neutralized by being put on the periphery of the analysis.

Negri's reflections since the 1980s up to the end of the century oscillate between a persistent optimistic matrix and the apparition – in light of the experiences of the last decade – of a greater scepticism that makes him consider possible conservative scenarios. In this sense, assuming the permanence of the relations of domination opens a bifurcation of possibilities when 'the meat of the multitude is made up of a series of ambivalent conditions: they can lead to liberation or stay trapped in a regime of exploitation and control' (ibid.). This dilemma states as a necessary condition the existence of a 'political project' of the multitude, of the mobilization of *the common* to elevate its 'intensity'. In this sense, Negri distinguishes two levels of formation: the *ontological* multitude and the *political* multitude, the first *present* and the second *latent* in a process of construction. On the second plane he glimpses the historical possibility of intensive cycles of struggle (in opposition to the extensive, thematic, spatial, and the global).

Based on these political considerations, the theme of autonomy becomes less slippery and oscillating considering the fundamental statement that links empire and multitude and that assumes that 'the empire depends on the multitude, the multitude is potentially autonomous', a potential that classically translates into self-management and social and political self-organization. *Potentially* does not mean *possibly*, but that it is *autonomous potency*.

At the same time, the theme of *exodus* – as the distancing of the sovereignty of the empire and towards democracy – is best settled by establishing its conflicting link with the existing world when Negri speaks of the need to propose 'rearguard wars', recovering the biblical metaphor of the escape through the desert.

Finally, it is worth pointing out other polemical issues presented in *Multitude*, particularly the invocation of a post-socialist and post-liberal left that combines equality, liberty and democracy as synthesis of an emancipatory project; the emphasis on the reforms possible in the current context; and the insistence on love as a subversive value.

To finish this journey through Negri's works, we should point out that in *The Porcelain Workshop*, a compilation of lectures imparted in France that might lack substantial novelties in terms of his theoretical body of work, the theme of antagonism appears more frequently than in *Multitude* and does so with a clearly objectivist or structural meaning:

The new conditions of the antagonistic process: this last one charges against the world of real subsumption and presents it as a world where the antagonistic forces of power and resistance, capital and liberty, are at play. (Negri, 2006a: 35)

In this sense, the sequence – historical phase, corresponding antagonism and space of subjectivation – clearly distinguishes *antagonism* and *subjectivation* even though they are relationally articulated.

Before the challenge of a 'unity of action' on behalf of the multitude, Negri states:

The answer we propose is the following: what makes the multitude subjectively efficient and objectively antagonistic is the emergence in its core of the common (both from a productive point of view as well as a political point of view). (ibid.: 86)

Here we end the tour of the concept of antagonism. It is no longer a subjective property but an objective expression of the subject, a way of situating oneself before the Empire and not a way of being, of becoming. The potential of the concept is disarmed to the point of neutralizing its capacity to aid in understanding the historical processes of political subjectivation.[24]

In conclusion, in Negri's intellectual trajectory the concept of *antagonism* is far from acquiring a coherence and categorical stability. Nevertheless, the connotation of the 1960s defines antagonism as a process of political subjectivation – as conformation of the subjectivity from conflict, starting from the incorporation of the experience of struggle and insubordination – that maintains continuity with the Marxist tradition by displaying the subjective implications of the class struggle and attempting to capture the passage from structure to action. In this sense, the conceptual development he proposes is susceptible to articulation with the perspective of subalternity as long as this, as we have seen, gives an account of political subjectivation that derives from the experience of subordination as well as that of autonomy understood – as we will argue in the following chapter – as subjectivation related to the experience of emancipation.

3

Autonomy

The concept of autonomy, which appears frequently in the approaches of diverse anti-systemic movements and in the debate over alternatives to capitalism in present times, has among its precedents and political and theoretical origins a long tradition of Marxist thought.[1]

At the same time, its meaning oscillated between different connotations and only on limited occasions it was the object of systematic theoretical developments. The contribution of *Socialism or Barbarism* (SoB), a political group of clear Marxist revolutionary inspiration which, in France of the 1950s, put this concept at the centre of its political reflections, looked to associate and articulate the two main meanings that circulated in the previous Marxist debate: the idea of *autonomy* as emergence of the sociopolitical subject and *autonomy* as a characteristic of the process and the emancipatory horizon, that is, of the construction of socialism.

In this chapter, after outlining the origins and previous uses, we will analyse in depth the theoretical proposal that emerged at the heart of the SoB developments and, particularly, from its main leaders and ideologues, Cornelius Castoriadis and Claude Lefort. Later we will review how the echo of the idea of *autonomy* tainted the reflections and practices of the *autogestionario*[2] French movements of 1968 until the 1970s, and what their contributions were while trying to consolidate an experiential meaning of the idea of autonomy. We will end by outlining a synthesis and formulating a projection of the Marxist debate on the subjective implications of the concept understood as *experience of emancipation* and thus susceptible to a relation with the categories of *subalternity* and *antagonism*.

Autonomy, Independence and Emancipation

The presence and use of the concept of autonomy in Marxism is, without a doubt, diffuse and varied.

Because it is a word whose usage is more common and frequent than subalternity and antagonism, in its general linguistic connotation as positive synonym of independence, it is able to be used, by Marx and Engels, in numerous and different descriptive planes, which go from the self-determination of peoples to the loss of autonomy of the worker before the machine, passing through the relative autonomy of the State and the theorization of Bonapartism. On the other hand, a notion of autonomy, even in absence of the nominal references can be traced in Marx's reflections on living labour and the formation of worker subjectivity in the linkage between social being and social consciousness. Finally, the concept occupies a fundamental place when it explicitly designates class independence, the political autonomy of the proletariat, and *selbsttätigkeit* or self-activity.

At the same time, insofar as a specific meaning of autonomy detaches from the theoretical and political use of the concept by anarchists, the word is discredited before Marx and Marxists in its prescriptive quality, a guideline on the plane of definitions and the political project. In an article on the idea of authority, Engels clearly expresses this rejection of the libertarian idea of autonomy as guiding principle and absolute value:

It is absurd to speak of the principle of authority as an absolutely bad principle and of the principle of autonomy as an absolutely good principle. Authority and autonomy are relative things, whose spheres vary in the different phases of social development. If the autonomists limited themselves to saying that the social organization of the future will restrain authority till the strict limit where the conditions of production make it inevitable, we might understand each other; but, far from it, they remain blind to all facts that make the thing necessary and lash out with fury against the word. (Engels, 1873a)[3]

This rejection of the idea of *autonomy* as essence, method and shape of the struggles, and the emancipatory process will be a constant in the Marxist conception of politics as a correlation of forces, in which autonomy figures as relative data for the construction of the independence of the subject-class that has no value in itself but in terms of the conflictual relation it configures. However, beyond the polemic with anarchism, Marx and Engels accepted and promoted the idea of communism as the realization of a social and individual autonomy, even without calling it as such, in the form of 'a free association in which the free development of each one conditions the free development of all' and of a society governed by the principle of 'to each according to their capacities; to each according to their needs!', and the subsequent overcoming of the need: 'the kingdom of freedom' (Marx, 1985c: 129, 1985a: (III) 14, 1999: (III) 1044). From this angle, integral autonomy could be considered a finishing point, the self-regulation of future society, textually, the condition-situation of self-determination in which the subjects establish the norms they submit to, the positive negation of heteronomy and dependence. In this sense, Marx and Engels distinguished a principle of self-determination valid to characterize the objective but not the passages of the process of emancipation, understood as counterposition and struggle, that is, relational, and thus irreducible to totally separate and independent spheres or areas, which implied assuming the exteriority of the working class from the relation of domination and the conflict that passed through it.

On the other hand, the idea of self-management – a specific notion of worker autonomy arising in the mid twentieth century – does not figure in the Marxian set of ideas either and, nevertheless, Marx approached a related thematic, that of cooperatives, adopting a clearly polemical posture that, while recognizing the value of 'autonomous creations', did not trust their localized character and relationship to the State and the market because he considered that they could have anti and post-capitalist meaning only after the triumph of the socialist revolution and to the extent in which the cooperative model could extend to the scale of society as a whole (see Bourdet, 1977: 57–74).

However, in a more general and lax meaning, as synonym of the *independence of the proletarian class*, the notion of *autonomy* appears in a constant and reiterated manner in the centre of the political preoccupations of Marx and Engels in relation to the formation of class as a political construction. In this direction, the *Manifesto* recites: 'the proletarian movement is the autonomous movement of an immense majority in the interest of an immense majority' (Marx, 1985c: 120).[4] In these general terms, as a qualifying adjective more than a noun, the idea of *autonomy* circles the political thought of Marx and Engels as a fundamental passage of the process of emancipation that will only happen if it is the work of the workers themselves, that is, the expression of their autonomous power. The concept appears in a prescriptive sense – being the expression of the existence of the class *for itself* – and is inserted in the process-based logic that is expressed with more precision in the idea of *autonomization* and the *construction and exercise of power* than in *independence* or plain *autonomy*, assuming, with Thompson, that the class (subject) does not form to struggle *afterwards* but it forms *in* the struggle. Even in the absence of a conceptual explanation, this meaning opens the door to the valorization of the processes of subjectivation relative to the incorporation of the *experience of emancipation*, starting with its dawning, the condition of independence relative to the emergence and formulation of class.

In summary, even in the midst of the suspicions derived from the polemics with anarchism, the idea of *autonomy* appears as an important piece in the Marxian categorical machinery: as principle of political rupture, as expression of the emergence of the power of the class *for itself*; and, in a second plane and with more conceptual ambiguity, as a form of the future communist society.[5] Let us take a look at how, on these bases, the subsequent Marxist debate will take up this problematic once more.

The theme of autonomy has been unquestionably the one that, among the three that interest us, has generated more debates and polemics within Marxism due to the semantic opening of the word and its greater degree of conceptual oscillation.

Mabel Thwaites Rey writes in light of the Argentine experience of 2001–02 and points out five possible connotations of the concept: autonomy of labour before capital (self-management), autonomy of the social subject before the party or union organizations, before the State, before the dominant classes (ideological) and, finally, social and individual autonomy (as a model of society) (Thwaites Rey, 2004: 17–22). This typology can be reordered in light of the corresponding Marxist debates. The first definition is without a doubt fundamental, but it could and should include a wider horizon than self-manage-ment that encompasses processes of autonomization of living labour that, as we saw from Marx's intuitions, develops Italian workerism in general and, in particular, Negri under the concept of *self-valorization*. The second definition, anarchist in origin, disappears in the face of Marxist approaches to the role of the union and the party and moves to the problem of the relationship between 'spontaneity and conscious direction', to use Gramsci's formula. The third is of another nature – tac-tical-strategic, in terms of the confrontation with bourgeois domination – and thus it is not equivalent at the theoretical level insofar as, in a broad sense, there exists a consensus of principle that corresponds to the formation of class *for itself* and the party as expression of the political autonomy of the workers before the State and the dominant classes and as melting pot of its ideological autonomy – the fourth sense noted by Thwaites Rey. On the other hand, the fifth dimension, the most problematic and less generalized within Marxism, is still linked to the first, that is, to self-management in terms of the social but, at the same time, it is deployed outside Marxism, as individual autonomy, both in the libertarian strands but fundamentally in liberalism and also in the field of psychology and psychoanalysis.[6] Finally, in this typology the notion of *autonomy* is missing as a process of political subjectivation related to the experiences of emancipation that we will trace and which cannot be summarized in the idea of class independence in its classic and traditional sense. It is linked to the theme of the model of society as well as that of self-management.

The Marxist uses of the concept of *autonomy* can be summarized in two strands: (1) autonomy as *class independence* – subjective, organizational and ideological – in the context of bourgeois capitalist domination; and (2) autonomy as *emancipation*, as *model*, *prefiguration* or *process* of formation of emancipated society. The first, since Marx, constitutes an indisputable pillar of Marxist thought. The second is not a common patrimony of Marxists but has been instead developed by some strands and authors. In the possible articulations between both we find the core of the contemporary Marxist debate and the path of a potential aperture and conceptual consolidation.

We should not forget also, at the nominal level that the word *autonomy* appears closely associated to the cultural and territorial problematic of local autonomies and the problem of self-determination of peoples and local autonomies. This use constantly appears in Marxist literature and contributes to the loss of specificity of the concept in other theoretical plans. To offer an example, Paul Lafargue's article entitled 'Autonomy' is centred on the theme of the State and territory and, only in the last instance, refers to the productive decentralization with polemical tones that associate proposals of the petite-bourgeoisie to those of the anarchists. In general, Lafargue defends centralization against the autonomies and, with a completely French irony, criticizes the imprecise character of the concept: 'There are as many autonomies as there are *omelettes* and morals, it is not an eternal principle, but a historic phenomenon' (Lafargue, 1981).

At the same time, the critical line against anarchist autonomy – based on the exaltation of spontaneity and direct action – will not cease to be a constant in the Marxist debate of the twentieth century. By way of example, the polemical forcefulness of the arguments of Leon Trotsky in an article entitled *The Lessons of the Commune* is illustrative:

> Passivity and indecision were favoured in this case by the sacred principle of the federation and autonomy …
>
> If particularism and democratic autonomy are extremely dangerous for the proletarian revolution in general, they are ten times more dangerous for the army. The tragic example of the Commune demonstrated this to us …
>
> By way of its agents, its lawyers and its journalists, the bourgeoisie has planted a great amount of democratic, parliamentary, autonomist formulas that are no more than the shackles with which it ties the feet of the proletariat and hinders its advancement. (Trotsky, 1921)

In effect, one sole meaning of autonomy, that of *class independence* inherited from the *Manifesto*, constitutes a theoretical pillar and constantly appears in a passive sense in terms of a fundamental passage of the construction of the revolutionary movement. For example, Rosa Luxemburg in *The Crisis of German Social Democracy* writes:

> Its role, as vanguard of the militant proletariat, is not to lay at the orders of the ruling classes in defence of the current classist state, nor to silently stray waiting for the storm to pass, but to continue in the political autonomy of class, which in every great crisis of

bourgeois society hits the ruling classes, pushes the crisis beyond itself. (Luxemburg, 1915)[7]

In view of the processes of political subjectivation, Rosa Luxemburg's intuitions are particularly fruitful insofar as, even without passing through the concept of autonomy that was reserved for the debate on the question of nationalities, she insists on the 'self movement' of the class and spontaneity as a resource – 'the spontaneous coordination of the conscious political acts of a collectivity' – pointing towards experience – 'the daily struggle' – as a fundamental factor of dialogue between social being and social consciousness.[8] At the same time, in the midst of the polemics generated by her views, Rosa Luxemburg will be one – if not the main – source of inspiration of the Marxist strands that incorporate the idea of autonomy as emancipation with more emphasis.

In effect, the debate raised by the views of Rosa Luxemburg became essential to the extent that the theme of spontaneity produced and produces short circuits in Marxism. To the extent that, with the exception of the 'opening' developed by Rosa Luxemburg, the views that associated autonomy with lack of consciousness dominated and that, from Kautsky to Lenin, all upheld the need for its overcoming by way of an external intervention of the party, of the conscious vanguard. Trotsky's trajectory – from councilism to centralist Bolshevism and finally to a pluralist Bolshevism – in this debate is a sample of several shades which the assessment of the combination between spontaneity and consciousness and its strategic and organizational translation can undertake (Mandel, 1990; see also Mandel, 2003).[9]

The dominant trend towards the identification between spontaneity and autonomy – *versus* anarchism – led the theme of class autonomy within contemporary Marxism as principle of separation to become an accepted assumption while the idea of *autonomy* as emancipation, as objective or as process of progressive self-determination turned into the patrimony of specific perspectives or currents. In the latter sense, with some exceptions, the concept of *autonomy* has not been an object of specific theorizing even when it has been present as constant reference, with diverse scopes and degrees of aperture.

In this line, the so-called *councilism* – inspired by Rosa Luxemburg's intuitions – would be the Marxist strand that would articulate the idea of class *autonomy* in terms of its concrete production as expression of power and self-determination, not so much as principle of subjective existence – of political foundation of class – *for itself* or on terms of its expression in the party form, but as valorization of the action of the masses, of the 'conscious spontaneity' and, in particular, of the immediate appropriation of the means of production.

In this strand, the concept of autonomy is linked to the practices and the experiences of self-determination undertaken in the workers' councils. We saw the appearance of this approach in Gramsci's pre-prison thought, in the *Ordine Nuovo* phase, just as we will see its theoretical expansion in the reflections of *Socialism or Barbarism* promoted by Cornelius Castoriadis and prolonged in the French debate of the 1970s on self-management.

The councilist Marxism inspired by the model of the *soviets* of the Russian revolutions from 1905 to 1917 forms a line of thinking that crosses the history of twentieth century Marxism.[10] Its origins start with the reflections of Lenin and Trotsky.[11] It finds in Rosa Luxemburg an important theory. It passes by other Bolshevik theorizations on the management of the socialist economy between 1918 and 1921 as well as by the reflections associated with the experiences of occupations of factories in Hungary in 1919, in Italy between 1919 and 1920, in the general strike of Britain and the factory delegates between 1918 and 1920, and in the Councils in Germany in the same years. It develops in the contributions of the Trotskyists of the 1930s, of Mao on the *soviets* in Tsinkiang and Kiangsi, of the Spanish Revolution, of libertarian communism and, particularly, of the Dutch strand of the Communism of the Councils headed by Anton Pannekoek and Paul Mattick, possibly the most systematic and radical in this field (see Bricianer, 1975; Mattick, 1976).[12] After World War II, councilism will find other branches in the practices of self-management as institutional form in Yugoslavia and Algeria but also as forms of resistance in the workers' rebellions in Poland, East Germany and Hungary (see Mandel, 1973). Finally, in the 1960s, the flourishing of the Marxist debates will enliven the councilist preoccupations in Italy and, as we will see, in France.[13]

The entire theoretical production of councilism revolves around the idea of the social and political autonomy of the working class as a set of practices and experiences of self-determination that are deployed in the direction of the occupation and self-management of factories.[14]

At the same time, this centrality does not translate into a theorization of the concept of *autonomy* as such. Let us take a look at some conceptually significant texts from the work of Anton Pannekoek, the biggest exponent of the most radical councilism, of councilism as a distinct and separate political strand.

In a 1938 text, in a paragraph that clearly illustrates the anti-party stance of this strand, emphasis is put upon the notion of *self-activity*:

The old ways of organization, the union and the political party, and the new way of the councils (soviets), belong to different phases in the development of society and have different functions. The first have to secure the position of the working class among the other classes within capitalism and belong to the period of expansive capitalism. The last must secure the complete domination of the workers to destroy capitalism and its class divisions, and belongs to the period of capitalism in decline. In an ascending and prosperous capitalism, the organization of councils is impossible because the workers are completely occupied with the betterment of their condition, which is possible in that period through unions and political action. In a decadent capitalism that navigates the crisis, these efforts are useless and the faith in them can only obstruct the increase of self-activity of the masses. In such periods of high tension and increasing revolts against misery, when the strike movements are propagated through entire countries and hit the roots of capitalist power, or when, following wars or political catastrophes, the governmental authority crumbles and the masses act, the old forms of organization fail against the new forms of self-activity of the masses. (Pannekoek, 1938: 294–5)

In 1946, in *The Workers' Councils*, the only book by Pannekoek and the culmination of his thought, the notions of *self-determination, self-liberation, self-government, self-regulation*, and *self-education* are repeated and linked to one another:

The great decisive step in the progress of humanity, the transformation of the fledgling society, essentially consists in a transformation of the working masses. It can only be achieved through action, rebellion, with the effort of the masses themselves. Their essential nature is the self-liberation of humanity...

The workers' councils are the form of government that in future times will replace the forms of government of the old world...

The self-determination of the workers regarding the action of struggle is not a requirement suggested by theory, by arguments of feasibility, but an affirmation of the fact that arises from the practice...

Furthermore, to a large extent, for the first appearance of new forms of self-organization of the workers in struggle, known as *soviets*, that is, *councils*...

And this change also corresponds to an economic change that is not imposed by an order from outside, but it is the result of the self-determination of working humanity, who with all liberty regulates the means of production according to their own ideas. (Pannekoek, n.d.)

In this text, the concept of *autonomy* appears on only two occasions:

The forces of solidarity and the devotion hidden in them only wait for the perspective of great struggles to appear in order to transform into a predominant principle of life. Furthermore, including the most repressed layers of the working class, who only join their comrades hesitantly wishing to lean on their example, will soon feel that the new forces of community also grow in them and will also perceive that the struggle for freedom asks for their adhesion and the development of all the powers of autonomous activity and trust in themselves that they possess. Thus, overcoming all the intermediate forms of partial self-determination, progress will decidedly follow the way of the organization of councils...

The self-liberation of the working masses implies autonomous thinking, autonomous knowledge, acknowledging truth and error by one's own mental effort. (Pannekoek, 1938)

In both cases, the word does not occupy a central place, it is an adjective and not a noun, even when the problem it alludes to is the axis around which the councilist conception of Pannekoek turns.

The determination that the concept will not be an object of theorization on behalf of the Dutch Marxist is corroborated by the fact that, years later, in an epistolary exchange with *Socialism or Barbarism* – that explicitly championed the idea of *autonomy*, Pannekoek will not abuse the term, circumscribing it to the idea of 'autonomous power' and 'autonomous action' in the first letter and to the 'autonomy of decisions', 'self-government' and 'self-management' in the second (see Socialisme ou Barbarie, 2009a).

At the same time, an explicitly autonomist strand will arise from councilist Marxism, based on the theoretical developments of Negri and Castoriadis, which defends the principle of autonomy as criteria of organization of the movements in their organizational dynamics and their emancipatory projections. For example, Harry Cleaver understands autonomy in a broad sense, in terms of all the historic movements that boosted emancipatory struggles that were not put into practice in state, institutionalized or bureaucratic forms. In this sense, autonomy designates all expression of resistance to domination to spontaneously manifest itself, without mediations (see Cleaver, 2009). From a similar perspective, George Katsiaficas defines the field of autonomous movement departing from the Luxemburgian and Gramscian idea of 'conscious spontaneity':

> In contrast to Social Democracy and Leninism, the two main strands of the left in the twentieth century, the Autonomous are relatively free of rigid ideological burdens. The absence of all central organization (perhaps even any type of primary organization) helps to maintain the theory and the practice in constant exchange. In fact, action precedes the Autonomous, not the words, and is the accumulation of decentralized actions, generated by small groups in function of their own initiatives, which blocks a systematization of the totality of movement, the first step in dismantling any system. There does not exist a unique organization that can control the direction of the actions that are taken from the base. Even when the Autonomous do not have a unified ideology and there is no manifesto of the movement, their statements make it evident that they fight 'not for ideologies, not for the proletariat, not for the people', but (in the same sense feminists approached it the first time) for a 'politics of the first person'. They want self-determination

and the 'abolition of politics', not the leadership of a party. They want to destroy the existing social system because they consider it the cause of the 'inhumanity, the exploitation and daily monotony'. (Katsiaficas, n.d.)

Obviously, definitions of this nature come so close to libertarian communism and anarchism they come into collision with tenets of Marxism. At this threshold, the borders between strands become porous.

In fact, today, this meaning is used by political strands that call themselves *autonomists* and assert themselves less than Marxism or open up their theoretical frame to contribute to the confusing proliferation of neo and post-Marxisms, whose parameters escape precise and rigorous definitions.

The idea of autonomy as horizon of emancipation appears again with a surprising frequency and intensity at the start of the millennium, associated with a return of the libertarian thought and anarchism coinciding with anti-globalization mobilizations but also with a new wave of neo or post-Marxist reflections.[15] It appears explicitly, on the other hand, in the Zapatista project in Mexico since 1994, linked to the thematic of territorial and sociocultural indigenous self-determination more than to the formation of anticapitalist subjectivities and, with an explicit opening towards an integral emancipatory horizon, in the Argentine movements of 2001, closer to the classic preoccupations over autonomy as liberation, generating a particularly fertile theoretical production and set of empirical studies on the corresponding processes of political subjectivation.[16]

We have already analysed Negri's ideas in *Multitude* and beyond those there is an outstanding and widely recognized example of the thinking born from these experiences. John Holloway assumes the challenge of understanding the dynamic of subjectivation in very similar terms to those we are highlighting.[17]

In his most famous book – *Change the World Without Taking Power* – Holloway develops an important and polemical theoretical reflection, starting from the analysis of domination as a *fetishization* – the process of separation of the producer from its product – and by assuming the Spinozian distinction between *power over* and *power to*, as counterposition between subordination and *non-subordination*:[18]

It is important to keep in mind that all capitalist societies rest on the subordination of the insubordinate workers, therefore on violence: what distinguishes capitalism from the other class societies is the shape subordination takes, the fact it is mediated by freedom. (Holloway, 2002: 258)

The *power to* is, for Holloway, the measure of emancipation understood as self-determination, as autonomy:

Our struggle is clearly a constant struggle to escape from capital, a struggle for space, for autonomy, a struggle to loosen the leash, to intensify the disarticulation of domination. (ibid.: 270)

In a recent essay, this author explicitly assumes a 'negative' autonomist stance by rejecting the workerist approach for being 'positive', that is, for stating a subjective recomposition when Holloway maintains, on the contrary, the need for an *anti-identitarian* subject, a movement of permanent negation, a negative dialectic.[19]

On the other hand, Holloway's conception points to an idea of *process* where autonomy is a project and a movement:

There is no autonomy, no possible self-determination within capitalism. Autonomy (in the sense of self-determination) can only be understood as a project that continuously takes us against and beyond the barriers of capitalism …

Every step foreshadows the goal: social self-determination …

The impulse for self-determination connotes a constant movement, a constant search, an experimenting. (Holloway, 2006: 5, 8, 11)

In this sense, autonomy is *experimentation* but not an *experience* to the extent it is not, does not even end up *being*. The real would be, for Holloway, the anti-power, the struggle. This translates into a negation – the *scream* – that is present in the interstices of the daily struggles:

The struggle for autonomy is the rejection of domination, the no that reverberates one way or another, not only in the work places but, ubiquitous, in all society. (Holloway, 2002: 271)

At the same time, the idea of 'beyond' implies an exit – by way of negation – of the interiority of the relation of domination.

From this standpoint, the suggestive theoretical itinerary traced by Holloway – albeit sharing the main conceptual coordinates – operates a theoretical leap insofar as it fuses the inside and outside, the *counter* and the *beyond*, the *power to* with *anti-power*, the negation with the affirmation. In this sense, the polarity between subalternity (*fetishism* and *power over*) and autonomy (*emancipation* and *power to*) subsumes the *power against*, simplifying the passage of the conflict and making obvious the specificity of antagonism. Like Negri,[20] interiority and exteriority overcome each other.[21] The *counter* and *beyond* – insubordination and no subordination – fuse and confuse. As we will see in the final chapter, a theoretical operation which obstructs the visibility of one of the three fundamental dimensions insofar as, on one hand, in analytical terms, it distinguishes domination and emancipation diluting the specificity of antagonism; and on the other, in terms of the real process, articulates struggle and emancipation, but separates and isolates domination (the fetishization or subalternity), eliminating its influence and permanence in the processes of political subjectivation,

More than a victim of the ghost of essentialist idealism that Holloway eludes to by insisting on the relational character of the class struggle, his approach is directed to exalt the emergence of a subjective potential of a clear anti-systematic orientation more than to create conceptual tools that allow the deciphering of contradictions that run through the construction of political subjectivities.

Without the pretension of mentioning and analysing all the expressions of councilism and their extension into contemporary autonomism – which would deserve a currently non-existent monographic treatment – much less the totality of the implicit references in the problem of autonomy, we can synthesize, in first instance, the Marxist debate in relation to two dimensions or meanings of the notion. The first – generalized – of social, political and ideological independence of the subject-class and the second – less diffuse – that places autonomy as emancipation, understood as process, foreshadowing or model of the society. Within this bifurcation, there emerge distinctions and articulations that add complexity to the debate. For example, both meanings – as independence and as emancipation – include an ambiguity to the extent that they designate both the data – the means or the end – and the process.

In effect, the connotation that puts autonomy as independence sits on a real triple determination (social, political and ideological) that Marxism has postulated as:

- Autonomy-independence as data or as event – as starting point or point of arrival;
- Autonomy-independence as condition or instrument for struggle; and
- Autonomy-independence as process of subjective construction.

This last trend is the least explored and will be one of the directing threads of the following sections.

At the same time, the meaning that links autonomy and emancipation – more polemical within Marxism – can be disaggregated in the same way and open a branch of analysis of the subjectivation processes we are interested in highlighting. We will come back to this issue in the conclusions of this chapter, in light of the analysis of theoretical contributions produced by the group Socialism or Barbarism in France in the 1950s and the self-managed French movements in the 1960s and 1970s.

Autonomous Subjectivation in the Reflections of Socialism or Barbarism

The reflections elaborated in the core of the group Socialism or Barbarism in France during the 1950s and 1960s have great theoretical relevance to the extent that they articulate the notions of *autonomy* as *independence* and as *emancipation* in terms of the set of the corresponding subjective dynamics, which constitute an original perspective at the heart of the Marxist debate and a fundamental referent to develop the connotations and the subjective scope of the concept towards the theoretical exercise we will undertake in the last chapter. Let us take a look at the main features of the thought generated by SoB in parallel with their historic trajectory to emphasize the juxtapositions between theory and political practice.

Socialism or Barbarism was a political group established in France that was active between 1949 and 1967. Like many organizations of revolutionary orientation in Western Europe, due to its small size and limited mass influence it did not achieve the political impact it had intended, not only because it was unable to launch and accompany a revolutionary process but also because it did not take root in French society and particularly in the field of the left, dominated in those years by the French Communist Party (PCF).[22] Nevertheless, the trajectory of the SoB stood out for the depth and the quality of the theoretical reflection that it generated and disseminated through the magazine of the same name, inspired by Rosa Luxemburg's formula in 1915 in the *Junnius pamphlet* on the crisis of social democracy. In the magazine, throughout the forty issues published between 1949 and 1965, there appeared theoretical themes and approaches that anticipated the diverse problematic propelled by the movement of 1968 – which paradoxically emerged the year after the dissolution of the SoB – and which constituted a significant – albeit debatable – contribution to the Marxist debate. In particular – beyond the valorization of the place this group occupied in the panorama of the French left and the political stands it undertook[23] –the originality of the reflections on the revolutionary subject and, in them, an attempt to develop the Marxist theme of autonomy stand out. This small set of militants – among which intellectuals that would later be known globally, like Cornelius Castoriadis, Claude Lefort and Jean-François Lyotard – accomplished in the plane of thought what it could not at the political level in terms of the objective enunciated in the subtitle of the magazine *Socialism or Barbarism*, which defined itself as an *organ of critique and revolutionary guidance*.

The origins of the group Socialism or Barbarism go back to 1946, during the post-World War II period in France and the era of reconstruction, of Keynesian capitalism, of the development of Gaullism and the powerful French Communist Party. The direct precedent of SoB was the Chaulieu-Montal tendency (after the pseudonyms for Castoriadis and Lefert respectively) that acted as the minority inside the French Trotskyist party – the Internationalist Communist Party – and the Fourth International.[24] In 1949, a year after the Second World Congress of the latter – in which Castoriadis (Chaulieu) was a delegate – the tendency would break with Trotskyism to form an independent group centred on the magazine, under the name Socialism or Barbarism.

The rupture of SoB with Trotskyism, at the end of the 1940s, originates from a polemic surrounding the characterization of the Soviet Union and the corresponding political line both at the international and national levels.[25] In contrast to most attendees at the Fourth International that characterized the Soviet Union as 'degenerate worker State', which had to be defended before capitalism and fascism, the founders of SoB maintained it was a regime of domination of an emerging class, the bureaucracy, that exploited the workers in a similar manner – albeit not equal – to the bourgeoisie, to the extent it was not the owner of the means of production but controlled them. Thus no defence of the USSR – albeit coincidental – was acceptable. This consideration, even when it acknowledged the validity of Trotsky's thesis on the 'degenerate worker State' and the defence of the USSR at the moment of its formulation, departed from the analysis of the context of the post-World War II period in which it was evident that Stalinism had not only not been defeated – as Trotsky predicted – neither at the external level by the war, nor at the internal level by an anti-bureaucratic revolution but that, on the contrary, it came out of the world war triumphant and consolidated as a stable, apparently lasting, regime.[26] This diagnosis translated into a condemnation without qualifications of the USSR, in opposition to what *Pabloism* proposed regarding the mass Communist Parties.[27] This fundamental difference of appreciation, along with the political critiques of the national and international order of the French Trotskyist party, led the group to a break with the left and to the creation of the magazine as an organ of diffusion of its ideas.[28]

From the *Editorial* of the first issue, SoB would reinforce the thesis of the bureaucracy as a new form of exploitation without private property, giving it a bigger scope insofar as it affirmed that it was assuming 'the handover of the traditional bourgeoisie in the decline of capitalism', as the statist tendencies that travelled across the Western world pointed towards.[29] This approach implied linking the critique of bureaucracy as dominant class in the countries of so-called real socialism to the critique of the 'worker bureaucracies' of the communist and Social Democratic parties and unions that favoured – by perfecting and rationalizing exploitation – the integration of the proletariat to capitalism in Western Europe (Chaulieu, 1949).

From the critique of *bureaucratic capitalism* a fundamental conclusion was arrived at:

> Parallel to the eviction of the traditional forms of property and the classic bourgeoisie for state property and for bureaucracy, the dominant opposition in societies gradually stops being between possessors and non-possessors to be replaced by the existing one between leaders and performers in the process of production. (Socialisme ou Barbarie, 2007: (2) 23)

Despite the arguable affirmation of its determining or mostly dominant character that displaced the capital-labour contradiction in its proper economic dimension to a second plane, SoB correctly emphasized an emerging contradiction – bureaucratization as a form of domination – that referred the analysis of the specific problem of power, the power to make decisions, that is, to political, social and economic democracy as the central axis of revolutionary reflection and action. The first level of this tension remained the management of the productive process. The group would assume, therefore, as fundamental banners, the workers' control of the economy – the 'economic dictatorship of the proletariat' – and the councilist form, inspired in the Russian soviets and other similar experiences.[30]

> ... the objective of the socialist revolution cannot be simply the abolition of private property, abolition that the monopolies and bureaucracy do themselves gradually with the only result being a betterment of the methods of exploitation, but essentially the abolition of the fixed and stable distinction between leaders and performers in production and in social life in general. (ibid.: (2) 31)

Along with the centrality of the relationship command-obedience – leaders and performers – as a key aspect of post-World War II capitalism, it is significant that this quote mentions the appearance of 'social life', which would acquire more importance in the SoB's subsequent analysis along with the theme of 'daily life':

The experience of bureaucratic capitalism allows seeing what socialism is not and cannot be. The analysis of the proletarian revolutions, but also of the daily struggles and the daily life of the proletariat enables talk of what socialism is and should be.[31]

The theoretical implications linked to the concept of *life* – *social* or *daily* – joined the trajectory of SoB. Despite there not being objects of explicit distinction, these notions referred, in the thought of SoB, to two separate but articulated dimensions: social life as a wider whole than the simple experience of exploitation in the factory – and therefore related to domination and resistance in general – and daily life as experience, as the immediate reality of the workers' existence.

This last dimension dominated the first stage of SoB's reflection and was seen as the field of production of the irreducible and irrepressible capacity for struggle and spontaneous and creative class resistance, just as it was narrated in the magazine by worker activists, particularly by Daniel Mothé, Renault worker and subsequently recognized sociologist of labour, who had joined SoB years after its foundation turning into one of its main leaders and ideologues.[32] Later, in the last stage of the magazine, the emphasis would be put upon the field of social life, on the forms of resistance to domination from life understood in a broad sense that included different subjects (students, young people, women, etc.) and different libertarian subject matter.[33]

In the first stage, it would be Claude Lefort (Claude Montal) who would theorize the idea of worker struggle in everyday life under the category of 'proletarian experience' in a long essay in which he proposed a series of methodological approaches to a theme he considered both central and slippery to the extent he doubted the capacity of theory to capture the reality of subjects in a permanent process of transformation:

This (the proletariat) is subjective in the sense that its conduct is not the simple consequence of its conditions of existence or more profoundly that its conditions of existence require of it a constant struggle to be transformed, that is, a constant detachment from their immediate fortunes and that the progress of this struggle and the elaboration of the ideological content that allows this separation make an experience through which class is constituted. (Socialisme ou Barbarie, 1952: (11) 77).[34]

In this baroque formulation, Lefort articulates and sequences fundamental elements of SoB's approach: the proletarian subject, its real existence, the struggle, the separation, the revolutionary ideology (the project), the experience, the constitution of class as an ongoing process. The circularity of a reasoning that begins with the subject to end with him accounts for a centrality but also for an aim oriented towards the construction of a class *for itself*, of the political subject that is constituted from experience by way of a separation, a rupture, a schism.

In this article – that also acted as an internal political document – Lefort planned the theoretical and strategic centrality of the understanding of the processes of political subjectivation from the perspective of experience, situated in the intersection between spontaneity and consciousness. This angle of observation and analysis is of fundamental importance because it will dye SoB's thought and reflections on the notion of *autonomy* that will be developed by Cornelius Castoriadis.

From this view focused on the subject – on the experience of daily life – follows a severe critique of objectivism, posing an arguable yet understandable antinomy in light of the debates and political positions that covered the socialist and communist movement during those years:

... it is definitely the objective analysis that is subordinate to the concrete analysis because it is not the conditions but the men who are revolutionaries, and the last issue is to know how they appropriate and transform their situation. (Socialisme ou Barbarie, 1952: (11) 78)

In this affirmation – which anticipates the tonalities of the revolutionary voluntarism of the 1960s – the critique of 'the Marxism of the productive forces' is glimpsed as well as its contradiction with the relations of production, whose main references are the 'Preface' to *A Contribution to the Critique of Political Economy* and *Capital* by Marx, which Castoriadis will resist so he will confuse it with the whole of Marxism towards the mid 1960s.

Despite this outcome, which we will review later, in these passages we clearly notice how the SoB's perspective, critiquing 'Stalinist' Marxism for its objectivist and determinist character, inverted its logic to such an extent that it led to the extreme subjectivist and relativist counterargument: there are no more 'conditions' and all that is left are the appropriation and transformation of reality. This logic of inversion was theorized by Castoriadis (signing with the pseudonym Pierre Chaulieu) in 1957 in a text that presents the most complete formulation of SoB's vision.

Castoriadis argued that the order of the sections of this article gave precedence to the reflection on socialism over the critique of capitalism because reality could only be critiqued from its possible opposite, from its possible alternative, that is, capitalism and its crisis could only be understood from the most complete vision of socialist society:

> … the content of our ideas leads us to maintain that none of the deep sense of capitalism and its crisis can be understood if not from the more general idea of socialism. Because everything we can say is finally reduced to this: socialism is the autonomy, the conscious direction of men of their own lives; capitalism – private or bureaucratic – is the denial of this autonomy, and its crisis results from necessarily creating the tendency of men towards autonomy and at the same time being forced to suppress it. (Chaulieu, 1957: 159)

In addition to the inverted logic in this paragraph, there is an idea that became the axis of SoB's reflection and an original stance within the Marxist debate: 'socialism is autonomy'. This idea makes up the main field for the class struggle in capitalism to the extent that this intends to negate it without managing it, leaving its potential as a subversive tendency intact. The logical inversion is translated to an analytical perspective: capitalist domination can only be seen and understood from autonomy.

Before advancing in the exploration of the idea of *autonomy* in SoB, we must talk about the context in which it developed. Since 1953, and especially since 1956, the protest movements in Eastern Europe – first in Germany, in Poland and to a larger scale in Hungary – provided some fresh political breath to SoB and inspired the direction of their reflections. Exalting the spontaneous character of the rebellions and the emergence of the workers' councils in the East, the *socio-barbarians* saw or wanted to see the signs of a self-management programme as the embryo of the antibureaucratic revolution they championed (see, for example, Lefort, 1956–57). At the same time, the convulsions in the processes of decolonization contributed to the optimism of the group. In particular, the Algerian war – for its direct relationship with France and for the ambiguities of the PCF – called the SoB's attention, expressed in Lyotard's visions, to expect revolutionary processes propelled by the autonomous action of the masses (see, for example, Lyotard, 1959–60, 1961). In effect, parallel to these events, the group grew and the magazine extended its circulation enjoying a certain recognition within the French left, with which an organizational optimism was added to the contextual optimism, considering that the events and the increase in militants and sympathizers were an acknowledgement of their labour and confirmed the relevance of their theses.[35]

In this context, the idea and the project of autonomy flourished as a characterization of socialism, understood as starting and end point, as instrument and as process. Autonomy was associated with the exercise of the collective free will – in permanent conflict with the heteronomy of alienation promoted by modern capitalism – and emerges in SoB as the means and end of the spontaneous struggle of the proletariat in its daily life and in all aspects of social life, beginning with the most immediate area of exploitation which is the workplace and leading to a new organization of society, to the emancipation of the proletariat:

> Socialism can only be established by the autonomous action of the working class, it is nothing if not this autonomous action. Socialist society is nothing but the organization of this autonomy, which it also presupposes and develops. (Chaulieu, 1957: 168)

Autonomous action is the *beginning*, the *middle* and the *end*, it is the *condition*, the *instrument* and the *result* of socialism. Resuming the classical terms, class independence – understood as practice of self-determination – is not data but a process of emancipation that ends in socialism, a process characterized by the experiences of emancipation.

Abusing the categorical imperatives to strengthen the originality and the polemical character of its affirmations, SoB puts autonomy as property or a characteristic of the subject and the action at the core of the political dynamic and, at the same time, deploys it as an emancipatory process that passes *by* but does not end *in* socialism, rather, socialism widens and organizes. This approach articulates the notion of autonomy – independence of class with that of autonomy – self-determination as emancipatory horizon. Autonomy is not only a resource or a simple stage for emancipation, it is a process propelled by a resource and a resource developed by a process.

The concept of *autonomy*, and here lays the originality of SoB's perspective, is settled in the idea of *experience* that Lefort had proposed in 1952. Autonomy is, therefore, an emancipatory process of subjective character that is realized to the extent it deploys the subjective emancipation from the experiences of self-determination. In other words, autonomy represents the process of subjectivation relative to the experiences of emancipation.

In this sense, the systematic valuation – including the exaltation and idealization – of spontaneity on behalf of SoB is justified insofar as autonomous practice is expressed in it, it turns into autonomous experience which, in turn, is the base for new practices and autonomous actions. This cycle of production and reproduction of autonomy is the key to the revolutionary process and the deployment of emancipation. Autonomy is, therefore, conceived by SoB as an emancipatory horizon that is constructed in the present by struggle and looks towards a new social form. In this sense, it is formulated as a foreshadowing and performative device of socialism understood as 'real movement': performative to the extent that autonomy guides the struggles and foreshadowing because these anticipate the shape of future society, that is, it 'represents' socialist society.

Keeping with its belief in the autonomous capacity of the revolutionary subject, SoB argued the need to eliminate the so-called 'transition to socialism' with the immediate dissolution of all bourgeois forms (for example, the wage differentiation) and of the State in general under the principle in which socialism is freedom, that is, autonomy of the associated producers.

For SoB, the origin of the bureaucratization in the USSR is identified with the loss of autonomy of the soviets before the party and the

State. Thus it was concluded that the expropriation of the capitalists was just the negative half of the proletarian revolution and the other positive part had to be the economic dictatorship of the proletariat that promoted and realized the dissolution of the State from the beginning.

Faithful to the *soviet* tradition, the concrete forms of autonomy are outlined by Castoriadis in relatively 'classic' terms of worker management by way of the factory councils which would articulate themselves nationally in a General Assembly and a Government of Councils (Chaulieu, 1957: 167–8). Nevertheless, this institutional formulation is considered by Castoriadis, coherently with SoB's approach, as an 'adequate' form and not 'miraculous', being that no legal solution guaranteed what only the autonomous action of the class could manage. Regarding this, SoB's position was explicitly against the 'statutory fetishism' but also against 'anarchist spontaneity'.

On the other hand, even while maintaining direct democracy from the 'social cells' of the workplaces from transparency, information and knowledge, Castoriadis defended the need for a certain level of centralization that did not delegate but was an expression of workers' power (ibid.: 168). The problem of autonomy was traditionally and logically related to the theme of political organization, that is, the theme of the party. Even when SoB – in tune with its origins in Trotskyist Bolshevism – defended the historical role of the vanguard and organization in parties for the diffusion of consciousness and the objectives of the antibureaucratic struggle, it was considering its immediate dissolution within the 'autonomous organisms of the class' in the revolutionary process:

> Such an organization cannot develop unless it prepares its encounter with the process of creation of autonomous organisms of the masses. In this sense, while one might say it represents the ideological and political direction of the class in the conditions of the regime of exploitation, it must also be said and above all that it is a direction that prepares its own suppression, by way of its fusion with the autonomous organisms of the class, once the entrance of the class as a whole in the revolutionary struggle produces, in the historical scene, the true direction of humanity, which is the whole of the class itself. (Socialisme ou Barbarie, 1949b: (1) 34–5)

In spite of the mythical use of the idea of the 'whole of the class' as the subject of history, SoB assumed the problem of its internal organization and proposed a workers' democracy based on internal pluralism (factions) and the revocation of mandates in the interest of a direct exercise of power that would avoid all forms of delegation and bureaucratization.

Within the organization that intended to combine the antibureaucratic critique, *councilism* and the Bolshevik tradition, it is not by accident that the theme of the party was an object of polemics and ruptures.

Since its foundation in 1949, the need for a form of political organization – differentiating itself explicitly from the anarchists – was posed within the SoB. It would accompany and guide the autonomous organizations of the masses so they could assume the revolutionary project, before which the party would dissolve (Socialisme ou Barbarie, 1949a (2)).

At the same time, the emphasis and interpretations of this approach were different within the group. Particularly, Claude Lefort (Montal) insisted, invoking Rosa Luxemburg, in an anti-Leninist stance that, without denying the role of the vanguard, encouraged the idea of the political organization as instrument – a 'provisional detail' tending to dissolve into worker power – of the revolution and not as its 'direction' (Montal, 1952).

By 1958, the nuances became irreconcilable differences and Lefort separated definitively from SoB precisely because of the rejection of the idea of the party that Castoriadis was promoting, whom Lefort accused of incoherence with the thought of SoB, of vanguardism and of promoting a microbureaucracy that assumed the right to direct a class as if it were a separate entity. Maintaining an argument against the exteriority of the Leninist vanguard, Lefort reinforced the autonomist argument: 'The role of politics is not, therefore, to teach but, rather, to make explicit what is inscribed in the state of tendency in the life and the conduct of the workers' (Lefort, 1958). The same year, Lefort founded the ILO (*Informations et Liaisons Ouvrières*, which would later be called ICO, *Informations et Correspondances Ouvrières*).

Castoriadis' answer (now using the pseudonym of Paul Cardan) endorsed the idea of a new form of political organization that did not discard the historical line of SoB based on the trust in the autonomous action of the proletariat.[36]

It is interesting how in these articles, in which Castoriadis traces the SoB's new line, a theme that had been previously blocked, due to the enthusiasm over autonomy, now appears. The theme of the party and organization emerged out of a preoccupation that was used polemically before the autonomist orthodoxy of Lefort that had been previously glimpsed in the letters to Pannekoek:

> If this activity directed towards the autonomy of the proletariat is not accepted, it is because autonomy is granted an absolute meaning, metaphysical: it is necessary for workers to reach certain conclusions without any type of influence...
>
> Autonomy or liberty are not metaphysical states, but social and historical processes. Autonomy is won through contradictory influences. Freedom emerges through the struggle with and against others. (Socialisme ou Barbarie, 2007: (28))

The nuances implied a theoretical clarification of the relative and process-based character of autonomy and a recuperation of the Leninist principle of exteriority that could be justified not only theoretically but due to a lesser confidence in the emergence of spontaneity and the autonomy of the masses.

In effect, in 1959, after the successful institutional coup d'état by De Gaulle and once the wave of rebellions in Eastern Europe had finished, the scenario demanded that account be taken of certain inertias within the worker movement. In this sense, Castoriadis acknowledged the 'manifested immaturity of the proletariat before socialism' considering that the degeneration of the workers' organizations could not be given without the complicity of wide sectors of workers: 'nobody can lastingly betray persons who do not want to be betrayed' (Socialisme ou Barbarie, 2007: (28) 219–20). The observation of the depoliticization, the apathy, the acceptance or insufficient reason resulted in an emphatic affirmation: 'the proletariat has the organizations it is capable of having' (ibid.: (28) 220).

This disenchantment – which deep down revealed a gap in SoB's thought, blinded by the faith in the revolutionary vocation of the class, by the autonomy of the worker subject – will be the *humus* in which the abandonment of Marxism on behalf of Castoriadis, the end of SoB and the suspension of the publication of the magazine will grow.

Under the sentence of the disappearance of the 'properly said political activity' in a context of depoliticization and privatization of society, SoB ended its cycle, according to Castoriadis, 'to avoid the sectarian obsession, the pseudo activist hysteria and the delirium of interpretation' (Socialisme ou Barbarie, 2007: (28) 220). In the *Editorial* from issue 35, January 1964, the stances that had been gestating since 1959 were summarized.[37] In this synthesis, Castoriadis decreed the 'end of classical Marxism' as a consequence of three events that modified the context in which it had emerged and developed: the transformations of capitalism, the disappearance of the workers' movement 'while an organized class movement explicitly and permanently questioning capitalist domination', and the absence of revolutions both in the first as well as the third world despite the convulsions linked to decolonization. These are the novel facts that led Castoriadis to consider that Marxism was in ruins as a concrete system of thought and a programme of action.

In order to uphold this diagnosis, Castoriadis used the principles elaborated by SoB in and from Marxism, now presented against the same in a more extreme version. By this logic, Marxism was considered dead for failing to acknowledge the centrality of the division between leaders and executioners and for insisting on the material division in the field of production; for not recognizing that the fundamental dominant class was the bureaucracy and not the capitalist one; that the 'system' was the bureaucratic organization and not the market; that labour was not an object, a simple commodity; that class was not a fact, but an active subject of the struggle. The *Editorial* recited:

> For the classic conception, the proletariat suffers history until the moment it makes it blow up. For us, the proletariat makes history, in given conditions, and its struggles constantly transform capitalist society at the same time that they transform themselves. (Socialisme ou Barbarie, 1964: (35) 281)

Another critique formulated in consonance with SoB's elaborations was directed against the Leninist model of the party:

> For us, the workers' autonomy stands in the middle of all, the capacity of the masses to direct themselves, without which every idea of socialism immediately becomes a mystification. (ibid.)

Marxism was accused of emphasizing the development of the productive forces and the objective factors, which led to an economic determinism. For Castoriadis, there was no contradiction between the development of the productive forces and capitalist economic forms or capitalist relations of production as demonstrated by the fact that in the capitalism of that time one could have full employment, a rise in salary and shorten the work schedule. Thus was declared the end of the 'theological stage', the decadence of the closed theoretical systems, of the 'complete and definitive theory' in the face of the triumph of fragmentary and provisional knowledges.

In this essay, Castoriadis put forward a very pessimistic characterization of the political situation in which the unification of categories of workers in a process of proletarization that did not polarize but rather established a pyramidal hierarchy by the differentiation of tasks, the fragmentation of the work process and the creation of new specialties, looked difficult. On the other hand, the growth of the service sector suggested that, while there were more *workers*, these were not *proletariat*. The lack of concrete definition of the subject led to its definition in terms of the attitude of the arrangement faced with the struggle: 'the only real difference is between those who accept and fight the system in daily life' (ibid.: 287).

Regarding the form of domination, the recourse to violence was always less necessary insofar as mechanisms of cooptation via redistribution, reformism and pseudo democracy operated efficiently. Barbarism was presented as a 'developed nightmare': 'With the monopoly of violence as a last resource, capitalist domination lies in the bureaucratic manipulation of the people, at work, in consumption, in the rest of life (ibid.: 288).

So the deep-rooted contradiction was between *exclusion* and *participation* at all levels of life in the midst of a crisis of values and the personality of modern man. The themes opening SoB's last stage appeared, themes that would tie in with the humanist and libertarian preoccupations of the movement of 1968 and, at the same time, were related with the psychoanalytic experience of Castoriadis and his subsequent intellectual trajectory, outside Marxism and any political movement.

It is surprising to find in this text that, in contradiction, the pillars of revolutionary optimism and the Marxist analysis of SoB had not been renounced and some of its fundamental postulates reaffirmed:

> The functioning of capitalism guarantees then that there will always be 'revolutionary occasions', but does not guarantee their outcome, which cannot but depend on the degree of consciousness and autonomy of the masses. There is no 'objective' dynamic that guarantees socialism, and to say one might exist is a contradiction in terms. (ibid.: 290–1)

The revolutionary perspective now moved in the future, there 'will be' occasions, in an implicit relinquishment in the present, assuming the current impossibility. At the same time, the principle according to which, in the context of a conflictual structure such as capitalism, the only solution to the crisis emerges from the subjective factor embodied in the tendency or aspiration of the masses to autonomy was reiterated.

The 1964 Editorial summarized all the elements that Castoriadis had developed since the end of 1959 and that created strong polemics and a schism in 1963 (Gottraux, 1997).[38] Simultaneously, Castoriadis will go on disaggregating these theses in a long essay called 'Marxism and Revolutionary Theory', which was published by instalments in numbers 36–40 (between April of 1964 and June of 1965) – the last issues of the magazine before its closing – and which he re-edited as the first part of his best known book: *The Imaginary Institution of Society* (Castoriadis, 1975).

The first section is titled 'Marxism: A Provisional Balance' even though by the tone of the arguments it is presented as definitive, as a death sentence and burial of an obsolete school of thought. The author declared that it was no longer a self-critique looking to break the ties of orthodoxy but 'to choose between continuing to be a Marxist or being a revolutionary' (Castoriadis, 1975: 21).

In the diagnosis, out of the two components of Marxism – class struggle and economic determination – the second is presented as the dominant and, therefore, the essence of Marxism in which the closing wins over the opening.

As an indication of the crisis in his thought, in his farewell to Marxism, Castoriadis recuperated tones and themes of his own Marxist reflection when he clarified in a note that autonomy means 'revolution of the working masses establishing the power of the Councils' and, in another passage, that worker management is a valid means of socialization with other spheres and, thus, the bridge to social totality.

However, a clear shift of focus is evident manifested in the appearance of thematics that will become central in Castoriadis' subsequent reflections, which explains its inclusion as the first part of the book *The Imaginary Institution of Society*. These are the themes of desire, the I, of the psychological relation conscious-unconscious, the imaginary, the sociohistorical, and the relationship instituted-instituting that Castoriadis recuperated from his education and professional practice as psychoanalyst precisely in those years. While there is a series of elements that give continuity with the reflections developed by SoB, Castoriadis' subsequent trajectory excludes not only a Marxist focus and perspective but also a thematic series and could hardly be read from the logic of the 'unity of course' as Philippe Caumières, on the contrary, affirms:

> To find in the SoB militant strong intuitions that could not be developed because they were caught in a schema of thought that became obsolete. But to want to liberate them from the revolutionary pathos would mean to abandon the project of autonomy. (Caumières, 2007: 101)

We would have to see whether Marxism was or is obsolete as a field of open and diversified thought or rather the rigid scheme of thought that Castoriadis presents as Marxism, passing from the defence of Marxism against Stalinism to the assimilation of one with the other. On the other hand, while it is true that in SoB there were given more intuitions than finished theoretical developments, these were inserted in a theoretical fabric that – even in its opening and branching – gave them meaning. In particular, the idea of autonomy acquired consistency to the extent that it articulated the independence of class to socialism in a process of emancipation anchored in the development of subjectivities forged from experiences and practices of self-determination.

The subsequent development Caumières refers to has to do with the formulation of a theoretical apparatus that Castoriadis would develop in the subsequent decades within the framework of a professional intellectual trajectory. This apparatus, beyond evaluation of its solidity and scope, is susceptible to critiques from the perspective of the reflection of the SoB insofar as it is proposed as finished theory even when it intends to have a fragmentary and provisional character – following *postmodern* trends.

On the other hand, as Caumières points out, it stops adhering to the 'revolutionary *pathos*' as an attitude in the face of the concrete implications linked to the subjects in their struggles, to the political compromise oriented towards the real transformation. From a militant reflection, Castoriadis stops theorizing the concrete political conflict to submerge himself in eminently philosophical reflections. Even if he might have gained academic consistency and – with it – acknowledgement, he lost the perspective of an intellectual militancy that allowed him to focus on concrete political problems from the viewpoint of collective action.[39] The pertinent critique of Daniel Bensaid is directed by this sense:

> But what is autonomy? Autonomy of whom or of what? And who holds the exorbitant power to define it? Autonomy for autonomy would only make formalism out of autonomy. And nobody could be against the principle of an indeterminate autonomy. The issue becomes more urgent precisely at the time in which its content and ways are trying to be determined, whether in the sense of a communicational intersubjectivity or when autonomy, very differently, is proposed as radical councilism ...
>
> This invocation to a sudden awakening seems to rest on one hypothetical exit of an indeterminate will or on the aim of the emergence of an event or miraculous happening. (Bensaid, 2007: 20–1)

In effect, with the abandonment by Castoriadis of the Marxist perspective, the solidity of the autonomy of the concrete subjects in concrete struggles melts in the metaphysical air of abstract autonomy, as formal transcendental property. This translates into the extirpation of autonomy from the political field.

To finish, let us go back to the heart of SoB's thought to evaluate its range and limits. Aside from reproducing the arguments, the Editorial previously mentioned and the preceding articles, the long text that was a farewell to Marxism by Castoriadis presents some points that, paradoxically, make the idea of autonomy more precise and profound. In particular, it seems linked to the notion of praxis:

> We can say that, because of praxis, the autonomy of the other and the others is at once the end and the means; praxis is what points at the development of autonomy as the end and uses autonomy as a means to that end...
>
> What we call revolutionary politics is a praxis that has as its object the organization and the orientation of society in light of the autonomy of all and acknowledges that this presupposes a radical transformation of society that will not be possible because of the deployment of the autonomy of men. (Castoriadis, 1975: 112, 115)

The three pillars of SoB's thought appear here explicitly. In first place, autonomy as praxis, which alludes to experience and political subjectivation. In second place, the articulation of its double nature: as a means and an end, as process and as event. In third place, the circularity and interdependence between present and future, between the orientation of today's struggles and the shape of society tomorrow is mentioned again. Autonomy is at the beginning and end of the process, in classical terms it is class independence and socialism, and in this manner it becomes the whole of the process to the extent in which human beings – based on their autonomous capacity – are at the forefront.

At the same time, alongside an intuition and an original and enriching approach, we can glimpse elements of a certain conceptual confusion derived from the absence of a clear distinction between *autonomy* and *autonomization*, between emancipatory *horizon* and *process* of emancipation. A necessary distinction to fully visualize the articulation outlined by SoB:

> We want to show the possibility and make explicit the sense of the revolutionary project, as a project of transformation of society present in an organized society and oriented towards the autonomy

of all, this transformation being achieved by the autonomous action of men just as they are produced by the present society. (ibid.: 116)

The last part of the quote reveals one of the most problematic passages of SoB's formulation: 'men just as they are produced by the present society'. Following SoB's reasoning, are men alienated by heteronomy or the carriers of autonomy? Both figures appear in SoB's analysis as opposing types without clearing up the coexistence or the passage from one to the other, assuming autonomy as an intrinsic quality that magically appears or disappears. Now, whether one assumes the viability of the passage or the existence of the quality, the SoB's approach is based on automatism, on a mechanical device. In the reflections within SoB, the emphasis on autonomy as a real movement leads to a mere acknowledgment of the alienated and heteronomous ties (we would say *subaltern*) as social facts that autonomy tends to surpass, without giving them a specific weight and place and constitutes a fundamental theoretical and political problem.

As evidence of this, the pessimistic considerations of the depoliticization and the privatization of life from 1959 onwards appear as exterior to the logic of SoB's autonomist thought, as its contradictory opposite, an unacceptable interference and, in some way, devastating to the extent it dismantles not only the optimism that regulated the design but the design itself, ending in the abandonment of Marxism and the group's dissolution.

In theoretical terms, the aim of autonomy blurs subalternity, unbalances the approach, puts it in the field of an autonomist essentialism that obstructs the capacity to visualize the complexity and the profundity of its subaltern counterpart located within the relations of domination, with which the process is dissolved in a leap towards autonomy. In this sense, the absence of such notions as *relative* autonomy – that Gramsci, for example, implicitly uses to refer to *integral* autonomy – or *autonomization* contributes to create an absolute notion, an essentialism and an imperative that encourage the conceptual and theoretical confusion that underlies SoB's approach.

However, marginal to these considerations, SoB's reflection remains relevant because it offers a Marxist elaboration of the concept of *autonomy* that explicitly combines fundamental dimensions: the *beginning* of independence, the emancipatory *horizon* and the *process* with the corresponding subjective implications. *Data*, *instrument* and *process* melt into a single perspective.

In this articulation, the perspective of analysis of the processes of subjective construction linked to the dimensions of emancipation and power is particularly significant at the conceptual level: the perspective of autonomic subjectivation, anchored in the notion of *experience*, a result of the dialogue between social being and social consciousness. Albeit this, by itself, leaves other aspects of the subjective formation uncovered, at the same time this meaning potentially situates the concept of *autonomy* beside the notions of *subalternity* and *antagonism* as a fundamental facet of the uneven and combined construction of the political subjects in the framework of domination, through conflict, on the way to emancipation.

The Autogestion Movement in France: Autonomic Theory and Practice

The concept of *autonomy* would have in France a moment of *verification* through a series of autonomic experiences, a process that assumed the shape and name of a *self-management movement*. Reflections over the concept of *self-management* understood as the theoretical and practical translation of autonomy and as a field and vector of political subjectivation proliferated.

In effect, the reflection over autonomy put forward by Socialisme ou Barbarie would find fertile ground in the France of 1968, that is, the cycle of mobilization and social struggles that began in 1961, passes through the epicentre of May–June 1968, extends until the end of the 1970s and culminates with the electoral victory of the coalition of the left headed by François Mitterrand in May of 1981, which marked the *zenith* of the accumulation of forces of the left and, at the same time, the end of a cycle (Artiéres and Zancarini-Fournel, 2008).

Within this process, the theme of autonomy would be propagated from its translation and dissemination in terms of *self-management*, a concept and an operative political proposal that intended to summarize a series of aspirations and autonomic social experiences that would acquire a surprising diffusion both in the plane of practices as well as in theory-making in the France of these years.

In practice, the fragmentary struggles of the first half of the 1960s converged, after the experience of mobilization against the intervention of the USA in Vietnam, in the outbreak of May 1968, in which the student movement disrupted the sociopolitical order. The students expressed politically a generational malaise translating it into rebellion, critique and political creativity before a country stuck between Gaullist conservative paternalism and the routine opposition of the PCF.

In spite of the economic development of the Glorious Thirty,[40] the Fifth Republic that emerged from the Algerian War did not offer the young ideal horizons that would overcome the productivist and consumerist universe. A deep malaise transformed into libertarian desire was at the origin of the student mobilization and in its vindications that implicitly appealed to autonomy in the face of a society in which, behind appearances, alienation was the structuring modality of social relations.[41]

In times of nostalgia, where neoliberalism opposes the hypothesis of the return to state regulation of the market, the radical critique of the *golden age* of capitalism and of the social State constitutes the most durable legacy of that experience. Rebelliousness, expressed as rejection in the confrontations of the *quartier Latin* and in the iconoclastic attitudes of the students, translated into an alternative by way of the self-management practices that were inaugurated in universities and schools, within which the student leadership propelled, even in the midst of contradictions, a participative vision of social relations and *public speaking* or *right to speak* without precedent.

In June, the working class entered the scene by striking and occupying factories that added an explosive ingredient, the social extension of the movement, the potential worker-student alliance, the mobilization of the powerful union apparatus and French left-wingers (see Vigna, 2007). The PCF and the CGT, in spite of their repudiation of the groups of the extreme left, had to accompany the worker mobilization that gestated from the student movement so as not to leave to the French Democratic Confederation of Labour (CFDT), recently radicalized, the monopoly of the workers' protest. A sector of the socialists, after their disastrous governing and parliamentary experiences in the Fourth Republic (particularly in terms of the colonial politics in Indochina and Algeria), saw in the movement an opportunity to recuperate the presence and visibility in the face of a communist party surpassed by the protests. In particular, the Unified Socialist Party (PSU), the most radical socialist group made up of diverse sectors (including left-wing Catholics and dissident Trotskyists), was the one that, with the most coherence, attempted to embody and to politically channel the values of 1968. Even Mitterrand himself, up and coming as leader of a new socialist generation, found in the conjuncture an opportunity to advance in the federation of the socialists he had been propelling and that would materialize in 1971 with the historical Congress of Epinay that would give birth to the *new* Socialist Party (see Portelli, 1998).

The biggest novelty in the reconfiguration of the field of politics in France since 1968 is the appearance or the strengthening of a series of organizations on the extreme left. The existing Trotskyist groups (the Internationalist Communist Organization (OCI) and Worker Struggle (LO)) were joined by a new organization – the Communist League (LC) – that emerged from the student experience of the Revolutionary Communist Youths (JCR), situated to the left of the PCF around the figure of Alain Krivine.[42] After an initial Guevarian bias, the LC assumed a clear Trotskyist identity at the Fourth International (Salles, 2005).[43]

The Maoist groups which, in principle, disdainfully perceived the student mobilizations, became involved when the workers' struggles occurred through the participation of the radicalized youth in factories. The phenomenon of the *établis* – thousands of young people who were proletarianized by entering the factories – showed the extension and marked the entrenchment of Maoism in France. A spontaneist and movementist strand – ironically called *mao-spontex* – regrouped in the Gauche Prolétarienne (GP), attracting many intellectuals like Jean-Paul Sartre and Michel Foucault, as well as the prominent disciples of Louis Althusser and, also, succeeded in founding newspapers of wide distribution like *La Cause du Peuple* and, finally, *Libération* which, purged of leftist radicalism, is one of the best-selling journals in France today.

With the convocation of elections in June which backed up the electoral weight of the 'silent majority' in favour of de Gaulle and conservatism in the face of the 'vociferous minorities' of May, the year of 1968 stopped as an *event* but continued as a *process*. Its extension in time took the shape of a rainbow of struggles of workers, students, and feminists, for civil rights and against repression. The common denominator of them all was the synthesis of the triad social justice–democracy–liberty, in a word: *autogestion*.[44] A word that indicated a *form* as condition for the realization of a *content* – emancipation – and at the same time pointed at a series of practices and experiences of subjective appropriation, at a process of political subjectivation established in the exercise of self-determination.

The first explicit political mention of autogestion goes back to May 1968, when the CFDT launched the slogan and included it in the heart of its programme. Immediately after this, the PSU made it its own and turned it into the banner of its differentiation from the PCF.[45] The Mitterrandian PS recuperated it to the extent to which its most structured internal current, CERES, maintained the centrality of self-management even though, contrary to the PSU and the CFDT and, in resonance with Marx's considerations on cooperatives, it considered that its realization necessarily passed through a change of government and structural transformations of the economy and the State, that is, in an integral scheme and not in the shape of partial and local experiences. The passage of the Rocardian current (headed by Michel Rocard) and Gilles Martinet from the PSU to the PS in 1974 would reinforce the self-managerial positions to the degree that the socialists, in 1975, assumed a thesis on self-management as the programmatic axis. The revolutionary left would be more sceptical over the issue, even though, contrary to the orthodox rejection on behalf of the Maoists, French Trotskyism showed a greater sensibility towards the incorporation of the topic of autogestion. The LCR, rearticulated after is dissolution by law in 1973, was attentive and its main ideologue, Ernest Mandel, would publish an anthology in three tomes on the control of workers and self-management to mark its Marxist anchoring and its Bolshevik origin. On the other hand, Michel Pablo, main leader of the Fourth International, would create an autogestion group after leaving this organization and became consultant to the government of Algeria when constitutional reforms introduced autogestion (ascending planning alongside descending) to this Arab country, starting with the government of Ben Bella until 1965 when Boumedienne came into power and undertook a process of counter-reform (see Béroud et al., 2003).

The same PCF, after disposing of the theme as an 'empty formula' in 1968, towards the end of the decade, when the problem (as well as the struggles that upheld it) started to decline, adopted the autogestion perspective. Regarding this late opening, some historians note the lack of conviction, the opportunism linked to the will to incorporate the self-management movements and its echoes, and the intention to show the PCF's disposition to follow the politics of convergence of the lefts, embodied in the common programme of 1972 and focused on the alliance with the PS that, precisely in those years, endured a problematic impasse (see Dandé, 2003). This late approach of the communists did not modify the fact that autogestion was hoisted in France fundamentally by the anti-Stalinist left, anarchosyndicalists, councilists, Trotskyists, libertarians and Christian Socialists.

Beyond the ideological incorporation on the part of the diverse segments, the reality of the autogestional longings expressed in the concrete struggles determined the opening of the left regarding the thematic. The symbol of this convergence was, without a doubt, the LIP experience in 1973, a strike transformed into self-management under the slogan 'we make them, we sell them, we pay ourselves', around which all the left, beyond its differences, mobilized (see Vigna, 2007). Other similar experiences, workers' experience as well as from other productive, territorial, artistic and student sectors produced the same effect at more reduced scales (see, respectively, Cuane, 2003; Pucciarelli, 2003; Legois, 2003; Morder, 2003). The communitarian phenomenon that accompanied the autogestion problem spread across the French social fabric, including the countryside, with the prominent experience of the Larzac, a region where decades later the antiglobalization movement headed by José Bove emerged.

The sequence of autogestion workers' experiences extended in time until the 1980s, and in space, mainly in the provinces: the dock workers in the whole of France, the textile workers in Cerizay, the agricultural workers in Pedernec, the automotive workers in Talbot-Poissy. At the university level, autogestion left a long-lasting settlement based on the establishment of *co-management* and translated into the experimental project of the Vincennes campus of the University of Paris where a big part of the radical intellectual left regrouped.

Nevertheless, in the midst of this practical and ideological proliferation, the autogestion banner was an umbrella term under which hid diverse interpretations that referred to different and, to some extent, divergent and conflicting theoretical and political stances. On one hand, the interpretations of self-management bifurcated between one meaning focused on the themes of social control and direct democracy, opposed at the beginning of the delegation, and a meaning that assumed representative democracy and participative democracy as complementary. On the other hand, the notion of *management* was susceptible to an integral translation that encompassed life as a whole according to the ideals and the slogan of 1968 but, at the same time, could be translated in merely technical terms, linked to particular aspects of life associated or limited to productive realities, essentially working class. Evidently, the subversive scope of the first hypothesis – of global character – was sensibly reduced in the second version, of sectorial type. In the third place, as a corollary to the former, at the ideological level, the notion of autogestion tended to be a substantial part of both socialist political projects of varying radicalness and of simple democratic-radical ideologies.

At heart, the debate underlined the disjuncture between one conception of self-management as *means* and another as *end*. The stances of the PCF and the PS were representative of this debate. They assumed, following the traditional Marxist attitude, that self-management only had meaning after the conquest of power (electoral) and the nationalization of the fundamental sectors of the economy in a Jacobian perspective, particularly theorized by the CERES (centre for Socialist Studies, Research and Education) strand within the PS (see Breheier, 2003), while the PSU, the CFDT and the Rocardians stated that autogestion was a vector of social transformation (see Georgi, 2003b) – and a political culture – that had to be encouraged immediately and, furthermore, it was the condition for the subsequent electoral and institutional ratification (Hatzfeld, 2003). This last position appeared from the search for a theoretical-political foundation for a radical socialist anti-State third way that surpassed the social democratic, as well as the dictatorship of the proletariat, management of the State-focused projects of the PS and the PCF.

If the left as a whole saw in autogestion a form of rejection of capital, the differences appeared in relation to the idea of autogestion as rejection of authority, be it State, union or party. This was linked to the placement of the autogestional theme in the linkage between economy and politics, that the autogestion socialists wanted to fund and that the Social Democrats and communists wanted to distinguish by leaving the monopoly of politics to the party and the socialist State. In the context of this debate, the notion of *civil society* would appear not only as a liberal formula but as an emancipatory hypothesis, literally translated into the principle of self-government, that is, autogestion. In another problematic intersection closely linked to the former, the radical left associated autogestion with the revolutionary perspective, while the social democratic left linked it to reformist solutions.

However, beyond the different interpretations over its scope, within the Marxist thought of the time, opposite to Althusserianism and structuralism, the notion of autogestion implied generally a perspective that tended to articulate the principle of the independence of class within the process of emancipation, that looked for an operative form that allowed to channel and to potentiate the autonomy, the capacity for self-determination, of the subject. In this sense, whether autogestion was presented as a prefigurative and prescriptive model of emancipated society or as its gradual realization, its value as political experience remained intact, its impact in a process of autonomic subjectivation that assumed itself as the vector of every humanist transformation project.

At the strictly nominal level, beyond the problematic affinity with the workers' councils studied and sanctified by the post-Red October Marxism, the word *autogestion* was imported to France from the Serbo-Croatian and the Yugoslavian experience, where the need to differentiate from the Stalinist model had translated into an implementation of a self-managed model established in the Law of the Workers' Councils in 1950 and sanctioned in the Federal Constitution in 1953 (Dezés, 2003).

The periodical meetings in Korcula, Yugoslavia, in which the French autogestionists actively participated, led to the birth of the *Centre International de Coordination des Recherches sur l'Autogestion* in 1976. Since 1975, the repression in Yugoslavia of the *Praxis Group* – which embodied the libertarian current of socialism in this country – made the problems that accompanied the Yugoslavian experience more evident, which included not only the absence of political pluralism but also the regional tensions, the contradictory opening to the market, the economic stagnation, and the need to resort to IMF (International Monetary Fund) loans.

After 1968 and throughout the 1970s, magazines and books on the theme of autogestion proliferated in France. One of the ideologues of the CFDT, Pierre Rosanvallon, maintained that *the era of autogestion* had begun, which had the virtue of being born as a social movement before becoming a doctrine (Rasanvallon, 1976).

The magazine *Autogestion*, whose 70 numbers came out between 1966 and 1986, reunited self-management intellectuals from different strands of critical Marxism: Trotskyists like Pierre Naville and Michel Pablo, former SoB members like Yvon Bourdet and Daniel Mothé, heterodox Marxists like Henri Lefebvre, libertarian communists like Daniel Guérin and libertarians without a banner like Georges Gurvitch, who died before the magazine started to circulate.[46] The trajectory of the name of the magazine is symptomatic, and since 1970 it included socialism (*Autogestion et Socialisme*) and, since 1980, changed to the plural: *Autogestions* (see Veil, 2003).

Henri Lefebvre, possibly the best known among the intellectuals of the magazine, tangentially approached the self-management thematic but his ample intellectual production turned around similar topics. The humanist Marxism of Lefebvre, radically averse to State socialism of the soviet type and to structuralism, assumed as the axis of social critique the analysis of alienation and developed a focus on daily life as centre of the emancipation starting from the idea of the *self-production of life* (see Lefebvre, 1966, 1968).

The works by Lefebvre on the social production of space and, particularly, on the city and urban problems were pioneers of a crucial problematic that Marxism had subordinated to the problems of the factory (see Lefebvre, 2000).[47] Between sporadic direct interventions on the issue, Lefebvre stated that autogestion was a way, in addition to an objective, and it was the form *par excellence* of the spontaneism of the time, just as anarchosyndicalism was in another, a form of appropriation of life. The attention given to the daily practices and the option to 'change life' that propelled Lefebvre – which would later be the campaign slogan for the Mitterrand socialists – brought him closer to the *situationists* to the degree that he initiated a direct collaboration with Guy Debord.

By the end of the 1970s, in another intervention focused on the idea of self-management, Lefebvre criticized the Yugoslavian model for being an established system while true autogestion could only be a permanent construction, 'a perpetual struggle and perpetually reborn', a 'movement and not an institution' (see Trebisch, 2003). These considerations clearly point to an understanding of self-management as a process of political subjectivation, as a subjective construction built on the incorporation of experiences of autonomy, of self-determination, of emancipation, albeit a relative one.

Other members of the magazine anchored their reflections on autogestion in the critique of alienation. For example, Pierre Naville, sociologist and Trotskyist, starting from the critique of alienation, contributed to the formation of French self-managerial Marxism from his studies on the negative impacts of technification and authoritarian planning (see Cuénot, 2003). Two other defenders of autogestion, Víctor Fay and Víctor Leduc, have a similar theoretical trajectory,[48] starting from the recuperation of Marx's thought and, in particular, from the thematic of alienation passing by the critique of the USSR to uphold autogestion as a model of emancipation.

Fay defined it as a 'realistic utopia', putting forward an interesting hypothesis of transition from which, in capitalist countries, the workers' control of production was the antechamber of integral self-management that could be realized after the conquest of power. Like the majority of French autogestion intellectuals, Víctor Fay combined an affinity for the Yugoslavian model with the critique of its limits, in the first place, getting inspiration from Rosa Luxemburg's thought, the bureaucratic weight of the party over the mass movements. Starting from the critique of alienation that produced the increasing technologization of production, Fay opposed the institutionalization derived from the state policies of nationalization and planning by setting it against the idea of the workers' control of production and assuming self-management as a model of social experimentation, of trial and error, without coercion but without excluding the possibility of internal and class conflicts throughout the process.

Víctor Leduc, starting from more philosophical studies, proceeded in the same way to recuperate Marx's thought as the theoretical support of the autogestion project and as an antidote against alienation, opening to problems like the radical reduction of the work schedule, the self-management of social time and elaborating a radical critique of the division of labour (Ravenel, 2003).

Both perceived autogestion as the framework for the deployment of processes of subjectivation rooted in autonomy, in the experience of emancipation.[49]

The antithetic relation between alienation and self-management clearly marked the placement of the autogestion theme at the level of an emancipatory mechanism – in the same manner in which alienation is a mechanism of domination as well as affirmation of subjectivity – just as alienation is its negation.

In sum, the autonomic eagerness born from the mobilizations of the 1960s and 1970s in France translated into a multiplicity of experiences and self-management theorizations. From 1981, the limits of the institutionalization of socialist reformism were measured in the hollowing out of the idea of 'changing life' – the electoral campaign slogan – towards a governmental conservatism in full continuity with the statist French tradition (see Halimi, 2000: 479–626). The autogestion cycle was over in France.

At the international level, this closing coincides with the enthusiasm and the subsequent disappointments generated by the emergence of *Solidarność* in Poland, the last experiment of workers' councilism in the countries of Eastern Europe that, at the beginning, reanimated the hopes for a libertarian socialism founded in the organized participation of the social sectors, workers first.

In the 1980s, autogestion stops being a political project in France and, in the experiences where it survives, becomes – in the best of cases – a 'pedagogical utopia', according to an expression by a French historian (see Proust, 2003), with all the limits and the scope this implies, without the possibility that learning would allow an emancipatory project at the level of society to mature nor to activate expansive processes of political subjectivation.

The problematic of autonomous learning that circulated in those years – contrary to the idea of cutting edge teaching – was linked to the subjective processing of the experiences that constituted the heart of the process of political subjectivation that propelled the autogestion movement in its concrete development.

On the other hand, in addition to the sum of the experiences – a set of dynamics of politicization and mobilization oriented towards the idea and the practice of autonomy – the French self-managerial cycle left an important theoretical legacy that, with the pioneering reflection on autonomy put forward by Socialisme ou Barbarie, strengthens and projects the concept in the field of analysis of the processes of political subjectivation.

Conclusion

The SOB's reflections on *autonomy* and its theoretical and practical translation into *autogestion* in the movements of the 1970s in France developed the scope of the concept and allow the specification of its content.

On one hand, they articulate its meaning as class independence based on its separation from the dominant class – the birth of the subject – assuming the subjective implications of its permanent formation with the emancipation in its quadruple dimension: as *means*, as *end*, as *process*, and as *prefiguration*. On the other, as counterpart to this process-based extension, they associate autonomy with a determined form of political subjectivation that detaches from practices and experiences of liberation, forged in the dialogue between spontaneity and consciousness.

Regarding the first aspect, we must remember that the association of autonomy with emancipation carries the debates relative to its location between present and future, between the emphasis on the value in itself of the autonomic struggles of today and the accent on autonomy as future societal self-regulation. This last emphasis does not necessarily imply the existence of a model, but the acknowledgement of the political role of an abstraction, a *myth* – in the line traced by Georges Sorel (see Sorel, 1972) and by Antonio Gramsci and José Carlos Mariátegui – an echo from the past, as Walter Benjamin would suggest, a horizon of the future and a possible utopia, or the *not yet* as suggested by Ernst Bloch.

On the other hand, as an attempt to articulate between temporalities, the hypothesis of *prefiguration* is highlighted. In this case autonomy does not designate only the form of the emancipated society of the future – the end – or the meaning of the struggles of the present – the process – but it characterizes their sense and orientation as anticipation of emancipation, as representation in the present of the future liberation. In this sense, whether or not it is presented as an abstract model, as a defined project or myth, autonomy starts to exist in the concrete experiences that prefigure it, giving life to an emancipatory process that acquires materiality if we understand it, as Marx and Engels understand communism, as a 'real movement that nullifies and surpasses the current state of things'.[50] In this direction, autonomy can be thought of as a synonym of communism, a synonym that points to the *method* and to the libertarian and democratic *content*, a procedural utopia that corresponds to the substantial or material utopia proper to communism.[51]

Be it an abstract referent or concrete experience, autonomy guides a real process: autonomization, the way to integral autonomy, plagued by partial or relative autonomies, which supposes the rejection of every autonomization that entails an idealization of a metaphysical property of the subject.

In these terms, the idea of autonomy as a contradictory process of emancipation is sustained by Mabel Thwaites Rey as follows:

> Autonomy is a process of permanent autonomization, of continued understanding of the subalternized role that imposes upon the system the popular classes and the need for its reversal, which has its marches and counter-marches, its fluxes and refluxes. (Thwaites Rey, 2004: 20)

On the other hand, if autonomy is, by definition, the capacity to establish norms, it is power and, therefore, it can be deduced from the relations of power, it is power understood as relation and not as thing or object, a relation between subjects. Autonomy emerges and is forged in the intersection between relations of power and the construction of subjects. In this intersection, autonomy appears as part of the process of construction of the sociopolitical subject, that is, as the condition of the subject that, by emancipating, dictates its own norms of conduct.

In this sense, thinking through democracy as 'self-determination of the mass', Zavaleta writes:

> … the act of self-determination of the mass as constitutive moment carries in its heart at least two tasks. There is, in effect, a foundation of power, which is irresistibility converted into incorporated dread;

there is, on the other hand, the foundation of freedom, that is, the implantation of self-determination as a daily custom. (Zavaleta, 1989: 87)

Going back to the double meaning *independence-emancipation*, avoiding its temporal petrification – that is, one precedes and is conditioned by the other – we can assume them to be faces of the same coin, simultaneous manifestations of a same process.

It has been assumed in the Marxist debate that the independence of class is a *sine qua non* condition for the maturation of a class struggle in which the interests of the oppressed are represented, the class *for itself*. However, it has also been considered that this condition is the result of a process of subjective construction, that is, of a first stage of emancipation, of exit from subalternity. In this sense, considering this the first step in the conquest of autonomy that does not necessarily have to be circumscribed to the emergence of the subject in a context of domination is justified, in its delimitation – Sorel would say *schism*[52] – but rather it prolongs in time, in the circumstances of the conflict until it becomes the shape of emancipated society *par excellence*.

With this process-based connotation the idea of *autonomy* enters into the Marxist repertory as a fundamental category for analysis and the understanding of the processes of political subjectivation corresponding to the experiences of independence and emancipation and, in this way, is potentially situated on a par with the concepts of *subalternity* and *antagonism*.

4

Articulations

Having situated the frame of reference for the concepts of *subalternity, antagonism* and *autonomy*, and after reviewing their development in the context of Marxist perspectives of analysis of processes of political subjectivation, in this final chapter we attempt to offer an assessment in light of their possible articulation within a conceptual triad.

To support this possibility we start from the diagnosis of its disarticulation – that is, of its separate genesis, development and existence – and of the identification of its main causes. In this direction, in the first part, resuming elements from the first chapters, we will outline a panorama of the political and theoretical interferences that impeded the meeting between the analytical perspectives focused on each one of the three concepts.

In the second section, which opens the properly theoretical trajectory of the argument of our proposal, we will maintain that, in spite of their uneven conceptual consolidation, if we pay attention to their origin and location within a common analytical framework, it is possible to think of them as *homologous* categories.

In the third section, the acknowledgment of the differentiated explanatory scope of each category will allow us to establish their *specificity* and, on that basis, to move forward to the justification of the pertinence of their articulation.

Finally, in a fourth and last section, departing from the synthesis of the identified affinities and differences – that pose them, respectively, as *homologous* and *specific* – we will maintain the *complementarity* of these categories and, in light of it, the possibility and relevance of their articulation in a tripartite scheme susceptible to capture and interpret the *synchrony* of the combinations that configure the political subjectivities as well as to characterize the *synchrony* of the process of their permanent formation. We will finish this journey by pointing out the centrality of antagonism as a fundamental axis and passage within the conceptual triad.

Disagreements

Before we argue the relevance and viability of their articulation, let us see the reasons for which the concepts of *subalternity, antagonism* and *autonomy* were created and developed separately presenting them as *alternative*.

Definitely, a decisive factor of disagreement was the political distance between the strands of thought that promoted them, a distance frequently crossed by the competition to elaborate the most adequate and efficient revolutionary strategy in terms of corresponding time and space. In fact, outside the relative absence of explicit debates, it is possible to identify with sufficient clarity the points of rupture, the distances and the confrontations as well as their theoretical consequences.[1]

A particularly visible political contrast – insofar as it crosses the same national context – is given between the Negrian workerist elaboration and the Gramscian communist thought transferred from the 1930s to the decades of the post-World War II period, by way of the political translation of the Togliattian leadership, as a framework for PCI politics.

The difference in eras and political agendas when they were being forged, beyond what the two Antonios – *Nino* and *Toni* – declared that propelled the proletarian revolution, is evident. Antonio 'Nino' Gramsci, in the years of fascism, arming himself with the 'pessimism of intelligence' to compensate for the vanguard's 'optimism of the will'[2] of the prior decade, searched – from jail and with the ebb of the revolutionary movement – for the keys that would open the roads for the resurgence of a revolutionary perspective that grouped the popular majority that, focused on the convergence of the subaltern classes, was adapted to the reality of the countries of advanced capitalism, in which bourgeois hegemony in civil society armoured the State.

On the other hand, in another time, Antonio 'Toni' Negri, riding the wave of mobilization that covers the beginning of the 1970s through to the end of that decade, thought from the 'optimism of intelligence',[3] about the keys to guide the revolutionary will, in the midst of the ineluctable transcendence of conflict, towards the roads of the imminent communist triumph, headed by a working class 'without allies' and propelled by its political vanguard.

Two moments, two hypotheses of subjective formation and two communist strategic options. In effect, *workerism* as a whole spurned, or even rejected, Gramsci's thought in virtue of the 'Gramscianism' of the PCI, mechanically associating one thing to the other, something that – as demonstrated, for example, by Perry Anderson's reading of the Italian Marxist's work (see Anderson, 1981)[4] – occurred with other sectors of the new left of the 1960s and 1970s in their opposition to all reformism.

The disagreement between Gramsci's and Negri's thought appears as the theoretical counterpart to the political confrontation in Italy between the prudent cultural rooting of the PCI starting from the post-World War II period and the daring radical irruption of the new revolutionary left since the 1960s. A disagreement that was an important factor, not to say decisive, of a historic – theoretical and practical – defeat that would be fought at the end of the 1970s and sanctioned in the 1980s with the consolidation of neoliberal hegemony, institutionally embodied by the government of Bettino Craxi. It was a defeat whose prolonged effects have maintained Berlusconism since the mid 1990s to date and from which the Italian left has not recovered.[5]

Beyond this Italian short-circuit, the other theorizations we have highlighted also emerge historically from strategic bets that tend to be opposed. This is how the reflections on autonomy and self-management in France were born of the two waves of mobilization and tendential revolutionary optimism: the first – in the 1950s – accompanied the wars of liberation in Indochina and Algeria that directly impacted French policy and had, as backdrop and international reference, the libertarian movements in Eastern Europe. The second – between the 1960s and the 1970s – was headed by students and workers in France and had as backdrop and international reference the Cuban and Vietnamese revolutions. The radical movements that put forward the ideas of *autonomy* and *self-management* could not, nor did they want to, integrate the cautious Gramscian strategy, in good measure embodied by the French communists of the PCF, who were accused of having renounced the revolution to encourage an unending conquest of a hegemony that translated into conformism, the acceptance of structural dualism and the consequent worker-boss negotiation of Fordist capitalism.[6]

At the individual level, Gramsci's own political itinerary, simplified between the workerist autonomist *ordinovista* emphasis and the national-popular subaltern nuance of the *Notebooks*, exemplifies a historical, theoretical and political oscillation that, while not irreconcilable, translates concretely into orientations and perspectives that tend to polarize, as demonstrated by the practical applications that were made in their name: the *war of movement*, that is, the insurrectional hypothesis of the factory councils at the end of the decade of 1910 and the *war of position*, that is, the process of progressive political, territorial and cultural rooting of the Togliattian *new party* in the post-World War II era.

Something rather similar in terms of the theoretical-political divergences happens with Castoriadis' passage from the revolutionary Marxism of SoB to liberal-democratic intellectualism between the 1950s and the 1970s, with the parallel deployment of the concept of autonomy, which includes an implicit rejection of the perspectives of antagonism, as revolutionary scenario, as hypothesis of open, frank and violent confrontation and as itinerary of formation of political subjectivities. As we have shown, the continuity of their hopes for autonomy is marked by an epistemological rupture insofar as the depoliticization of the category ends up relegating it to an abstract field in which the political subjects and their concrete struggles are diluted.

Finally, as the third example of the persistence of disagreement, the 1980s marked, with the end of the era of radicalization and the subsequent conservative turn, the orientation of Negri's thinking without this favouring the opening towards the problematic of subalternity. In effect, even though the defeat of the anti-systemic movements of the 1970s weighed on his reflections – which would have allowed the assimilation of the analytical virtues of the focus on *subalternity* – this was blurred by the persistence of an unwavering verbal optimism that caused his attempts to theorize the new conditions of the social struggles not to produce a conceptual approach nor a theoretical opening in this direction. It is not by accident that his thought would flourish again – and find enthusiastic readers – once the end of the tunnel had been glimpsed, in the dawning of a new era of mobilizations and protests, between the mid 1990s and the beginning of the millennium, between the Zapatista uprising, the French strikes and the antiglobalization protests in Seattle.

The 1980s were an era of the ebb of mobilizations and hegemonic reconfiguration. They offered a possibility of theoretical articulation to the extent that they could not maintain the optimism and much less the triumphalism that underlay the antagonistic and autonomic essentialisms and opened the door to an incorporation of the perspective of subalternity. However, insofar as the reflux was forged in a scenery of open defeat of the revolutionary movements in the world, the 1980s translated, at the theoretical-political level into a *lost decade* to the extent that they triggered – as an expression of the so-called 'crisis of Marxism' – a theoretical diaspora and an exodus of political reflection. Even if the focus on subalternity were to come back into favour, more able to explain the defeat and its sequels than the concepts of *antagonism* and *autonomy*, the bedrock and the elemental conditions of elaboration for any approach or articulation among the perspectives carrying the diverse concepts were missing. In effect, as much as it could explain the defeat, the subaltern focus also adapted to the era because it easily lent itself to empirical dissolution, in the postmodern relativist way.

As backdrop, the emptying of political thought, passed through the conservative triumph that, mounted on the sequence of frustrations from the prior decade, had managed to embed in common sense the mistrust over the force of the subjective factor and the fatalist acceptance of the inexorable weight of the structures, deploying the theme of subjectivity at the edges of the system, favouring the exaltation of the *margins* and *exteriority* as the only stronghold of relative freedom, of autonomy.

Currently, in view of a new epochal passage particularly sensitive in Latin America, initiated in the mid 1990s and penetrated by the tension between the crisis of neoliberal hegemony and the reappearance of mobilizations and socio-political movements, the proper conditions for an articulation of theoretical approaches that permit the visualization of nuances, superimpositions and contradictions that cover the processes of political subjectivation currently in progress are present.

Nevertheless, beyond the affiliations and phobias of the authors and the movements that promoted them in the first instance in their more systematic use and in their application to discourse and political practice, these concepts keep backing essentialist focuses that tend to oppose each other, as much by their analytical emphases as by the political projects they put forward.[7]

Apart from these historical-political considerations, there are factors of another kind to be recognized in the origin and the cause of the disagreement between the perspectives of subalternity, antagonism and autonomy. These lie in the fact that the theoretical forge of these notions, as is proper to Marxism, is produced in the intersection between the understanding and the transformation of reality, that is, it emerges from the interweaving of descriptive, interpretative and prescriptive aims. This interlocking has the virtue proper to praxis insofar as it allows the combination of concerns and theoretical and political tasks and emerges from the concrete necessities of the same compression of the world and action.

Subalternity, *antagonism* and *autonomy* emerge as concepts to the extent they offer a glimpse at answers to political-strategic questions in terms of the horizons of visibility and of historically determined projections. This double conditioning – *strategic aim* and *historic horizon* – constitutes the genetic code, the DNA of each one of them. They are the spine of Gramscian communist thought, of the *socio-barbarian* ideology synthesized by Castoriadis – subsequently deployed by the French autogestion movement – and of Negri's workerist thought. To the extent that they present themselves as the categories from which the horizon of visibility of perspectives loaded with political will is organized, subalternity, antagonism, and autonomy constitute *precepts*.

In this way, both the wealth as well as the limits of the approaches put forward by the authors and currents we have reviewed, arise from the reduction that their starting points produce, from the contexts and the subjective referents, real or ideal, they think from. In addition to the general validity of this principle, in our case, the thinkers that, more systematically, propelled the use of the categories of *subalternity, antagonism* and *autonomy* are, not coincidentally, *organic intellectuals* of political movements. Because of this thinking within the movements, we have insisted on accounting – simultaneously to the analysis of the work of their ideologues – for the body of ideas that accompanied the struggles and the subjects that headed them. Subalternity, antagonism and autonomy are born then as *precepts*, instruments of struggle, conceptual tools that, to the extent they seek to understand the processes of political subjectivation, fundamentally work to project them.

Nevertheless, despite the advantages it implies, this dialectical origin is the carrier of the germ of the dualist vice, of the tendency to polarization and the possible rupture of the balance between understanding and strategic elaboration. In effect, the transformation of the concepts in banners includes the tendency to place its prescriptive content first, which ends up consuming, or at least subordinating, the descriptive and interpretative scope. Put differently, the prescriptive weight of political-strategic thought can produce a certain level of blockage in the descriptive and interpretative plans. In Marxism, the risk of the *over-politicization* of the theory is always latent,[8] the tendency to place the needs, urgencies and political-strategic wills before the essential methodological cautiousness and vigilance of the unstable and precarious search for explanatory and interpretative clues that allow the deciphering of processes and social relations.[9]

As we have seen, this stress towards *overpoliticization* travels the theorizations on the concepts of *subalternity, antagonism* and *autonomy* we reviewed in the previous chapters. We could say at first sight that it is more present in the revolutionary urgencies and second thoughts of the experiences of workerism, of *Socialisme ou Barbarie* and of the French autogestion movement than in Gramsci's reflection from prison. However, not only is triumphalism – as a political device – a factor of theoretical blockage but also defeatism leads to the loss of visibility and to theoretical closing.

In this sense, from his historic moment and in terms of his strategic aims, Gramsci did not give – because he did not want and could not give – the same importance to the antagonistic and autonomic expressions of the political subjectivations than to the subaltern ones. Negri did the same by emphasizing the antagonist ones and Castoriadis the same with the autonomic. Neither one denied the existence of historical counterweights, but all theorized from a perspective that marked a way of illumination that simultaneously overshadowed other angles.

Apart from the prescriptive drive of the political struggle, at a strictly epistemological level, the theoretical perspectives that are the object of our analysis are subject, as conceptual structures, to the tension between the simple hierarchization of dimensions/aspects between the primary and the secondary, the central and the peripheral, and the subsequent drift towards essentialism. The tendency towards essentialism is fed by well-known methodological vices. One of them is produced when the lag between the scope of the explanatory and interpretative capacity and reality tends to be fulfilled expanding the theory, artificially extending its reach. In these cases, an explanatory *hypertrophy* of hypotheses or concepts, an inordinate growth eager to cover the unmanageable or, alternately, a *reduction* of the reality so that it fits with the concept is generated. The verification of the hypothesis becomes a struggle with reality in which, on several occasions, the latter is folded in to the needs of the theory, hypertrophic or reductionist.[10]

We have seen how these tensions towards the overpoliticization of the theory and the explanatory *hypertrophy* of the concepts traversed the gestation and the deployment of the concepts of *subalternity, antagonism* and *autonomy*, transforming approaches, focuses and perspectives into *essentialisms*, that is, analyses whose generalizing pretensions overflew into absolutist, totalizing and all-encompassing visions from the assumption of having captured the essence of the problems, presuming to explain through synthesis the entirety of the phenomena, or resorting to simple resources of identification of the part with the whole, in the literary style of the synecdoche.

In this complex framework of political and theoretical tensions we are able to understand the disagreement between the perspectives in which the concepts of *subalternity, antagonism* and *autonomy* appeared; a disagreement that, translated to a competition – be it potential or effective, explicit or implicit – presents them as alternatives in the theoretical as well as in the political.

However, the assessment of the disagreement does not negate the possibility of raising combinations that find their justification in the theoretical *homologation* of the concepts we are working on.[11] That is, it recuperates the scope of the three concepts as analytical tools susceptible to highlighting the experiences of subordination, insubordination and emancipation that cross through the processes of political subjectivation.

Homology

Beyond the previously traced balance, it is possible to maintain the hypothesis of theoretical *complementarity* of the categories of *subalternity, antagonism* and *autonomy* from the logic of their conceptual construction and the correspondence of the levels of analyses in which they are situated. Despite the fact that different points of view led to separate itineraries, we can think of a path of convergence to the extent that there exists a shared theoretical cornerstone: the centrality of the intersection between relations of power and construction of the subject.

To move forward on the hypothesis of the relevance and viability of a tripartite focus that articulates them, it is necessary to demonstrate their *complementarity*. As we put forward at the beginning of this chapter, this exercise argues that these categories are *theoretically homologous*. By *theoretical homology* we understand here a common characteristic of those concepts that are determined by, and derived from, the same factors, which leads to recognizing their location at the same level of analysis. That is, even when their uses, applications and their interpretations might be different, they have the same theoretical origin, built on similar analytical purposes.[12]

The *homology* between the concepts of *subalternity, antagonism* and *autonomy* refers to the Marxist roots of their emergence and development and settles in the delimitation of the field of analysis in which they move and operate. This origin/development/delimitation that homologizes them, is revealed in four fundamental identity-defining passages among which, due to the first two being immediate consequences of the Marxist forge of the categories and the explicit position taken within it, we will focus on the last two, in whose development we will find decisive tools to sustain the articulation between the perspectives derived from the three concepts.

In the first place, the concepts of *subalternity, antagonism* and *autonomy* emerge from understanding enterprises that suppose the centrality of the problematic of the subject in history. This unfolds, in Marxist logic, around problems we have emphasized in the previous chapters: the social and political subject, the class *in itself* and *for itself*, the relation between spontaneity and consciousness, the movement, the party, the organization, and so on.

In the second place, always in accordance with the fundamental principles of Marxist thought, the categories in question are forged in a doubly articulated level of understanding of the social reality: structural and process-based. From the Marxist viewpoint, this implies the understanding of the nature of the subject from its position in the structure and its construction as a process of subjectivation; that is, the understanding of a course of internal configuration in terms of the assimilation, processing or incorporation of given experiences in the context of structural conditionings.[13]

In the third place, as we have seen, the three categories are forged, in a more or less explicit manner, to designate forms of *experience*, which implies their placement on a common terrain that answers, just as E.P. Thompson notes, to an open conception of the relation between social being and social consciousness and between spontaneity and consciousness. In this conception a point of intersection and subjective activation in the 'disposition to act' is glimpsed that detaches from the assimilation of experience, in the articulated sequence between spontaneous emergence and conscious projection. This problematic is at the polemical heart of the Marxist debates and, even without fully solving the dilemma and untying the dualist knot that characterizes it, it clearly states the explanatory challenge and illuminates the fundamental issue: the intersection between spontaneity and consciousness as the red thread of the processes of political subjectivation.

In the fourth place, the shared field of analysis is formed from two axes or coordinates that permanently appear in contemporary Marxist debate. In effect, it is possible to synthesize the ensemble of Marxist elaborations around the subject in terms of two correlative axes: domination/conflict/emancipation and *power over/power against/ power to*. In each of these axes, between the elements that comprise them, sets of dialectical relations focused on contradiction are established.

Beyond their evident correlativity, while the axis domination/ conflict/emancipation alludes to a triad of *conditions* of existence that indicate the relational field in whose frame the processes of political subjectivation develop, the axis *power over/power against/power to* accounts for the *manifestations* of existence of subjects through the exercise of force and action.

If the first axis clearly can be deduced from an analytical triangulation proper to Marxist thought, the second one, less evident, appears from its translation on the plane of the forms of power as manifestations of the agential emergence of subjectivities, beginning from the polarity stated by the philosopher Baruch Spinoza, and adopted by Negri, Holloway and Enrique Dussel (see Dussel, 2006: 23–33), but incorporating at its core the proper form of power that emerges from conflict and that has been a preoccupation and a central theme in Marxism: *counterpower*.

Susceptible to attracting the *conditions* and *manifestations* of existence of the subject, the matrix delineated by these axes underlies all the uses of the concepts that worry us. This is the case, of course, when they articulate theoretical approaches, that is, where they have consistency and operate as analytical categories and not as mere discursive resources.

A specifically Marxist way of representing the relationship between *structure* and *action* is configured in the said matrix, where the structure is always one of domination until, because of conflict, alternative social relations are structured and the action is always an expression of power, oriented towards conservation and transformation. All the approaches we have reviewed, implicitly put forward a characterization and an ordering of these elements, emphasizing one or the other, but always in mutual reference, as far as they constitute themselves reciprocally.

Outlining the rationalizing logic of the three approaches we can elaborate the following parallel formulations:

a. The focus of subalternity assumes the relations of domination as a field of emergence, formation and development of political subjectivities – characterized by the exercise of *power over* – and as a factor of the experiences of subordination. In the backdrop of this perspective lurk, as projections of subaltern subjectivity, antagonism and autonomy as experiences of insubordination and as emancipation respectively, *power against* and *power to*.

b. The focus of antagonism assumes the relations of conflict and struggle as a field of emergence, formation and development of the political subjectivities and as a factor of the experiences of insubordination – characterized by the exercise of *power against*.

In the backdrop of this perspective lurk, respectively as precedent and as projection of the antagonistic subjectivity, subalternity as experience of subordination and autonomy as experience of emancipation, *power over* and *power to*.

c. Finally, the focus of autonomy assumes the processes of liberation as a field of emergence, formation and development of the political subjectivities and as a factor of the experiences of emancipation – characterized by the exercise of *power to*. In the backdrop of this perspective lurk, respectively as precedent and as recourse to autonomous subjectivity, subalternity as experience of subordination and antagonism as experience of insubordination, *power over* and *power to*.

The common frame of reference for the categories of *subalternity, antagonism* and *autonomy*, which are located in different intersections of similar coordinates that are arranged in the same axes, can be visualized schematically. If the former is true, that is, if we can homologize these categories from a series of coordinates and shared axes that configure a framework of analysis, then it is possible to acknowledge the *specificity* of each one of them within this frame, the feature of distinction that permits the sustenance of their *complementarity*.

Specificity

To define the *specificity* of the concepts of *subalternity, antagonism* and *autonomy* we must start from their degrees of *consolidation* as analytical categories. We assume as given, in the first instance, a determined explanatory potential such as it can be deduced from their use by the authors and the strands studied in the previous chapters. Apart from this potential, if we account for the degree of consolidation of the categories, the review of their trajectories throws an unequal panorama. This is evident, above all, if we consider – in linguistic terms – these concepts as *significants* which have a certain degree of consensus over their *significance* and a certain precision in their use in relation to relatively homogeneous and concrete *referents*.

In the case of the concept of *subalternity,* its adoption by the Gramscian branch and the School of Subaltern Studies translated into a relatively stable definition and a relatively precise usage.[14] The frequent and imprecise use of the term in common discourse has been compensated for by the existence of a field of study whose definition and development tends toward its formation into a school reunited around a specific focus. However, as we have seen, the consensus on the relevance and the reiteration of the use of the concept hides a degree of oscillation around its meaning and this opens up to a possible *hypertrophy*. Put differently, its definition maintains an opening that possesses a level of ambiguity and, consequently, its use tends to spread until it dilutes the specificity of the phenomena it presumes to name, illustrate and characterize. In this context, the consolidation of the concept has been given by the consensus that surrounds it, but it appears incomplete if it is subjected to a rigorous reading of its internal consistency and the precision with which it is used.

The concept of *antagonism* lacks the consensual consolidation that derives from the existence of a definition encouraged by a school or current of thought articulated around it. The passage brought about by Antonio Negri from its mainly structural Marxian origin to a clearly subjective meaning suggested and defined by Marx himself, pointed towards a determined meaning but, as we saw, did not consolidate the precision of the concept in terms of the referents to which it applied. On the other hand, its reiterated use in Marxism as synonym of conflict and contradiction, as well as the semantic fluctuation within the same Negrian theoretical trajectory, finds the concept of *antagonism* in a theoretical limbo.[15] Thus, contrary to the category of *subalternity*, that of *antagonism* lacks stability in its meaning and its use. Finally, in contemporary Marxist discourses, the word *antagonism* keeps appearing as synonym of contradiction and conflict more than as synonym of struggle and, even less, of subjectivation of the struggle, of experience of insubordination.

The concept of *autonomy* appears as the most slippery from the point of view of its consolidation. As we saw, its linguistic opening multiplies its possible application to deeply diverse realities. Its use in Marxist debate includes a great diversity of meanings and referents. Nevertheless, considering its more or less consistent use in terms of the processes of political subjectivation, the range of oscillation can be reduced to two main meanings: as principle of subjective independence and as subjectivation related to experiences or desires of emancipation. While a generalized consensus surrounds the first, the second lacks an equivalent agreement. However, we saw how the reflections that emerged at the heart of Socialism or Barbarism point to an articulation between both where the second – as process – comprises the first.

In summary, the theoretical consolidation of the concepts of *subalternity*, *antagonism* and *autonomy* is uneven but, nevertheless, throws a shared panorama of absence of consensus around its meanings and of weaknesses in terms of the precision of their use. In effect, we saw how the same bodies of theory within which these concepts flourished – that is, in which they assumed theoretical quality and density – leave margins of oscillation that do not allow the formulation of finished definitions from the simple heritage of traditions, mechanically recovering the works and authors that inaugurated them. However, at the closing of every chapter we have seen how, beyond their limitations, each one of these traditions adds and contributes in the direction of the theoretical consolidation of the categories.

In this sense, the operations of delimitation and distinction that we will undertake with the objective of establishing the *specificity* of the categories of *subalternity*, *antagonism* and *autonomy* refer, in the final instance, to the intuitions and reflections of the authors that developed them, but presume to surpass their limits to take advantage of the heuristic scope of the concepts and, in a second moment and on that basis, to establish a relation among them. This relational aim is raised as possible to the extent that the *homologous* character of the categories has already been discussed. The *specificity* of one category in terms of the others is relevant insofar as these are located at the same level of analysis which, consequently, makes their articulation possible.

Because we are dealing with a crucial passage, before moving on to *specifying* the concepts, some methodological notes become pertinent. In this sense, we should underline that, while it may seem at first an arbitrary and mutilating eagerness to define, the effort to look for greater conceptual precision constitutes a necessary step, a methodological recourse that does not correspond to the theoretical conclusions we will reach but that makes them possible to the extent in which it allows the delineation of pertinent articulations. In the following paragraphs we will define and differentiate the field of influence of the categories by posing definitions that underpin their specificity, without which they are destined to float in relative ambiguity, suggestive and useful to guide hypotheses but insufficient for deeper analytical purposes. We thus assume that it is possible to delimit, in an open and general way, the categories of *subalternity*, *antagonism* and *autonomy*, without betraying but instead including and benefiting from the theoretical referents we have reviewed.

The specification of the content and the scope of the categories thus constitute an exercise that intends to maximize their *semantic availability*[16] without abandoning the theoretical horizon in which they appeared, for which they have meaning, and in which they can operate. It is not about posing fixed meanings, of semantically closing the field of action, of every category, nor of syntactically tying certain uses, but about turning them into tools susceptible to articulation in an appropriate manner in the face of the phenomenal field of the processes of political subjectivation.[17] In this sense, delimitation and distinction do not imply the repudiation of relations, impurities, intersections, and juxtapositions, but, on the contrary, establish criteria to recognize them, assuming that – as we will insist later on – the processes of subjective configuration can be visualized as uneven combinations of *subalternity*, *antagonism* and *autonomy*.

We can now continue their specification from the formulation of three definitions that highlight the differentiation of the concepts.

a. The specificity of the notion of *subalternity* refers to the subjective formation inherent in and derived from relations and processes of domination, constructed in terms of the incorporation of collective experiences of *subordination*, characterized fundamentally by the combination between the *relative acceptance* and the *resistance within* the frame of existing domination, projecting towards a renegotiation or adjustment of the exercise of the *power over*;

b. The specificity of the notion of *antagonism* refers to the subjective formation inherent in and derived from relations and processes of conflict and struggle, constructed in terms of the incorporation of collective experiences of *insubordination*, characterized fundamentally by the *contestation* and the *struggle* (or rebellion) *against* the existing domination, projecting towards the establishment and the exercise of a *power against*; and

c. The specificity of the definition of *autonomy* refers to the subjective formation inherent in and derived from relations and processes of liberation, constructed in terms of the incorporation of collective experiences of *emancipation*, characterized fundamentally by the *negation* and the *overcoming* – *going beyond* – of the existing domination, projecting towards the establishment and the exercise of *power to*.

We will now disaggregate the definitions to emphasize the common framework and the specificity of each concept.

The criteria of definition of the processes of formation of political subjectivities are the following: field, modality, expression, scope, and projection. That is, we assume that: *the subjective constructions derive from a determined relational and process-based field from which specific modalities of experience can be deduced that manifest themselves in different forms which refer to differentiated scopes and projections.*

In terms of these criteria, the specificity of each concept stands out according to a further three axes of differentiation that subsist within each of the following concepts:

1. Field: domination/conflict/liberation.
2. Modality: subordination/insubordination/emancipation.
3. Expression: acceptance and resistance/contestation and struggle/ negation and overcoming.
4. Scope: within/against/beyond.
5. Projection: renegotiation of the *power over*/establishment of the *power against*/establishment of the *power to*.

Let us have a look at the borders defined by these criteria of delimitation.

On the first point, the differentiation refers to the specific fields that frame and condition the general characteristics of the relations and the processes of subjectivation. In this sense, the distinction between *domination* understood as a relatively stable frame, *conflict* as a field of tension that destabilizes it and is able to dismantle it, and *liberation* as its overcoming and as the establishment of a new balance, is evident.

At the second level, referred to the format of experience, the qualitative experience is evident to the extent in which the modality of *insubordination* marks an evident rupture with *subordination* being its negation, just as the positive character of *emancipation* marks a clear discontinuity with the fundamentally negative character of the insubordination.

Referring to the third aspect, which alludes to expression as a form of experience, the acceptance-contestation-negation line expresses the *position* facing domination, while its correlate resistance-struggle-overcoming refers to the corresponding *action*. In relation to the passages, *acceptance* is clearly distinct from *contestation* – the integral questioning – even when the relative character of acceptance deserves to be made clear to the extent in which it implies its reverse, a certain degree of *non-acceptance*. The difference between *relative non-acceptance* and *contestation* corresponds to the distance between the *partial* questioning of domination – within its accepted borders, sustaining and defining itself in its perimeter – and the *integral* questioning – that is, of the parameters, the rules and the form of the domination itself. The difference between *resistance* and the *struggle*[18] can be qualitatively established in terms of a restrained but precise and specific definition of resistance, by associating it to a defensive action within the framework of the relative acceptance of domination.[19] Obviously, the expansion of *resistance* tends to overflow into *struggle*, understood as offensive, open and honest expression. The passage of differentiation between *contestation/struggle* and *negation/overcoming* is marked by the distance between the negativity of the antagonism and the positivity of autonomy, between interiority and exteriority in light of the relation of domination.

In effect, the fourth point translates into terms that scopes the previous criteria to the extent that it explicitly establishes the differentiation between the inside and the outside of the domination as well as the transitive character of the passage from antagonism. *Within* and *beyond* refer with clarity to the interiority of subalternity and the exteriority of autonomy. Yet it is even more problematic to define *against* in these terms. On one hand, in the first instance, it is unarguably internal to the extent in which it emerges and manifests itself in the context of an existing domination. On the other, in the second instance, it carries an idea – a desire and a hypothesis – of exteriority to the extent that it questions the domination and alludes to its overcoming. Put differently, it is concretely internal and potentially external.

On the fifth criterion, the projections in terms of the exercise of power are defined according to their differentiated balances. The renegotiation of *power over* does not imply the appearance and the establishment of a different field of power that is negative, like *power against*, or positive like the *power to*. In this sense, *subalternity* as a dimension of subjectivity would be projected, for example, onto the restoration of a violated order of justice or on the tendency towards adjustment of the relation of domination, be it by way of the negotiation among parts, of systemic regulations, of reforms, of concessions, of changes or by the simple restoration of the order before the emergence of the demand and the injury. On the other hand, antagonism would designate the emergence of a *counterpower* that surpasses subalternity, contesting the existing order in forms of open conflict like rebellion, revolt and insurrection, but including other less easily typified manifestations that surpass resistance. Finally, autonomy would designate the creation of self-regulated fields by the subject, by means of the construction of new social relations beginning with the ones that appear from the birth of a 'disposition to act' as subjectivity *for itself* – in the passage between spontaneity and consciousness – at the outer margins of the structure of domination, whether or not they tend towards the establishment of a new social order from the generalization of self-regulation and the *power to* as a format of social relations.

This differentiation of fields and forms allows the establishment of criteria and should not be confused with a typological pigeonholing in which to insert concrete subjective manifestations. It is only from a differentiation based on the definition of the specificity of the analytical scope of the categories that we can embark on the task of recognizing the *articulations* and *superimpositions* that, in all, structure the *complementarity* of the categories.

Complementarity

We have seen how each concept, defined according to their specificity, is susceptible to illustrating or understanding an *aspect*, a *dimension*, a *level* or a *field* of the totality of the reality of the phenomena and dynamics of subjective configuration. Aspect, dimension, level, and field allude to the coexistence of diverse forms or modalities, in temporal terms, to *simultaneity*. Each category points out, illustrates, identifies a part of the whole. Their virtues, therefore, are not limited to accounting for a distinguishable and recognizable form of a field of the real but, instead, deprived of their all-encompassing and reductionist ambitions, they can coordinate according to their *specificity*, in a *complementarity* that will be defended as hypothesis at two levels of articulation: one *synchronic* and another *diachronic*.

This coordination can structure a *synchronic* articulation in which each concept illustrates a *simultaneous* aspect of the real configuration of the socio-political subjects. This way, synthesizing, the notion of *subalternity* can be an analytical instrument able to capture the anchoring of the processes of political subjectivation in the field of domination and its gestation in the practices of resistance – in the tension between relative acceptance and relative rejection of the *power over* – the notion of *antagonism* can capture the subjective deployment – real or potential – that is realized in the struggle and the corresponding formation of a *power against*; while the notion of *autonomy* can capture the weight or the influence of emancipatory experiences in the configuration of subjectivities and their deployment in terms of the *power to*.

This triple focus is justified to the extent in which we acknowledge that political subjectivities are uneven combinations of *subalternity*, *antagonism* and *autonomy*. Put differently, the configuration of the socio-political subjects is given by *the combination of* and *the tension between* three fundamental components. The combinations result, therefore, from diverse contributions of each component; a historically determined configuration implies specific weights and measures.[20]

Before we develop the corresponding arguments, we should make clear that the conceptual exercise we propose can be characterized as a construction of Weberian ideal types in dialectical tension (Weber, 2006: 34–41). In this sense, any temptation to pigeonhole by type that is unable to accept that the intersections and superimpositions be put before the typical definitions disappears.

It is the *degree* of subalternity, antagonism and autonomy that characterizes a concrete subjective formation in a certain time. Assuming the *inequality of the combination*, deciphering its composition implies an operation of *relative deliberation* that establishes the weight and the value of each dimension before the others.

This operation can be guided by three considerations or general ordering principles:

1. The *permanent coexistence* of the three dimensions, that is to say that, at every moment, even though they are ordered and articulated in a different way, each one plays a role, albeit minimal but never irrelevant. In this sense we exclude the possibility of the absolute absence of an element;

2. The possibility that one dimension will colour the others, that is, that it will rise to an *overdetermining, structuring* and *ordering factor* in relation to the others; and

3. As counterpart, the possibility of uneven combinations in which an ordering factor does not stand out – or is not recognizable – but also the impossibility of a perfect equivalency of the three dimensions.

The first point is relatively obvious to the extent that it can be deduced from the argument against essentialism we have maintained throughout the text. However, it is pertinent to mention that it translates into a designation of the permanence of the elements. This means that, even in the moments of greater strength and visibility of a dimension, the rest do not disappear. Subalternity, antagonism and autonomy have, in the last instance, *a minimal niche of irreducible permanence.*

In effect, regarding the second point, assuming the persistence of the three dimensions it is possible to recognize that the uneven combinations that characterize the processes of political subjectivation are configured from an element that is built on an *overdetermining, structuring and ordering factor.* This can be visualized in three combinations where the order of the factors determines a form of subjective configuration:

a. SUBALTERNITY/Antagonism/Autonomy: subalternity operates as an overdetermining factor by ordering a combination in which political subjectivation is constructed and fundamentally structured by the experiences of subordination, which frame antagonism – that remains as a glimpsed possibility by the extension and widening of resistance in struggle – and autonomy – that is glimpsed as an embryonic experience in the formation of the subject itself and as horizon or utopia that stimulates the process of subjective formation;

b. ANTAGONISM/Subalternity/Autonomy: antagonism operates as an overdetermining factor by ordering a combination in which political subjectivation is constructed and fundamentally structured by the experiences of insubordination, which frame subalternity – that remains as inertia related to the genesis of the subjective formation and with the environmental permanence of the relations of domination outside the field and the experience of conflict – and autonomy – that is glimpsed, like in the previous case, as embryonic experience in the formation of the subject itself and as horizon or utopia that stimulates the struggle as well as the process of subjective conformation; and

c. AUTONOMY/Antagonism/Subalternity: autonomy operates as an overdetermining factor by ordering a combination in which political subjectivation is constructed and fundamentally structured on the experiences of emancipation, which frame antagonism – that remains as a defensive recourse or to move forward on the autonomic conquests – and subalternity that remains as inertia to the extent that all experience of emancipation is constructed against an already existing matrix and as process implies a gradual overcoming of the relations of domination, which means that these continue to exist to some extent.

The ordering operated by the overdetermining factor frames the others and tints the process of subjectivation with its colours.[21] The persistence of the secondary factors is measured by the centrality of a factor around and from which these acquire a determined meaning, weight and character. The central factor shapes the specific form of subjectivity and gives it its characteristic and distinctive feature.

Regarding the third item, we must consider that the previous ones imply that it is possible to decipher the processes of subjectivation, even when we know that historical reality presents hybrid formations that are not easy to deconstruct with pre-established keys for reading. However, this same consideration implies ruling out the laboratory hypothesis of a perfect equivalency of the three dimensions. At the same time, this hypothesis does not correspond to the logic of a combination between elements whose contribution is qualitative and does not lend itself to a quantitatively measured equivalency.

The operation of *deliberation* goes hand in hand with another fundamental methodological resource: the analysis of the links, superimpositions and articulations between subalternity, antagonism and autonomy, which we will study as *tensions* to highlight that they configure inflexion points in the constructions of political subjectivities.

We consider, in effect, that the *tensions* subalternity/antagonism and antagonism/autonomy constitute the greatest explanatory challenge as they constitute the perspectives of subjective activation and generation. The concatenation of the elements and their relational logic are the focal issues of political subjectivation and, thus, the explanatory knots to untie.

There are two significant *tensions*:

1. Subalternity/Antagonism: the tension between the experiences of subordination and insubordination is presented as the point at which the location of the process of subjectivation is defined, within or at the limits of the relation of domination and its possible crystallization as *power against* or the re-establishment of a *power over*; and

2. Antagonism/Autonomy: the tension between the experiences of insubordination and emancipation is presented as the point in which the location of the process of subjectivation is defined, at the limits and/or outside the relation of domination and its possible crystallization as *power against* and/or *power to.*

These two lines of tension are crossed by the antinomic polarity of affirmative or positive order between domination-emancipation and *power over* and *power to.*

This first interpretative level, of *synchronic* order, allows us to evidence the *simultaneity* and the *superimposition* of elements that remained isolated, each one of them turned into exclusive angles of the approaches we have reviewed.

At the same time, this *synchronic* perspective should acquire certain mobility to account for the process-based character of the subjective configurations and not petrify the analysis on an ahistorical level that has obviously very little to do with the concrete dynamics of political subjectivation.

The hypothesis of *synchronic* articulation is, thus, only the first level of the interpretative *recomposition* of the analytical *deconstruction* that implies the differentiation between the concepts of *subalternity*, *antagonism* and *autonomy*. Another complementary passage is situated at the level of its *diachronic* articulation. The point is to take the observation of the uneven combinations we located in a photographic plan, as representation and key to reading a specific moment of subjective formation, to the cinematographic plan, to recognize how a determined configuration moves in time, transforming and reconfiguring.

At this level, the hypothesis is that, once the configurations have been established in a moment of their existence, the process-based relation between the elements forms possible sequences among them that characterize the process of subjective configuration.

In this case, we call *subaltern*, *antagonist* and *autonomic* the subjective configurations in which these dimensions appear as over-determining and ordering just as we previously argued. This implies recognizing, behind the nominal synthesis, the uneven combination that corresponds to them. We can establish, in the first instance, at the abstract level, sequential lines and hypothetical movements within the processes of political subjectivation.

In a sequence corresponding to a *formulation of an emancipatory project* or an emancipatory teleology that is not foreign to Marxist thought and the imaginary of the concrete subjects in search of their liberation, we pass from *subalternity* – as the state to overcome – to *antagonism* – as a necessary conflictive and combative passage – to *autonomy* – as concretion, goal or end point.

According to the temporal reading that is established, past, present and future can be interchangeable in relation to each passage or structural and subjective condition, that is, to correspond to either subalternity, antagonism or autonomy. However, the interchange-ability is logically limited by the descriptive scope of the concepts. In this manner, subalternity can correspond to the past or the present but not – if we assume the point of view of the emancipatory project – to the future. From this same perspective, antagonism and autonomy can correspond to the present or the future but not to the past, unless they are understood as myths or mobilizing utopias, that is, devices that evoke and structure imaginaries to guide and project the struggle.

This same sequential order corresponds to a *genealogical observation of the subject* to the extent that it can only originate in the condition of subalternity to eventually move on to antagonism and autonomy. If, on the other hand, we assume the *perspective of the imaginaries* that emerge in the processes of political subjectivation, we can establish a sequence in which autonomy is situated in the last as well as the first instance, as utopia that operates as an activation device of the process and that glimpses the arrival point of the same. Nevertheless, once the process of subjectivation is underway, in its trajectory of existence, the wide variety of sequences or possible scenarios it embodies and in which it is susceptible to pass through, multiply and branch itself in three other potential movements.

In the first place, we must contemplate the possibility of *stagnation* in subalternity, in antagonism or in autonomy. The first scenario is historically more frequent and can extend in the long term, while the other two turn out to be unsustainable in the medium term being that struggle or insubordination cannot be permanent, just as emancipation cannot be stable to the extent we understand it as a process and not a state of things.

In the second place, there exists the possibility of the *ebb* of autonomy or antagonism in a return to subalternity, just like an ebb from autonomy to antagonism. These scenarios are historically frequent as a counterpart of the process of ascending flux that characterizes the emergence of the political subjectivities.

In the third place, we must consider the hypothesis that there is an *oscillation* between subalternity and antagonism without the materialization of autonomy, remaining as longing, projection or utopia, or between antagonism and autonomy in the unstable process of the consolidation of a new order.

In addition to the linear sequence, the possibility of these three non-linear processual sequences – which do not presume to be exhaustive – suggests the relevance of exercises of periodization that permit the decryption and disaggregation of the processes of subjective construction.

After having established the synchronic and diachronic articulations that allow the identification of combinations and sequences, the challenge of *crossing* the levels of analysis opens up. The analytical matrix, from its two fundamental dimensions, should be able to account for the *diasynchrony* of the real processes of political subjectivation. A key for *diasynchronic* reading can be found in the core of the matrix: *antagonism*.

The place occupied by antagonism within the conceptual triad locates it as an essential passage or a linkage between subalternity and autonomy. Synchronically and diachronically, it constitutes the axis or the passage – according to the respective emphasis – around which the sociopolitical subjectivities are configured. In this sense, antagonism is the *synchronic* element that re-establishes the *diachronic continuum*. This is evident by opening the specific definition of *antagonism*, expanding the field of insubordination and struggle, the subjectivation of conflict, and the construction of the *power against*. In effect, albeit dealing with the characteristic features of a specific form of subjectivation, struggle and the construction of *power against*, can meet – in embryonic form – in the subalternity and, in an expanded form, in autonomy: in the first case within the experiences of resistance; in the second, in the internal conflict of the experiences of emancipation. On the other hand, the *liminal* character we have previously talked about, referred to in relation to the limits of domination, situates it between interiority and exteriority. This ubiquity and this transversality grant antagonism a synchronic quality by placing it as the axis of articulation and, at the same time, it places it as the dynamic factor *par excellence*.

To attribute it a function in relation to the rest of the components does not dismantle its *homologous* quality at the level of analysis of the uneven combinations, rather it highlights – at another level – its dynamic character and permits the attuning of the synchronic and diachronic focus. By passing from the analytical-descriptive field to the explanatory-interpretative, antagonism becomes a privileged key for interpretation.

On the other hand, antagonism understood as an experimental passage, as a synchronic dynamic of the process of political subjectivation, is the dimension in which all essentialist pretension dissolves, by installing the *gerund* as temporality (Rodríguez de la Vega, 2005), in tune with E.P. Thompson's proposal: the political subject *is* not, rather it *is being* and it *is being* because it is *struggling*.

We come back to the Marxist core of the problem; the relations of conflict, antagonistic subjectivation and counterpower are the axes, the linkages of the subjective dialectic. A dialectic in which, to put it in Thompson's words once more, women and 'men are seen as the agents, always frustrated and always resurgent, from a non-dominated history' (Thompson, 1989: 146).

Afterword

Passive Revolutions in Latin America:
A Gramscian Approach to the Characterization
of Progressive Governments at the Start of the
Twenty-First Century

> Does the conception of 'passive revolution' have a 'present' significance? Are we in a period of 'restoration-revolution' to be permanently consolidated, to be organised ideologically, to be exalted lyrically?
>
> (Antonio Gramsci)

In this additional chapter added to the English edition of my book, I intend to sketch a line of interpretation at the start of the twenty-first century of Latin American progressive governments based on the Gramscian concept of *passive revolution* and its related parallels of *progressive Caesarism* and *trasformismo*.

The concept of *passive revolution* put forward by Antonio Gramsci in his *Prison Notebooks* has been the object of several specific studies that evaluate and highlight the value and the scope of the concept within the Gramscian conceptual scaffolding and its concrete application to the history of the Italian *Risorgimento* (cf. Voza, 2004; Mena, 2011; De Felice, 1988; Morton, 2010). The concepts of *progressive Caesarism* and *trasformismo* have been much less analysed, probably due to the fact that they are less recurring throughout the *Notebooks*, for having a lesser theoretical weight and for being, as we will later argue, subsidiary to the first (Liguori and Voza, 2009: 123–5, 860–2). Incorporating the contributions of these studies, yet remaining relatively at the margins of Gramscian debate between different interpretations, I am interested in finding to what extent it is possible to synthesize – from the *Notebooks* themselves – the constitutive elements of the category of *passive revolution* in light of the definition of an operational concept of general scope – a criterion of historical interpretation – sufficiently precise and resilient to be susceptible to application in relation to current historical processes, particularly Latin American ones.[1]

We will start from the textuality of the emergence and the creation of the concept in Gramsci's work to then move towards a wider categorical construction and to outline a brief exercise of analytical and interpretative application related to the debate over the characterization of the progressive governments that have surfaced over the last decade in Latin America.

I

The possibility of the application of these concepts to diverse historical realities is maintained to the extent it reflects the progressive expansion of the use of the notion that Gramsci traces throughout the *Notebooks*. In effect, the idea of *passive revolution* – borrowed from the work of the historian Vincenzo Cuoco – is traced and used by Gramsci at first to formulate a critical reading of a fundamental passage of Italian history: the *Risorgimento*. Later Gramsci would use it as a key to read the whole era of 'reaction–overcoming' of the French Revolution, that is, of mainly anti-Jacobin and anti-Napoleonic conservative reaction. The history of Europe of the nineteenth century will appear to him as an era of *passive revolution*. Finally, but not by chance since the analogy that inspires him is obvious, this extension of the concept is expressed in Gramsci's time and the idea of a passive revolution will be applied to Fascism, the *New Deal* and Americanism and Fordism to identify them as reactions to the revolutionary wave unchained by the Bolshevik October, when the same modernizing push – via corporatism and Fordist industrialism – happens in two faraway places, focused on the passage to a rationalization of the economy and society (Gramsci, 1981–99: Vol. 1, No. 1, note 150: 189; Vol. 2, No. 4, note 57: 216–17; Vol. 4, No. 10 (1): 114; Vol. 3, No. 8: 344). In this transfer to another time the concept reaches a level of canon or a criterion of general interpretation. Undertaking Gramsci's explicit intention to create a theoretical concept, we take as our point of departure the generalizing potential of the concept, from its possible historical and theoretical extension already rehearsed by its author.

Frosini maintains that Gramsci follows the connection of the passivity of subaltern classes towards a new form in the age of total mobilization and politicization, that is, the age subsequent to World War I. He is particularly interested in the contradiction between the activation of the masses and their moulding to the passivity of the totalitarian State, something completely new in the 1930s. Is there another epochal leap between the forms of 'passification' in Gramsci's times and ours, from a Euro-American to a Latin American perspective? Undoubtedly, new modalities of passification and depoliticization can be read in light of a new general and comprehensive key for interpretation, such as the condition of passive revolution. Let us see, after having shown and hinted on its analytical and interpretative resilience, what its constitutive coordinates are just as they appeared in the *Notebooks*.

The first time the expression 'passive revolution' appears is as a synonym of 'revolution without revolution', which clearly defines the point of ambiguity and contradiction that constitutes the core of the concept and its descriptive-analytical scope (ibid.: Vol. 1, No. 1, note 44: 106). In effect, the notion of *passive revolution* seeks to account for a combination – uneven and dialectic – of two tensions, tendencies or moments: restoration and renovation, preservation and transformation or, as Gramsci points out, 'conservation-innovation' (ibid.: Vol. 3, No. 8, note 39: 238). It is important to recognize two levels of reading: at the first, we recognize the coexistence or simultaneity of both tendencies, which does not exclude that, at a second level, we can distinguish one that becomes determinant and characterizes the process or 'cycle'. What Gramsci ends up naming as *passive revolution* refers to a relatively frequent historic phenomenon characteristic of an age that lends itself to the interpretation of another age in which the factors seem to link themselves in a similar manner. Gramsci writes in a crucial passage of the *Notebooks*:

> Quinet's 'revolution-restoration' as well as Cuoco's 'passive revolution' will express the historic fact of the lack of popular initiative in the development of Italian history, and the fact that progress would take place as a reaction of the dominant classes to the sporadic and inorganic rebelliousness of the popular masses as 'restorations' that accept a certain part of the popular demands,

that is, 'progressive restorations' or 'revolutions-restorations' or also 'passive revolutions'. (Ibid.: Vol. 3, No. 8, note 25: 231, text A; Vol. 4, No. 10, note 41: 205, text C)[2]

The equivalencies may be read, more so than synonyms, as important nuances of differentiation to the extent that they introduce another concept antithetical to that of *revolution* such as *restoration* and another differentiating criterion such as *progressiveness*, which we encounter again when Gramsci attempts to define the idea of *Caesarism*. In any case, beyond this approach of synonyms, Gramsci stays with the *passive revolution* formula because he finds it convincing to the extent that it expresses with greater clarity the sense of what he wishes to show. He chooses *revolution* as a noun – with all the polemical burden this choice implies and taking on a wide or non-political nor ideological version of the concept – and *passive* as adjective to clearly differentiate this specific modality of *revolution*, not characterized by a subversive movement of the subaltern classes but rather as a group of objective transformations that mark a significant discontinuity and a strategy of change oriented towards guaranteeing the stability of the fundamental relations of domination. Thus we will insist that the most outstanding and convincing aspect of the definition is the selection of the criterion of *passivity*.

The characterization of the noun *revolution* refers to the content and the scope of the transformation as inferred by the formula 'revolution without revolution' that Gramsci takes up as equivalent to that of *passive revolution*: revolutionary transformation without revolutionary irruption, without social revolution. The *quid* of the revolutionary or restorative content of passive revolutions substantially refers to the combination of doses of renovation and conservation and accounts for the more structural pitch of the formula and for the characterization of historical phenomena: the class content of the politics undertaken by the dominant classes. To what extent do they reproduce or restore the existing order or modify it to preserve it? To what extent do they 'accept certain parts of the popular demands'? How much and what part? The possible variations are diverse but delimited by two points: the *passive revolution* is not a radical revolution – in the Jacobin or Bolshevik style – and a *progressive restoration* is not a *total restoration*, a full reestablishment of the *status quo ante*. Gramsci writes:

It is about seeing whether in the dialectic 'revolution-restoration' it is the revolution element or the restoration one that prevails, because it is certain that in historical movement there is no going back and there are no restorations *in toto*. (Ibid.: Vol. 9: 102)

On the other hand, in terms of its dynamic, the conservative modernization implicit in any *passive revolution* is led from above. Here, above refers to the level of the initiative of the dominant classes as well as to the state elite, given that the State location or moment is crucial at the strategic level to compensate for the relative weakness of the dominant classes which resort, therefore, to a series of 'defensive' measures that includes coercion and consensus. One could argue, following on from Gramsci's examples and especially in relation to fascism, more coercion than consensus, more dictatorship than hegemony.[3] Nevertheless, it is evident that if Gramsci is creating an original concept and he textually constitutes it within the terms *revolution* and *passive*, one must deduce that he did not wish to emphasize any dictatorial feature nor any particularly coercive one as they tend to acknowledge or highlight the legitimacy and the inevitability of the process. Rather, it seems that Gramsci pointed to the constitution of a form of domination based on the capacity to encourage conservative reforms disguised as 'revolutionary' transformations and of promoting a passive consensus of the dominated classes.

Although the concept of *passive revolution* refers to the superstructural sphere it is evident that, beyond the sociopolitical dimension, in the example of fascism and Americanism and Fordism the reference to a capitalist consolidation by way of state intervention in economic life with a counter-cyclical function is clear. In this sense, the expression 'forms of government of the masses and government of the economy' used by Gramsci fully applies. He refers to the state interventionism typical of an age of passive revolution – an expanded State that includes civil society and intends to control the relations of production and the development of the productive forces through planning – which also alludes to problems typical to the USSR during those years.[4]

Pasquale Voza writes:

In the age of the passive revolution the notion of the expanded State, linked to the unprecedented processes of diffusion of hegemony, does not entail the default or the decrease of the notion of the State 'according to the productive function of the social classes', but it means a radical increase in complexity of the relation between politics and economy, a molecular intensification of the primacy of politics understood as power of production and of government of the processes of passification, standardization and fragmentation. (Voza, 2004: 204)

In addition to the ambiguous and contradictory content of the process in the sphere of the structural base and the identification of the State as the superstructural sphere through which the process is impelled, in Gramsci the concept is clearly and *principally* situated within the theme of the revolutionary *form*, that is the problem of subjectivity as an actor, of subversion as an act and of subordination-insubordination of the subaltern classes in the historical process in terms of the process of subjectivation, mobilization and political action. This is what is referred to by the idea of *passivity* or subordination of the subaltern classes and their counterpart, the initiative of the dominant classes and their capacity to reform the structures and the relations of domination to support the continuity of a hierarchical order.

In Notebook 15, Gramsci links the concept of *passive revolution* with that of *war of position* to suggest an eventual 'identification' – which leads us to think of it as a specific form of hegemony – and says that:

The interpretative criterion of the molecular modifications that in reality progressively modify the preceding composition of the forces and therefore become matrixes of new modifications can be applied to the concept of passive revolution (and can be documented in the *Risorgimento*). (Gramsci, 1981–99: Vol. 5, No. 15, note 11: 187–8)

In this sense, any passive revolution is the historical expression of determined correlations of force and, at the same time, a modifying factor of the same. In relation to its genesis, Gramsci notes that it is about reactions of the dominant classes to 'the sporadic, elemental and inorganic rebelliousness of the popular masses'. At the beginning of the process rests an action from below – albeit sporadic, elemental, inorganic and not 'unitary' – the defeat of a revolutionary attempt or, in a more precise sense, of a failed act, of the incapacity of the subaltern classes to impel or maintain a revolutionary project (Jacobin or typically from below according to the emphases found in different passages of the *Notebooks*) but able to outline or show signs of a movement that seems threatening or that apparently calls into question the hierarchical order. In effect, while the push from below is not enough for a revolutionary rupture it does manage to impose – indirectly – certain changes to the extent that some demands are incorporated and satisfied from above.

This precarious balance of forces is manifested in a commitment to formulae of various kinds. Attempting to generalize, Gramsci writes:

> We find other historical and political modern movements of the Dreyfus type, which are certainly not revolutions, but they are not reactions completely, at least in the sense that in the dominant field they also break suffocating national crystallizations and introduce in the life of the State and in social activities a different and more numerous personnel than before: these movements can also have a relatively 'progressive' content as they indicate that in the old society they were latent bustling forces that the old leaders did not know how to exploit, albeit 'marginal forces', but not absolutely progressive, as they are not 'epoch-making'. They become historically efficient due to the constructive weakness of the adversary, not because of one's own intimate strength, and thus they are associated to a determined situation of the balance of forces in struggle, both unable in their own field to squeeze a reconstructive will by themselves. (Gramsci, 1975: 1681)[5]

The passive revolution is in any case a movement of 'reaction' from above, which implies – subordinates and subsumes – the existence of a previous 'action' without this necessarily leading to the dichotomous simplification of revolution-counterrevolution, both poles being raised by Gramsci in a more nuanced manner and dialectically related. However, Gramsci conceived the passive revolution based on the paradigm of the active revolution or an 'anti-passive revolution' (Voza, 2004: 206),[6] just as he conceived the war of position in the face of the hypothesis of the war of movement and the permanent revolution. So, what one must keep in mind about Gramsci's notion is:

It is still dialectic, that is it presupposes, or better said, postulates as necessary, a vigorous antithesis [to avoid] dangers of historical defeatism, that is indifferentism, because the general approach to the problem can make one believe in fatalism. (Gramsci, 1981–99: Vol. 5, No. 15: 236)

Returning to our main argument, the correlated and subsidiary concepts of *trasformismo* and *Caesarism* that Gramsci addresses as possible and recurring devices of the concrete and historically identifiable passive revolutions lend credence to the conceptualization of *passivity* as a defining element of the criteria of interpretation *passive revolution*.[7] The category of *passive revolution* seems of a general order and includes more specific or particular mechanisms like *trasformismo* – 'one of the historic forms' of the passive revolution (Gramsci (1981–99, Vol. 3, No. 8: 235) – and *Caesarism* (Burgio, 2007: 82).

In the bundle of possible relations between antagonistic forces the hypothesis of 'catastrophic equilibrium' appears as a typical situation of the emergence of *Caesarism* as a specific modality of the passive revolution. *Caesarism* is a concept that Gramsci uses as a synonym of *Bonapartism* and by which, without nominally differentiating it from the first, extends its common meaning by introducing a possible positive reading of the phenomenon by means of the explicit differentiation between *progressive* and *regressive* modalities (Gramsci, 1981–99: Vol. 3, Vol. 9, notes 133 and 136; No. 13, note 27; Vol. 4, No. 9, note 136: 105–6). Gramsci assumes – following Marx – that in the face of a 'catastrophic equilibrium' Caesarism offers an 'arbitrational solution' linked to a 'great heroic personality' but suggests that this transitory exit 'does not always have the same historical meaning'. Another significant element of this definition in relation to the criterion of passivity and that indirectly evokes the 'sporadic and inorganic' character of the popular struggles, is that Gramsci points out that the catastrophic equilibrium can be the result of the divisions within the dominant class or of simple 'momentary' deficiencies, not always 'organic', that cause a crisis of domination and not a maturation or strengthening of the subaltern classes. At the same time he notes that the catastrophic equilibrium from where Caesarism emerges is always precarious and not lasting to the extent that class contrasts inexorably emerge (ibid.: Vol. 4, No. 9: 105–6). According to this outcome, the differentiating factor between progressive and regressive Caesarisms refers to the 'help' provided in each case to the subsequent triumph of a regressive or progressive force, but always with the 'compromises and limiting adjustments of victory': Caesar and Napoleon versus Napoleon III and Bismarck.[8] Another significant element is that Gramsci assumes that in the age of mass organizations (political parties and trade unions) there can be a 'Caesarist solution' without Caesar – without a heroic personality – by means of mass organizations or parliamentary means or coalitions. More than military, Caesarism tends to have a police nature, understanding by police something more than repression, such as a group of mechanisms of social and political control (ibid.: Vol. 4, No. 9: 102–3, Vols 4 and 5, No. 13: 65–8). However, outside these possibilities, the notion of *progressive Caesarism* is more efficient in its descriptive and analytical scope as it directly refers to the emergence and centrality of a charismatic figure that fulfils a specific political function in a context of catastrophic equilibrium and, in particular, from the viewpoint we are interested in emphasizing, impels and makes feasible a *passive revolution* operating as a balancing factor between classes and between conservative and renovating and passifying tendencies, channelling in particular the popular demands and undertaking – by delegation – the formal representation of the interests of the subaltern classes.

Along with *progressive Caesarism*, another Gramscian concept complements the theoretical structure of the notion of *passive revolution*. Using the neologism of *trasformismo*, Gramsci designates a process of molecular slippage that leads to the strengthening of the sphere of the dominant classes through a gradual drainage (absorption) by means of the cooption of the forces of the sphere of the subaltern classes or, vice versa, a weakening of the subaltern sphere by means of the abandonment or betrayal of sectors that opportunistically *transform* their political convictions and change sides. Let us look at the most significant passage in the *Notebooks* in this respect:

It can even be said that all state life from 1848 on is characterized by trasformismo, that is, by the creation of a ruling class more numerous every time in the cadres established by the moderates after 1848 and the fall of the neoguelfe and federalist utopias, with the gradual but continuous absorption obtained with diverse methods in their efficiency, of the active elements emerged from the allied groups and even from the adversaries that seemed irreconcilably enemies. The political direction became an aspect of the function of domination, while the absorption of the elites of the enemy groups leads to their decapitation and their annihilation for an oftentimes long period. Of the politics of the moderates there can and should be a hegemonic activity even before the taking of power and one should not only count with the material force that power gives to exercise an efficient leadership: precisely the brilliant solution to these problems made the *Risorgimento* possible in the forms and the limits in which it took place, without 'Terror', as 'revolution without revolution' or 'passive revolution' to employ Cuoco's expression in a slightly different sense from what he means to say. (ibid.: Vol. 1, No. 1: 106, Vol. 5, No. 19: 387)

Trasformismo then appears as a device linked to the passive revolution to the extent that it modifies the correlation of forces in molecular form dependent on draining forces and power – by means of cooption – to a project of domination in the interest of guaranteeing the passivity and of encouraging the demobilization of the subaltern classes.

Closely linked to each other, passive revolution, Caesarism and *trasformismo* form a useful and suggestive conceptual structure to interpret phenomena and historical processes, particularly those that are presented in a contradictory and discordant fashion.

II

Although the previous references speak for themselves in good measure and without the pretension of exhausting an exercise that would require an extensive and meticulous development to avoid the risk of theoretically pigeonholing historical realities full of specificities, I intend to leave open in the next pages a vein of analysis by postulating that the experiences of the progressive Latin American governments of the last decade can be read as *passive revolutions* and, hand in hand, in light of the complementary concepts of *progressive Caesarism* and *trasformismo*. One could even maintain that, methodologically, the establishment of a general pattern would be a condition for the recognition of the particularities. In this sense, the categories we propose are put forward as some analytical terms with regard to the formula 'progressive governments' that has conventionally been adopted and is currently in use.

In effect, even though an interpretative exercise that tends to assimilate different processes like the governments headed by Lula-Dilma, Hugo Chávez, Tabaré Vázquez-Pepe Mujica, Evo Morales, Rafael Correa, Néstor-Cristina Kirchner, Daniel Ortega, Mauricio Funes, Francisco Lugo and Ollanta Humala – that include the great majority of the countries of South America – can be imprudent, there are several relevant arguments that point to the possibility and the need to compare them to recognize common elements as well as differences. The debate on contemporary Latin America was oriented towards the characterization of these governments as a central interpretative challenge and there are always more analytical exercises and investigations that point in this direction. While the political-ideological branch of this debate has dislocated itself from some positions we might define as typical: support, critical support, opposition of the right, opposition of the left,[9] in the analytical field the biggest theoretical problem seems to be the synthesis of contradictions and ambiguities that mark these political experiences. The Gramscian concepts, by their dialectical character, seem to offer a possible articulation by accounting for the contrasts and tensions internal to the processes, without this excluding the possibility of taking sides or taking a political and ideological stand. At the same time, and as counterpoint in the theoretical-methodological field, the 'proof' of the interpretative scope of the concepts can be gathered from the possibility of this generalization. Put differently, if the group of these phenomena can be read in the form of passive revolution-progressive Caesarism-*trasformismo* these would lend weight to the explanatory capacity of these categories and their connections.

At this level of generality, as an open hypothesis that avoids falling into stereotypes that subordinate the reality to the theory, I wish to simply outline some preliminary ideas we can thus summarize:

1. The transformations occurred in the decade starting from the impulse of the progressive Latin American governments can be denominated *revolutions* – assuming a wide connotation and exclusively focusing on the contents mentioned in the previous

section—as they encouraged significant changes in an anti-neo-liberal and post-neoliberal sense, which can be visualized in a range of oscillation, according to the cases, between profound and substantial reforms and a 'moderate reformist conservatism' – using Gramsci's expression. Brazil could represent a point of reference for conservatism and Venezuela one for strong reformism with a structural scope.

2. At the same time, initially boosted by, but subsequently moving against the antagonistic activation of popular mobilizations and on the basis of their limitations, the direction and realization of the process was sustained *from above* – even when it incorporated certain demands formulated from below. At the level of class, at the height of government, progressive political forces reconfigured their alliances incorporating segments of the dominant classes, in terms of interests and orientation of public policies, as well as by the superimposition of new bureaucratic layers on top of the previous ones. On the other hand, in terms of the political dynamic and political procedure, the changes and the reforms were strictly encouraged *from above*, by means of the *State*, the government and, particularly, presidential power, using institutionalism and legality as the sole approach and instrument of political initiative.

3. The political forces installed on this governmental rung developed, encouraged or benefited from a *demobilization* or *passification* more or less pronounced of the popular movements and exercised an efficient social control or a hegemony over the subaltern classes that undermined – partially but significantly – their fragile and incipient autonomy and their antagonistic capacity, as a matter of fact generating or not counteracting a functional re-subalterniza-tion to the stability of a new political balance. The passive element became characteristic, outstanding, decisive and common to the configuration, in the ebb tide of an antagonistic politicization to a subaltern depoliticization, of the diverse Latin American processes (see Modonesi, 2010).

4. In the context of these *passive revolutions*, important phenomena of *trasformismo* operated to the extent that entire elements, groups or sectors of the popular movements were coopted and absorbed by conservative forces, alliances and projects and, particularly, 'moved' to the terrain of institutionalism and the state apparatus to

operate or undertake the public policies oriented to redistribution, generally of the welfare type, like the corresponding processes of demobilization and social control or, eventually, of controlled mobilization.

5. The modality of *passive revolution* in Latin America emanates from the tradition of *caudillismo* and is presented under the form of *progressive Caesarism*, to the extent that the *catastrophic equilibrium* between neoliberalism and anti-neoliberalism was resolved through a progressive synthesis (that is, tendentially anti- and post-neoliberal) around a charismatic figure as a needle on a scale situated at the centre of the process. The progressive governments work around the figure of a popular *caudillo* that guarantees not only the proportion between transformation and conservation but that, in addition, enables and secures a fundamentally passive and delegative character, even though such a leader may sporadically resort to specific and contained forms of mobilization.

This line of interpretation is not oriented towards ignoring the importance of the current transformations nor disqualifying a group of governments – some more than others – that are encouraging processes that are to a significant extent anti-neoliberal and anti-imperialist – which could well be reflected in the ideas of revolution and progressiveness that appear in the concepts we are using – but to acknowledge a fundamental and, in effect deeply problematic, dimension like passivity and, worse yet, like the passification that accompanies and characterizes these experiences.

The idea of *revolution* suggested in the first hypothesis refers to a historical passage marked by the exhaustion and the (relative) overcoming of neoliberalism as a political-economic paradigm and as the dominant model of the majority of the Latin American countries. The ongoing debate on anti-neoliberalism, post-neoliberalism, neodevelopmentalism, anticapitalism, and socialism in the twenty-first century is symptomatic of this general process although the positions, far from reaching a consensus, branch out not only in terms of political-ideological strands but also according to the different spheres and the different national experiences. At the same time, when evaluating the scope of the change of paradigms it is not the same to weigh and value the relaunch or stagnation of public and social spending as to acknowledge the scant revitalization of the internal productive sector or the prioritizing of the export pattern, which do not operate in the same manner regarding different products and different national economies and which traverses the entire region, regardless of the orientation of the governments. Regarding the Gramscian formula, this evaluation of the scope of the socioeconomic transformations concerns the structural dimension of the revolutionary character of change. All in all, assuming the most even-handed stand possible, we must acknowledge a twist – albeit a relative one – regarding neoliberalism as far as the national and social emphases that are reflected in a set of sovereignty-oriented and redistributive measures, whereas in the relaunch of industrial production, the insertion in the global market and the persistence and even the reinforcement of a primary-export profile – and the subsequent environmental costs – no substantial changes were observed, and there are even those who support the hypothesis of a regression. Whether this is not enough to be post-neoliberal, anticapitalist and socialist and whether this last threshold is feasible in the short term is a topic that surpasses the analytical exercise I wish to develop. Even within the range of oscillation between structural reforms and a 'moderate reformist conservatism', the ongoing processes do not stop us from marking a significant twist that goes beyond neoliberalism just as it was implemented in Latin America and which, following the Gramscian formula, we can define as a *revolution* in the limited and restrained sense previously mentioned.[10]

On the other hand, regarding the second hypothesis, there is consensus in acknowledging that the transformations go through an initiative that emerges from above and situates the state apparatus and state relation at the centre as the engine of the reformist and conservative practices. The following formulation from the *Notebooks* – *mutatis mutandis* – could well be applied to the Latin America reality:

> The ideological hypothesis could be presented in these terms: we would have a passive revolution in the fact that by the legislative intervention of the State and through the corporate organization, more or less deep modifications would be introduced in the economic structure of the country to accentuate the element 'plan of production', that is, the socialization and cooperation of production would be emphasized without touching (or limiting itself to simply

regulate and control) the individual and group appropriation of the profit. (Gramsci, 1981–99: Vol. 4, No. 10: 129)

It is indisputable that, with varying intensity, the progressive Latin American governments, counter to neoliberalism, again situated the State – and the public policies which emanated from it – as a central instrument of intervention in the social and the economic. Beyond the debate on the socioeconomic vices and/or virtues of a neodevelopmentalist illusion, the nationalization currently in vogue in Latin America corresponds to the model of *passive revolution* to the extent that it efficiently combines the capacity for innovation from above with control over the base. This does not imply an ideological condemnation in principle of the role of the State in the style of autonomism, but the plain and simple acknowledgement of the role it is fulfilling in the context of the experiences of the progressive Latin American governments. One of the most prominent challenges points at the use of social aid policies – which partially respond to demands formulated from below – to which all these governments have resorted in abundance and which, on one hand, operate a redistribution of wealth while, on the other, they not only do not guarantee the proper and durable means for the poor to achieve their welfare but, in addition, they operate and operated as powerful devices for cronyism and the construction of political loyalties. However, more than the evaluation of the socioeconomic achievements and class character of these processes, I am interested in highlighting the gap between movement-led mobilization and governmental passification, and to show the initiative from above, from old and new elites, from the State or political society and the corresponding top-down construction of passivity, of the subaltern classes, organized or not.

In this sense, in a manuscript published posthumously just a year ago, José Aricó clearly noted the critical edges of a progressive branch or version of the *passive revolution*:

The passive revolution can be exercised through the centralizing authoritarian tendencies, in a dictatorial state, but, as Gramsci claims, it is not separated from consensus, from hegemony, which is fundamentally what occurs in the Soviet Union. That is, either there is a social restructuration, a modification of social property from above through the dictatorship that operates on the set of classes that support it, or this process can be undertaken by a corporate tendency, that is a social democratizing tendency that fragments the set of classes, that divides them through a reform policy that stops the formation of a historical bloc able to reconstruct society on new bases. In this manner, every process of transition that is not directed, formed and governed by the full exercise of democracy as the decisive element of the formation of hegemony (democracy that means the process of self-government of the masses) acquires the character of a passive revolution, of a power of transformation that is exercised from the top against the will of the masses and that, in the last instance, always ends up questioning the concrete possibility of the constitution of socialism. (Aricó, 2011: 273–4)

This characterization can be applied to the populist or national-popular experiences of the past as well as to those that circulate in Latin America today. At the same time, so as not to revive the old debate on populism that produced several sectarian positions on behalf of the Marxist left, we insist on the decisive aspect of passivity, the opposite of the 'full exercise of democracy' that Aricó evokes, without which there is no revolution in the integral sense of the word: objective transformations impelled and accompanied by subjective transformations.

It is a fact that the Latin American progressive governments appeared after waves of popular mobilizations, with more or less temporal proximity or direct relation among the governments that emerged directly from political crisis (Argentina, Ecuador, Bolivia) and those that were born of relatively ordinary processes centred on elections (Uruguay, Brazil, Nicaragua, El Salvador, Peru, Paraguay, and also, with some exceptions, Venezuela).[11] At the same time, above the institutional ruptures provoked by the irruption of popular movements that occurred in the first cases, a certain cycle of protests or opposition to neoliberalism, more or less intense yet always significant and influential to the extent that it disrupted the correlation of forces, would be reflected in the subsequent electoral results.[12]

Since the mid 1990s, as has been widely studied and documented (more frequently by the different national plans than across the Latin American scale), after years of defensive retreat, there appeared on the political scene of the great majority of Latin American countries, actors and popular movements that quickly – more than a few times provoking political crises and overthrowing leaders – undertook a leading role and marked an antagonistic line between the field of defence of the neoliberal order and the anti-neoliberal struggles, politicizing again the practices of resistance, modifying the correlation of forces, positioning demands and occupying important places in the hegemonic dispute in the context of civil society.

Later, from the start of the century and the millennium, on the basis of this accumulation of experiences and forces, the movements went from displacing actions, expressed through the exercise of the action of struggle and street confrontation, that allowed them to exercise a power of veto, to project their political force in the institutional, and particularly, electoral game, propelling or only explicitly or implicitly supporting political parties and progressive candidates that more or less radically proclaimed themselves anti-neoliberals. As a result, a wave of electoral defeats for the supporters of neoliberalism occurred alongside the corresponding opening of one of the greatest processes of replacement regarding the ruling groups that the history of Latin America has ever seen – probably only comparable to the anti-oligarchic turn of the 1930s. In the first decade of the century there were so many progressive governments as had not been seen since the 1930s and 1940s.[13]

In actuality, save for the most recent cases of installation (El Salvador and Peru), the majority of these have already fulfilled a relatively extended temporal cycle that contemplated, in addition to three constituent processes, several presidential re-elections and renewals of mandates of rulers and legislators, and even, in the case of Argentina, Brazil and Uruguay, the replacement of the head of the Executive with the change of the command from Néstor to Cristina, from Lula to Dilma and from Tabaré Vázquez to Pepe Mujica, which implied certain adjustments and leaves open problems related to the charismatic and Caesarist leaderships.

In this field, the interpretative problem can be stated from the hypothesis that points out that the presence and the actions of the so-called progressive governments in Latin America benefit from/propitiate/promote a relative demobilization and depoliticization or, in the best of cases, a controlled and subaltern mobilization and politicization of the public sectors and the social movements and organizations. During the first years, particularly in Venezuela, Ecuador and Bolivia, when the right has looked for a way to foster social and institutional conflict to destabilize the anti-neoliberal governments, the indexes of the rate of conflict have kept relatively high. But since this offensive was halted and the conservative or neoliberal oppositions started placing their chips at the electoral level especially – when they did not pragmatically adhere or were happily articulated within an alliance with the governmental progressive forces waiting for the moment of revenge to arrive or for another political option to be more feasible – the qualitative decrease of the social rate of conflict has been evident and has been so registered by analysts and can be verified in different exercises of quantitative compilation. However, in the last two or three years there seems to have been an upturn towards a new increase in episodes of protest.[14] At the same time, the process of demobilization and passification, beyond the quantitative, is reflected in a clear passage from an antagonistic politicization to a subaltern one, which permits the avoidance of the more schematic features of the active-passive antinomy. In effect, while there are margins of action and mobilization of a subaltern matrix these are qualitatively different from those that appear from processes characterized by antagonistic and autonomous features. This qualitative gap allows us to speak, even in the presence of subaltern forms of action, of resistance and protest, of a general tendency towards demobilization and passification that registers in combined form a relative, variable and oscillating quantitative decrease of events but overall the subaltern depoliticization that accompanies and characterizes it.

As far as the causes, among the critical evaluations that, with more and more frequency, circulate in the countries where the progressive governments are, some of them are listed in variable order: the context of crisis of the political institutions and parties; the installation of governments and Caesars that vented their tensions and demands that catalysed the social organizations and movements in the previous years; the cooption and the voluntary and enthusiastic entry of rulers and militants of popular movements into the national institutions in view of translating the demands into public policies; and the pressure and cronyism regarding the actors of government and eventually the selective repression, among others.

The hour of the so-called progressive governments was also, beyond the evaluations of the results in terms of public policies and of a future historical balance, the hour of demobilization and depoliticization, of the failed opportunity to rehearse or to let flow a participative democracy based on organization, mobilization and politicization as vectors of a process of strengthening and empowering the popular classes. On the contrary, the political forces perched on the governments did not counteract, they made the most of and even encouraged the tendency of the corporate-cronyist withdrawal of a great part of the organizations and movements that had led the previous stages. We should not, however, lose sight of the fact that in the backdrop of the process, there are three organizing aspects of the ongoing mobilization in the countries we are contemplating: those encouraged from the governments and the political parties and trade unions that support them; those that are driven by the oppositions of the right; and those that appear from social dissidence and oppositions from the left.

As I have pointed out, the first two tended to decrease throughout the years in consistency with the creation of governability treaties (save for the electoral junctures and the routine mobilization that is related to it). The existence of the last type, increasing in the last years, could appear as disproof of the hypothesis of passivity. At the same time, above its qualitative valorization we must acknowledge that it is not about, save some exceptions and junctures (particularly Bolivia), quantitatively massive and prolonged phenomena, that is, neither intensively nor extensively do they manage to invert the general tendency that, rather, confirms the hypothesis of re-subalternization, that is of a reconfiguration of subalternity as the subjective matrix of domination, as condition for passive revolution. In this field there exists the possibility of relaunching a cycle of conflict, of initiatives from below that, as scarce and minimal as they might be, the popular struggles against the progressive governments have an enormous symbolic, political and strategic value to the extent that they are experiences that accumulate and can be maximized giving life to a new stage marked by popular leadership.

Additionally, as Álvaro Bianchi notes we should not assume that the passivity and consensus generated by a passive revolution is absolute or total:

The absence of popular initiative and an active consensus does not indicate the total passivity of the popular masses and neither does it indicate the total absence of consensus. In fact, there is a 'sporadic, elementary and inorganic' rebelliousness that, by its primitivism, does not eliminate the capacity for intervention of the dominant classes, but instead sets its limits and imposes the necessary absorption of a part of the demands from below, precisely those that are not contradictory with the economic and political order. Thus is the passive and indirect consensus of the subaltern classes created. (Bianchi, 2005: 16)

On the other hand, in this passage in which significant countertendencies flourish in the Latin American countries it becomes evident that the hypothesis of characterization by means of the concept of passive revolution implies unpacking it by differentiating project and process. It is worth asking to what extent the project is being achieved and, supposing it is not being fully but only partially so, whether that is enough to determine the process. At the provisional level we assume that it is and, thus, with the necessary caveats it is possible to recognize and analyse some features that, unfinished as they may be, allow the tracing of the outline and the profile of the passive revolution as the modality and operating form in the experiences of the Latin American progressive governments.

In reality, the most delicate and problematic issue of the application of these concepts is the class character that Gramsci emphatically and unequivocally attributes to the phenomenon of passive revolution. In the case of the Latin American experiences we are attempting to characterize, more so than in the examples used by Gramsci, it is not possible to emphatically affirm that the progressive governments are direct expressions of the dominant classes and the bourgeoisie, just as we would not be able to affirm the opposite, that is, that they strictly emerge from the subaltern classes and the workers. Nevertheless, between the mediations and contradictions across classes that, with different nuances and emphases appear in all these cases, some progressive aims as well as some conservative limits to the horizon of the transformation and the ideological shade of the project are clearly perceived and, in the latter two, an evident feature of class is glimpsed to which Gramsci evidently referred. Put differently, without saying we are dealing with governments directly or completely exercised by the dominant classes, they are governments whose performance does not frontally and systematically oppose their interests – some might even say they are accomplices – but they aim to create a hegemony that crosses classes, that breaks their unity to promote the breech of a progressive or nationalist segment of the oligarchy towards a conservative reformist project that takes place as a passive revolution.

On the other hand, it is impossible not to count the limitations that from the popular movements allowed the accomplishment of experiences of passive revolution, that is, to use Gramsci's words: there is a lack of unitary popular initiative and sporadic, elemental and inorganic rebelliousness. These are elements from which the possibility of passive revolution is configured and, at the same time, the current conditions for their continuity and extension in time, as is observed in the fragmentary and occasional phenomena of resistance and opposition from below that appear in the countries governed by progressive forces.

We must not lose sight of the contradictory and unfinished nature of the processes of passification of popular movements. There is a tension that crosses them and, as was evidenced in the long tradition of populist experiences, there exist convocations for controlled mobilization that can sometimes be surpassed. They may even overflow and, as Franklyn Ramírez points out, possible attempts have been made to 'neutralize' them precisely because of this tendency to overflow.[15]

This same author considers that we must acknowledge that, in the institutionalization phase, there are instances of direct democracy established in the three new constitutions (Venezuela, Ecuador and Bolivia). He asks whether we should not qualify the accusations of authoritarianism towards the progressive governments assuming there also exists, particularly in these countries, an 'aim to undermine the weight of the liberal institutions of representative democracy to open a greater dynamism of collective action from *los de abajo* [below] in the processes of control and public decision-making'. I believe this aim existed at the origin of the governments, in the agendas of the movements, but was gradually diluted in the practices of government even though it keeps discursively reproducing or remains a banner for some segments within the governmental coalitions, groups that are not sufficiently strong or influential to determine the general course.

Beyond the good intentions of some, it is true that, at least in the case of Venezuela, the design and practice of participative democracy has been situated high on the agenda at the symbolic level as well as at the level of public financing. But, this does not keep from recognizing that the mechanism has been flawed by the cronyism-based logic and the verticality emanating from the PSUV [The United Socialist Party of Venezuela], which leads us to ask whether the course of the Venezuelan process is defined from below, from the perspective of 'protagonistic democracy'.[16]

We must consider that the reflux of the spontaneous processes of participation linked to junctures is not mechanically solved by adding and superimposing mechanisms of institutional engineering of the participatory kind. At the same time, any form of institutionalization necessarily carries with it a degree of passivity and of passification, which does not mean the existence of institutional structures that contemplate and include participative instances – as long as they do not become empty of content, do not simply become bureaucratic links and turn into mechanisms of social control – is irrelevant.

Avoiding the Manichaeism natural to the dichotomy institution-alization-autonomy, the underlying trends towards political distrust, towards the crisis of the western political institutions that lead to the thesis of passivity as a societal tendency, appear.[17] Finally, the contradiction between the movementist and governmental moments finds its roots in the superimposition of these moments throughout the length of the process. Said differently, the same popular movements searched for and to different extents found the road to creating institutions under a perspective of construction of power that tended towards success.

Regarding *trasformismo* and *progressive Caesarism*, these are concepts that allude to phenomena that are so visible that the references made to them end up being obvious. It is evident that the installation of progressive governments produced phenomena of cooption from the state apparatus that drained important and even massive segments and groups of leaders and militants of the popular movements and organizations. This event is central to explain the passification, subal-ternization, social control, or controlled or heteronomous mobilization. Further, it is particularly notorious how the political form assumed by these facts refers to a *caudillista* format and, in the terms we are proposing, a progressive Caesarism that fulfils a fundamental function as it not only balances and stabilizes the conflict but it, additionally, affirms and endorses verticality, delegation and passivity as central and decisive characteristics.

The recurring, outstanding and determining element is then passivity or, in the terms of the heteronomous process and initiative, the passification or subalternization which in more common terms and in the logic of the Latin American decade is more appropriately called demobilization as it responds or follows a phenomenon of mobilization.

Returning to strictly Gramscian language, Fabio Frosini writes:

There thus exists a relation between realized hegemony, the subjects established by it, and the way in which the organization of social relations expresses or critiques a power, a particular class subordination. More precisely: if it is true that the difference between the 'passive' composition of the conflicts and their 'permanent' retreat marks the difference between bourgeois and proletarian hegemony, this will have consequences either for the way the hegemony establishes the subjects, or, consequently, for the nature of the latter. Not in the sense of a return to the 'old concession of the historical efficiency of the social forces' (Laclau 1996: 43), because the subjects, far from being something original or also a unitary ideological effect, are rather the contingent intersection between the set of conflicts and the form in which they are politically organized and then 'represented', that is transferred towards the imaginary sphere. (Frosini, 2011: 9)

Focusing the matter in the sphere of the processes of political subjectivation, we must acknowledge a reflux towards subalternity, a loss of antagonistic capacity and of the margins of autonomy of the actors and social movements that headed the social struggles in Latin America at the time of activation of the anti-neoliberal cycle. As counterpart, the tendencies towards institutionalization, delegation, demobilization, and depoliticization become evident (when not authoritarianism, bureaucratization, cronyism, cooption, and selective repression) that characterize the political scenarios dominated by the presence of progressive governments. The flourishing 'perversions' of projects of transformation which, beyond declarations of intention, are disregarding, negating or limiting the emergence and the flourishing of the political subjectivation of the subaltern classes, focusing on initiatives and dynamics from above that far from encouraging emancipatory democratic processes, reproduce subalternity as a condition of the existence of domination. Apart from the valorization of socioeconomic balances and the scope of public policies propelled by the progressive governments, the miseries of the historic forms of nationalism and partisanship appear, and far from operating as devices for the real democratization and socialization of politics they become obstacles and instruments of passive revolution. By benefiting from, controlling, limiting and, in the end, obstructing any deployment of participation, of conquest of spaces for the exercise of self-determination, of the formation of popular power or of counterpowers from below, a substantial element of any emancipatory hypothesis would not only be denied but the possible continuity of reform initiatives – not to mention a revolutionary radicalization – would be weakened to the extent that a fundamental political recourse for the history of the subaltern classes: the initiative from below, the capacity for organization, for mobilization and struggle, would be concealed or simply disappear.

Notes

Introduction

1. The processes of political subjectivation refer to the formation and development of sociopolitical movements. From the Marxist viewpoint, they are sociopolitical insofar as this articulation excludes and denies any hypothesis of absolute autonomy of the political or autonomy of the social, while recognizing specific domains within this unyielding and constant overlap. In this sense, I consider the designation 'social movements' to be so comprehensive it becomes ambiguous and, on the other hand, it results in a depoliticizing connotation specific to the time in which it was created and disseminated in the academic world and of the 'objects of study' to which it referred – the 1970s and sociocultural movements (Touraine, Melucci, etc.) respectively. At the same time, the analogy between the notion of *movement* and *subject* might result equivocal, since the first presupposes a level of internal consolidation – particularly of organizational character – superior to the latter. Inversely, the notion of *subject* presupposes an internal coherence at the level of the identity superior to that of *movement*, understood as a shared framework in which some diversity or plurality might coexist. Nevertheless, in this work's viewpoint, the reference to the *subject* belongs to the more general and abstract plane in which we distinguish and order the analytical elements, while the *movement* refers to the concrete benchmark in the application of the analysis.

2. In reality, Thompson (1981: 67–8) virulently attacks the structural theoreticism embodied by Althusser but does not reject a use of theory – a 'dialogue between concept and empirical reality'. Thompson's stance generated a riposte from Perry Anderson (1985) that prolonged a debate of profound historiographical implications.

3. Even though we will see in Chapter 3 how this notion had been moved forward in 1952 – nine years earlier – by Claude Lefort in the group Socialisme ou Barbarism. We assume that Thompson did not read the magazine in which the text by Lefort, called 'The Proletarian Experience', appeared. It would not be re-edited by its author until 1971, eight years after the book by Thompson on the English working class came out and where the historian formulated his own meaning.

4. Thompson (1981: 19) points out that the experience 'already includes the mental and emotional answer, be it of an individual or a social group to a plurality of events related between them or to many repetitions of the same event'. Later he adds: 'The experience appears spontaneously inside the human being yet does not appear without thought...'

5. Thompson (1981: 262) writes: 'We have found that experience has been generated, in the last instance, in the material life and has been

structured in a classist manner, thus is the consciousness determined by the social being.'

6. Thompson states (1965: 357): 'Class is a social and cultural formation (often finding institutional expression) which cannot be defined abstractly, or in isolation, but only in terms of the relationship with other classes, and, ultimately, the definition can only be made in the medium of time – that is, action and reaction, change and conflict. When we speak of *a* class we are thinking of a very loosely defined body of people who share the same congeries of interests, social experiences, traditions and value-system, who have a disposition to behave as a class, to define themselves in their actions and in their consciousness in relation to other groups of people in class ways. But class itself is not a thing, it is a happening.'

7. On the last page of *Time, Work-Discipline and Industrial Capitalism* he writes: 'And in fact, all economic growth is accompanied either by the growth or the transformation of a culture; and in the last instance, the development of the social consciousness, no less than the development of the spirit of a poet, could be planned' (Thompson, 2004: 89). For more on the implications and debate surrounding this formulation, see 'Rethinking the Structure and Superstructure' in Meiskins Wood (2000: 59–89).

8. When Thompson writes that 'the experience of class is *vastly* determined by the relations of production', it is inferred that it is not *totally* determined thereby, which can be corroborated in the emphases and aims of his work.

9. Anderson points out the incoherence between some of Thompson's passages, for example, when he emphasizes the separation by writing of 'the consciousness they have of this experience'. Nevertheless, it seems evident it is a methodological distinction insofar as the insistence lies in that 'we cannot put class here and consciousness there, like two separate entities, consecutive one from the other, as both must be taken together: the experience of determination and the handling of this in conscious ways' Thompson (1981: 158, 166–7).

10. Thus the famous and polemical formula of 'class struggle without class', which indicates the absence of a full class consciousness, even in the midst of an embryonic presence that accounts for a minimum degree of existence, without which there would be no struggle.

11. Thompson (1965: 357) writes: 'If we use this control – if we keep on remembering that class as identity is metaphor, helpful at times in describing a flux of relationship – then a very useful dialogue can be opened up between historians and those sociologists who are willing to throw across the time-switch again. If we do not use this control, we have a very blunt cutting instrument indeed.' He goes on (ibid.: 358): 'It is generally a fairly easy matter to locate opposing social poles around which class allegiances congregate: the rentier here, the industrial worker there. But in size and strength these groups are always on the ascendant or the wane, their consciousness of class identity is incandescent or scarcely visible, their institutions are aggressive or merely kept up out of habit; while in between there are those amorphous, ever-changing social groups amongst whom the line of class is constantly drawn and re-drawn with respect to their polarization this way or that, and which fitfully become

conscious of interests and identity of their own. Politics is often about exactly this – how will class happen, where will the line be drawn? And the drawing of it is not (as the impersonal noun nudges the mind into accepting) a matter of the conscious – or even unconscious – volition of "it" (the class), but the outcome of political and cultural skills. To reduce class to an identity is to forget exactly where *agency* lies, not in class but in men.'

12. Even though Thompson repeatedly emphasizes the social and cultural character of class formation – possibly to distinguish it from the closed political definition that the Marxists he sparred with used to advance – we will insist on the political character of processes of subjectivation built on relations of domination and conflict, which illuminate the concepts of *subalternity*, *antagonism* and *autonomy* that we are emphasizing.

Chapter 1

1. 'Colección completa facsimilar, 1919–1929 y 1924–1925' (*L'Ordine Nuevo*, 1976).

2. In Chapter 3 we will see the oscillations and articulations between the avatars of the notion of autonomy as independence and as emancipation in Marxism.

3. See, for example, among many articles, the editorial 'Il Consiglio di fabbrica', *L'Ordine Nuevo* (1976: Year II, 4–5: 1) in June, 1920. An illustrative selection in Spanish of the councilist texts published by Gramsci in *L'Ordine Nuovo* can be found in Vol. 1, April–June 1973 of the new *Pasado y Presente*, the magazine promoted by José Aricó in Córdoba, Argentina, see Gramsci (1973, Vol. 1: 103–35). To read further on the Latin American appropriation of Gramsci's thought, see Aricó (1988).

4. For a history of the interpretations and the debate on Gramsci's thinking in Italy, see Liguori (1997).

5. In Spanish, see Gramsci (2000: Vol. 2: 27).

6. In Spanish, Gramsci (2000: Vol. 6: 182). In the Spanish translation 'method' is translated as 'methodology'. Gramsci did not fall for this widespread confusion. The modifications presented by Gramsci in the second edition of the note are in cursives.

7. I present here directly the revised and corrected version by Gramsci in Notebook 25 in 1934. The differences with the first version of Notebook 3 (372–3), besides the already mentioned change between classes and groups, belong to the aggregate of 'consensus', which is explained by the importance this dimension acquired in the development of the Notebooks between issues 3 and 25. The same goes for the aggregates of points 1 and 2 which are the reflections of the historical analyses undertaken by Gramsci in these years. The modifications done by Gramsci in the second draft of the note are in cursives.

8. In Spanish, see Gramsci (2000: Vol. 2, 38–9).

9. Gramsci (1975: Vol. 12: 1376; author's translation): 'and also in the entire system of beliefs, superstitions, opinions, ways of seeing and operating that we glimpse in what is generally called *folklore*'.

10. See this tripartite scheme in Green (2007: 199–232).
11. This was the name of the magazine established by the founding group.
12. See, for a general review, Mellino (2008). For a Latin American perspective, see Lander (2003).
13. Beginning in the 1960s, Hobsbawm promoted the study of subalternity, see Hobsbawm (1963: 58–67), the text was published for the first time in Italian in 1960. Between 1959 and 1969 he published two classic texts in this genre: *Rebeldes primitivos* [*Primitive Rebels*] (Hobsbawm 2001), and *Les bandits* [*Bandits*] (Hobsbawm 1999).
14. This same article appears in Guha (2002).
15. In fact, the acknowledgment of this interdependence leads us to use the word 'indian' and not 'indigenous' to underline that this is a historical construction, a hybrid identity built on a concept of oppression and domination from resistance, not a pure and separate form.
16. Also in Guha and Spivak (2002).
17. The same article appears Guha and Spivak (2002) and in Guha (2002).
18. In his book *Los dominados y el arte de la Resistencia* [*Domination and the Arts of Resistance*], Scott (2000) maintains an approach very close to the perspective of subalternity (in fact, the author acknowledges having received comments and critiques from members of the SSG, as well as having been *unable* to incorporate them). Yet he does not use nor mention the concept and, starting from a single reference to Gramsci (the quote is badly translated, read in isolation and misunderstood in its literal sense) he makes a radical critique of the concept of *hegemony*, which he confuses with an absolute closure – between acceptance and resignation. Despite this theoretical setback, Scott's study has the virtue of analysing the embryonic manifestations –infrapolitics – of the hidden resistance of the subordinated as a fundamental platform to understand the bases of their subjective constitution. Although the author does not say so, it is a perspective completely consistent with Gramsci's approach, when the latter clearly described the process of subjectivation taking as a starting point popular culture as a melting pot of practices of resistance.
19. See, for example, the use of the concept *political society* in *Oltre la cittadinanza* (Chatterjee, 2006b). A similar compilation in Spanish was recently published in Argentina (Chatterjee, 2008).

Chapter 2

1. In *The German Ideology*, the concept of *antagonism* appears in relation to the opposition between country and city and between the interests of different professions; only on one occasion does it appear as antagonism between capital and labour and as class struggle.
2. As synonym of conflict, in the *Manifesto* it is used to designate the 'antagonisms between peoples' Marx (1985c: 126).
3. In this sense, in the 'Preface' to the Italian edition of 1893, Engels wrote: 'The revolution was a product of the proletariat everywhere: the labourers were the ones who put up the barricades and gave their lives fighting for the cause. However, only the labourers from Paris, after toppling the

Government, had the firm and decisive intention of toppling the entire bourgeois regime. But, even though they had a very clear consciousness of the irreducible antagonism that was rising between its own class and the bourgeoisie, the economic development of the country and the intellectual development of the French labouring masses had not yet reached the necessary level for a socialist revolution to triumph.'

4. As synonym of contradiction, in relation to the commodity and the conditions of life (Vol. 1, Ch. 3), as class antagonism (Vol. 1, Ch. 8), as antagonism 'between the exploiter and the primary matter of its exploitation' (Vol. 1, Ch. 11), as 'separation between the countryside and the city' and as 'contradictions of the capitalist use of machinery' (Vol. 1, Ch. 12), as 'a side' of pillage, as antagonism between the interests of capitalist groups, as contradictions of the process of capitalist production, as antagonisms of the field (Vol. 1, Ch. 13), as 'social antagonisms' (Vol. 1, Ch. 20), 'antagonisms of the capitalist production' (Vol. 1, Ch. 23), between economic and production systems (Vol. 1, Ch. 25), 'between the interest of every individual capitalist and that of the capitalist class as a collective' (Vol. 1, Ch. 15), as antagonism of wage labour (Vol. 3, Ch. 21), it refers to 'the antagonistic character of capital', to 'systems of production based on the antagonism between the labourer as direct producer and the owner of the means of production', to 'antagonism between the government and the masses' (Vol. 3, Ch. 23), to 'antagonism between the owner of the means of production and the owner of the force of labour', to the 'antagonistic character of the lords of capital over labour' (Vol. 3, Ch. 25), again to class antagonism, then to 'antagonism as public property before all the individuals who really intervene in the production', to 'antagonism of interests between the different companies', to antagonism 'between the nature of wealth as social wealth and as private wealth', again to antagonism between capital and labour (Vol. 3, Ch. 27) and to class antagonism and, finally, to antagonism between forms of value (Vol. 3, endnote Ch. 36).

5. Marx (2003: (3) 31–2), '… struggles whose first law is indecision; in the name of calm an unbridled and empty agitation; in the name of the revolution the most solemn speeches in favour of tranquillity; passions without truth; truths without passion; heroes without heroic acts; history without events, a process whose sole propelling strength seems to be the calendar, tiresome for the everlasting repetition of tensions and relaxations; antagonisms that only seem to get exalted periodically to blunt and decay, without being solved; pretentiously ostentatious efforts and awful bourgeois before the danger of the end of the world and at the same time the saviours of it weaving the pettiest intrigues and palatial comedies, which in their *laisser aller* remind us more of the times of Fronda than of Judgement Day; the official collective genius of France defiled by the artful stupidity of a sole individual; the collective will of the nation, how many times does it speak of universal suffrage, seeks its adequate expression in the inveterate enemies of the interests of the masses, until, finally, it finds it in the obstinate will of a filibuster. If there is a passage of history painted grey upon a grey backdrop, this is it. Men and events

appear like an inverse Schlemihl, like shadows that have lost their bodies. The same revolution paralyzes its own carriers and awards its adversaries only with passionate violence. And when at last, the "red spectre" appears, constantly evoked and conjured by the counterrevolutionaries, it does not appear touched by the Phrygian cap of anarchy, but wearing the uniform of the order, with red *zaragüelles*.'

6. Marx (2003: (3) 51), 'What the bourgeoisie did not understand was the consequence that its own parliamentary regime, that political domination in general had to fall under the general condemnation, as socialist. While the domination of the bourgeois class had not organized integrally, it would not have acquired its true political expression, the antagonism of the other classes could not have stood out either in a pure manner, nor could it, there where it stood out, take the dangerous turn that turns every fight against the power of the State into a fight against capital.'

7. We generalize under the banner of workerism a movement that includes the workerism of the 1960s as well as the workerism-autonomism of the 1970s. We will distinguish further on these two expressions and these two moments of one movement that can and should be read in its continuity as well as its ruptures.

8. To read further, see Borio et al. (2002); Balestrini and Moroni (1997) and, in Spanish, Albertani (2003: 169–99).

9. Regarding the history of Italian Marxism, the place this current occupies in a recent and pioneering attempt at synthesis is significant: Corradi (2005). On the other hand, workerism appears in the famous *Diccionario crítico del marxismo* [*Critical Dictionary of Marxism*] by Labica and Bensussan (1985: 816–17).

10. Agosti also finds a link between workerism in the 1960s and 1970s and the revolutionary syndicalism at the end of the past century, the thought of George Sorel and the councilism of the first postwar. See Agosti (2000: 509–12).

11. See the anthology *La ripresa del marxismo-leninismo in Italia* [*The Recovery of Marxism-Leninism in Italy*] (Panzieri, 1977).

12. See the Dossier 'Uso socialista de la encuesta obrera' ['Socialist Use of the Workers' Survey'], *Quaderni rossi*, AA. VV. (1965 (5): 67–269).

13. We are referring to the groups explicitly linked to the workerist tradition. Other relevant groups of the left associated were *Il manifesto* (appeared at the left of the PCI and got very close to the PO at the beginning of the 1970s) or *Avanguardia Operaia* (a Trotskyist organization that had an important presence in the Unitarian Base Committee of Pirelli in Milan, an outstanding labour experience where the workerist influence was perceived).

14. See a recent balance by Tronti in 'Noi operaisti' (2008: 5–58).

15. Tronti always maintained the need to fight the influence of social democracy within the PCI, to avoid its handover to the capitalist reform operation. See Tronti (1964a).

16. The text was written in the summer of 1977.

17. 'The antagonistic subject, that is, its multiplicity and its permanent referral to the dualist logic of confrontation and struggle. The thought

of the constitution must apply to the antagonistic subject: following that mobility, that freedom, that variously formed desire of life that return to the antagonistic subject its positive and negative hegemony: the negative of the elusive and fantasy, the positive of the strength and the collective link. Thus, the antagonistic subject is not constituted once and for all. It is temporarily constituted in a project of investigation and verification. The negative labour returns to the centre of analysis. But it returns outside the puzzle, as liberation, as displayed innovation. Beyond resistance' (Negri, 2006c: 75).

18. 'Time is the nature in which the vicissitude of subsumption is realized. Time measure is the negative ontology of the power of command and the time of life is the constituent ontology of rejection, of the alternative, of liberation. The set of all the possibilities that make up the existential contradiction of the collective subject opposes the negation of all the possibilities that make up the systemic tautology of the power of command. When the analysis finishes in this dimension of separation, the balance nevertheless demonstrates its value: and it is the ontological temporal foundation of subjectivity, the ontological matrix of antagonism' (Negri, 2006c: 122).

19. Published in Italian in 1991; quotes from the 1997 edition, own translation.

20. Published in Italian in 1995.

21. In the second part, he analyses and critiques the main liberal and communitarian postmodernist theories.

22. In the text, *antagonism* appears 39 times. To put an example of its blurring, on one occasion it refers to 'racial local antagonisms referred to the outbreaks in Los Angeles'.

23. The word *autonomy* appears 70 times with references such as: autonomy of the market, autonomy of the State in international relations, political autonomy, and autonomy of administration.

24. Altamira (2006: 337) writes in this sense: '... in Negri's thought antagonism plays a particular role: it means to destabilize and question the assumptions and standard conceptions of thought as well as the classic proposals that maintain the relation of thought with politics, that is, of the theory with the practice. In Negri, antagonism does not acquire the status of classic concept, in the traditional sense of the word, able to offer support for its political or historical analyses and philosophical writings, that is, to provide sustenance and foundation for an investigation of social and political behaviors in the context of the formulation of ontology of power.'

Chapter 3

1. The other historical vein of references for autonomy refers to anarchist thought and movements. Keeping in mind its Kantian origin and the philosophical development of the concept, referred to the independence of the individual subjectivity, which still occupies an important place in philosophical debates as well as in psychology and current psychoanalysis.

2. I use the adjective *autogestionario* to underline the aspect of promotion of the idea of *self-management* on behalf of political movements in opposition to the social movements that practised it. That is, I make a distinction between self-management as project and practice. Evidently, it is an operative distinction that does not ignore the intersections between one and the other dimension.

3. See also Engels (1873b).

4. The German word *selbsttätigkeit* in this fundamental passage has been translated as autonomy but also as self-activity, self-activation or self-constitution.

5. An erudite exercise in a libertarian reading of Marx is found in Rubel (2000: 284–327). See, in particular, regarding the theme of class, where he says Marx advances the idea of the 'self-constitution of class' (ibid.: 289). Another more recent autonomist reading of Marx of a similar concept can be found in Bonefeld (2008).

6. See, for example, the typically liberal synthesis proposed by Emma Norman after analysing various authors (Norman, 2007). See, on the other hand, the philosophical reflection of Raymundo Mier, who links autonomy with collective experience and action, without anchoring it to an antagonistic matrix and the conformation of concrete political subjectivities (Mier, 2009).

7. Disseminated in 1916.

8. See in particular the debate with Lenin over the Bolshevik Party in Luxemburg (1969: (II) 41–63; quotes from pp. 47, 48, 61). See also Luxemburg (2003; 1995). Daniel Guérin advances a communist libertarian problematization of her thought in *Rosa Luxemburgo y la espontaneidad revolucionaria [Rosa Luxemburg and the Revolutionary Spontaneity]* (Guérin, n.d.). For Luxemburgian readings, see Basso (1977) and Geras (1980).

9 In a parenthesis, Mandel attributes to Trotsky the concept of *self-organization* and uses it emphatically when he synthesizes his thought. In effect, it appears tangentially in the November 1911 text entitled 'Why do Marxists Oppose Individual Terrorism', published in *Der Kampf*, when the Russian revolutionary writes: 'The more "efficient" the terrorist acts and the bigger their impact, they limit more the interest of the masses in their self-organization and self-education.' Later, the concept disappears – albeit the problematic it intends to synthesize does not. For a much more systematic use of the notion of self-organization we will have to wait for Pannekoek.

10. A line that is pierced by polemics and conflicts, mainly focused on the lesser or greater role of the party, on the lesser or greater valorization of spontaneity.

11. About the *soviets* and in relation with the revolutionary scope of the exercise of power and the self-determination of the working class, linking itself to the issue of dual power, analysed by Lenin, Trotsky and, in Latin America, developed by the Bolivian René Zavaleta in *El poder dual en América Latina [Dual Power in Latin America]* (Zavaleta, 1974).

12. Pannekoek's texts can be found at: www.geocities.com/cica_web/consejistas/pannekoek/indice.html.

13. Important elements of the Italian debate can be reviewed in AA.VV. (1977).

14. In this text, we assume a broad definition of councilism that does not necessarily exclude the existence of a communist party. See, for example, AA.VV. (1977). See Rossanda (1973).

15. Samples of these tendencies can be found in Albertani (2004). An analysis of the return of anarchism in antiglobalization can be found in Epstein (2001). Elements of the debate between autonomists, anarchists and communists can be observed in the special issue of the magazine *Contretemps* (AA.VV., 2003).

16. See, for example, some texts in which explicit references to the idea of autonomy appear: Colectivo Situaciones (2003); Rebón (2007); AA.VV. (2007). In particular, see the evaluations of Argentinian autonomism by Hernán Ouviña, 'La autonomía urbana en territorio argentino', and Martín Bergel, 'Balance del autonomismo argentino', in Albertani et al. (2009: 245–84, 285–325). Finally, to understand autonomism in the context of recent Argentinian history, see the works by Maristella Svampa (2005, 2008).

17. For Holloway's intellectual trajectory, see *Los marxismos del nuevo siglo* [*Marxisms of the New Century*], by César Altamira, dedicated to *Open Marxism* (Altamira, 2006).

18. See Holloway (2002). This book was the object of an extensive debate and an intense polemic. We will not get into the peaks of the debate since it goes beyond the scope of our study. A significant part of the debate can be found in Holloway (2006).

19. Holloway writes: 'In capitalism subjectivity is in the first place negative, it is the movement against the negation of subjectivity (the anti-working anti-class)' (Holloway, 2009: 123–9).

20. The relationship between Negri and Holloway deserves a specific treatment. A critical approach, of Negrian inspiration, is found in ch. 4 of César Altamira's book, *The Marxisms of the New Century* (Altamira, 2006: 265–327).

21. Even when Holloway – arguing with the idea of Negrian *immanence* – insists on the 'fetishist' interiority and thus emphasizes the negation against every 'positive' affirmation: in the anti-power, the anti-politic, the anti-subject (Holloway, 2002: 241–5).

22. The PCF was the 'party of the executed' of the Resistance against the Nazi occupation, deeply rooted in French society, in the world of culture, in the popular neighbourhoods and the main representative of the proletarian movement, by way of the General Confederation of Work (CGT) which, in good measure, operated as its union. See the classic study – first published in 1968 – by Annie Kriegel, *Los comunistas franceses* [*The French Communists*] (Kriegel, 1978).

23. For a reconstruction of the history of SoB, see Gottraux (1997).

24. Born in 1944, clandestinely, by the fusion of three groups.

25. The politics of the PCI in France during these years was the object of harsh critiques on behalf of the Chaulieu-Monatal tendency, particularly the

slogan 'Government PCF-PS-CGT'. See 'Lettre ouverte aux militants du PCU et de la "IV Internationale"' (Socialisme ou Barbarie, 1949b).

26. See the Resolution of the tendency Chaulieu-Montal to the II World Congress of the IV International, 'La URSS et le stalinisme mundial' in *Les congrés de la IV Internationale* (Chaulieu-Montal, 1988); see also Pierre Chaulieu (Cornélius Castoriadis) (1946, 1947). These positions would bring Chaulieu and Montal closer to the Johnson-Forest tendency (L.C.R. James and Raya Duyaneskaya) of American Trotskyism, with which it would have a close relationship in the coming years. See 'La IV Internationale et la question russe' of the tendency Johnson-Forest in ibid. (1988: 221–6).

27. By *Pabloism* we understand the line proposed by Michel Pablo (Michalis Raptis) as leader of the Fourth International. For a synthetic history of the Trotskyist strands see Bensaid (2002).

28. The PCI's ambiguity before the PCF and the support of Yugoslavian communists aided in the rupture with Stalin. The dissidents maintained that, despite the rupture of Titism with Stalinism, there was no need to substitute one bureaucracy for another as the Trotskyist majority of the PCI and the Fourth International did.

29. 'Editorial' from March–April in *Socialisme ou Barbarie* (Socialisme ou Barbarie, 1949b: 22).

30. We have already mentioned the closeness of SoB with the councilist strand and in particular with one of its biggest exponents, the Dutch Anton Pannekoek, with which Castoriadis would establish an epistolary debate that would end, after acknowledging the general coincidences, due to the emergence of differences of appreciation over the role of the party and the vanguard. See the exchange in 'Pannekoek-Castoriadis Correspondence', *Políticas de la memoria* (Socialisme ou Barbarie, 2009a: 75-81).

31. Pierre Chaulieu, 'Sur le contenu du socialisme', *Socialisme ou Barbarie*, No. 22, July–September 1957 (in Socialisme ou Barbarie, 2007: (2) 157).

32. See, for example, Mothé '(1957). This strand of analysis was inaugurated with the publication of a text inherited by the relations of *SoB* with the Trotskyist tendency Johnson-Forest, see Romana (1950).

33. Daniel Blanchard, a former member of SoB, insists on this aspect in 'La idea de autonomía. *Socialismo o Barbarie* y el mundo actual' ['The Idea of Autonomy. *Socialism or Barbarism* in the Current World'] in Albertani et al. (2004: 151–63). Blanchard himself was the protagonist of this opening that would lead Guy Debord, founder of the Situationist International and bearer, before the workerist profile of SoB, of more open and sensible thematics and tones to artistic and literary lines to participate briefly in SoB.

34. Editorial (Claude Lefort), 'L'expérience prolétarienne', in *Socialisme ou Barbarie* (Socialisme ou Barbarie, 1952: 77).

35. In 1958, the group formed the organization Workers' Power that edited a newspaper with the same name; see Gottraux (1997).

36. See Cardan (Castoriadis) (1959a, 1959b). In Spanish, see fragments of this polemic in Socialisme ou Barbarie (2009b: 83–93).

37. See 'Editorial, Recommencer la révolution' (Socialisme ou Barbarie, 1964). This editorial summarizes Castoriadis' stand by the end of 1959

and published subsequently after a harsh debate within SoB, in a long essay titled 'The Workers' Movement and Modern Capitalism', published in ibid. (1961–62 (31–3)).

38. We must point out the polemical response in defence of Marxism given by Lyotard, who would subsequently be one of the fathers of 'postmodernism'.

39. The subsequent reflections by Castoriadis on the concept of autonomy are found in *Le monde morcelé* (1990: 38–71), written in 1987; *Domaine de l'homme* (1986: 513–23), written in 1981; and *Fait et á faire* (1997: 9–98), written between 1986 and 1987.

40. That is how the three decades of economic growth that began in the post-World War II period are known in France.

41. It is not by coincidence that the spark of the French May was a group of anarchist students, the Movement of 22 March headed by Daniel Cohn Bendit in Nanterre, a branch of the University of Paris recently constructed in the periphery of Paris, in a *bidonville*, a shantytown.

42. On the Trotskyist and Maoist dissent that broke with the Union d'Étudiants Communistes (UEC), see Dreyfus (1990: 141–53).

43. *La Ligue communiste révolutionnaire (1968–1981)* (Salles 2005).

44. See the only recent text that summarizes the theme: *Autogestion. La dernière utopie?* (Georgi, 2003).

45. The group associated with Michel Rocard maintained the self-managerial stand with the most consistency and coherence.

46. Another central character of the magazine was Albert Meister who, without being a theorist, was the biggest expert and proponent of the international experiences. In particular, within his wide work of dissemination there is an original critical study of the Peruvian experience between 1968 and 1975 during the military government of Velasco Alvarado that Meister discredited in 1981 for its authoritarian character 'in uniform'.

47. The first edition is from 1974.

48. Political as well insofar as they broke with the PCF and assumed Luxemburgian and councilist perspectives that brought them closer to the PSU, which they considered more open, plural and libertarian.

49. Contrary to this tendency, the postindustrialist André Gorz, starting from the principle of autonomy, showed the limits of autogestion, enclosed in the 'kingdom of necessity' of the irreducibly heteronomous material production, and maintained its reduction to a strictly essential minimum and its subordination to the expansion of the universe of autonomy, human, ethical, affective (Gorz, 1980: 142–55).

50. Karl Marx and Friedrich Engels, *La ideología alemana* [*The German Ideology*], ch. 1 'Feuerbach'. Opposition between materialist and idealist conceptions.

51. 'Association of free and equal producers', according to Marx.

52. Sorel (1972: 124): 'Si une classe capitaliste est énergique, elle affirme constamment sa volonté de se défendre; son attitude franchement et loyalement réactionnaire contribue, au moins autant que la violence prolétarienne, à marquer la scission des clases qui est la base de tout le socialisme.'

Chapter 4

1. It is indicative that between them, behind the political opposition, a field of explicit polemic of theoretical character has not been deployed – save some skirmishes outlined in Italy between Negrian workerists and Gramscian communists in the 1970s. There are no traces of theoretical polemics focused on the use of key concepts like the ones that interest us.

2. A recurring formula in Gramsci, who had picked it up from the French writer Romain Rolland, *Quaderni* (1975, Q1, Vol. 63: 75).

3. In an Appendix to *Fábricas del sujeto* [*Factories of the Subject*] (2006b: 295–317) titled 'A propósito del aforismo *Pesimismo de la razón, optimism de la voluntad* y de la oportunidad de darle la vuelta'.

4. More recently, in 2009 an article by Anderson – 'Italy: An Invertebrate Left' – generated a polemic over the interpretation of the role of the PCI in the history of the Italian left that evokes this historic controversy. Also see the important critique of Thomas (2009).

5. In the 1970s in Italy, the left as a whole had a presence and an extraordinary influence in a critical context of capitalism, of weakening of the Christian Democrat hegemony and of failure of the Social Democrat hypothesis propelled by the PSI. In retrospect, it has been without a doubt the most relevant historical opportunity from the post-World War II period to date. Outside the reasons of one or the other and the possibility/impossibility of convergence in respect of difference, we cannot ignore at the historical level that the defeat originates in good measure due to the incapacity to articulate a political movement capable of propelling a radical transformation, further acknowledging, as counterpart, the merits of the rights to mobilize instruments of consensus, manipulation and of repression to attain the victory of the conservative and reactionary stances and to guide the subsequent historical process.

6. Before Italy, beginning with the 'general rehearsal' of 1968, the French left found themselves before favourable circumstances, with a correlation of forces that seemed to oscillate in their favour. Like in Italy, the conservative rising and the corresponding historic right should not only be traced to the successes of the right but in the responsibilities of the left, incapable of taking advantage of the opportunity and of making the most of their potential by way of the convergence within an articulated political movement.

7. Just as, vice versa, determined political projects look for and find in the theoretical matrixes the justification of their political vein. Today this is particularly evident in autonomism, a relatively defined theoretical and political strand. Yet some traces that link the focus of subalternity to communist, postcommunist and Social Democrat stances could be found just like the focus of antagonism for sectors of the revolutionary left more attached to the insurrectional paradigm. Obviously, it is a hypothesis of theoretical and political correlation schematically put, whose treatment surpasses by far the frame of this work.

8. I use the idea of *over-politicization* to avoid two misunderstandings: the first is to avoid the confusion with the necessary politicization of the theory; the second is that if I were to use the notion of '*ideologization*' or

hyper- or over-ideologization, it could be read as a rejection of ideology, a theme and problem whose semantical and theoretical complexity is not the object of this work.

9. For example, this translates into notorious and diffuse intellectual practices that force the theoretical instruments into justifying aims, which sometimes get confused with realities – what Anglo-Saxons call *wishful thinking*.

10. This recurring operation in social theory is described by Horkheimer and Habermas in the following terms: 'The supreme principles of traditional theory define universal concepts under which all the facts of the field of the object of theory must be subsumed. In the midst there is a hierarchy of genres and species among which there exist everywhere corresponding relations of subordination' (Horkheimer, 2000: 58–9).

   'The lines of investigation in the theory of systems and the theory of action isolate and overgeneralize in each case one of these two concepts' (Habermas, 2001: 533). In another record, attributed by some to Hegelian idealism and by others to Lenin: 'by corroborating my hypotheses, I verified that the reality was wrong'.

11. Leaving aside the hypothesis of its potential political *compatibility* – and the obstacles that intervene – it is an aspect that surpasses the purposes of this study and that would need an *ad hoc* treatment, related to the study of projects and strategies of movements and political groupings.

12. A general definition of *homologous*, in biology, is the following: 'Said of the organs or body parts that are similar for their origin in the embryo, for their relations to other organs and for their position in the body, e.g., the anterior extremities in mammals and the wings in birds, even though in their aspect and function they might be different': *Diccionario de la lengua española* (Real Academia Española, 1992: 1120).

13. This Marxist problematic ties in with sociological treatments and, in particular, with the proposal by Pierre Bourdieu focused on the concepts of *field* and *habitus*. See Bourdieu and Wacquant (2005).

14. The theoretical Gramscianism can be recognized by distinguishing a *core* and a *circle*. The hard core dedicates itself to Gramsciology, the study of Gramsci's work. This mainly lies in Italy – not only around the Instituto Gramsci, but in the numerous intellectuals formed in the communist area – but it has its international, IGC (International Gramsci Society), that groups the great majority of Gramsciologists. On the other hand, we can identify a circle, a wider but softer and more heterogeneous universe of Gramscians, that is, those who use or develop concepts, categories or approaches derived from or inspired by Gramsci's thought, without being specialists on his work.

15. On the contrary, a convergence could be found around its use as synonym of conflict. In this sense, the clearly subjective use by Negri and Melucci would be exceptions that confirm the rule.

16. According to Bourdieu, Chamboredon and Passeron: 'as Freud would say, "the elasticity of the definitions", or as Carl Hempel affirms, "the semantic availability of the concepts" … constitutes one of the conditions of the discovery, at least in certain eras of the history of a science or the development of an investigation' (Bourdieu et al., 1998: 21).

17. These methodological annotations point to the separation of what Charles Wright Mills reproaches the 'grand theory' as an enterprise exclusively engaged with the 'association and dissociation of concepts': 'When we think about what a word represents, we deal with its *semantic* aspects; when we consider it in relation to other words, we deal with their *syntactic* characteristics. I employ these shorthand terms because they supply an economic and precise model to say the following: grand theory is drunk with syntax and blind for semantics' (Mills, 1961: 45, 52).

18. The differentiation could be clearer if we were talking about rebellion, since resistance can be understood as a form of struggle. At the same time, the notion of *rebellion* also appears as another form of struggle that tends to imply a certain degree of violence and the explicit disregard of authority, which reduces the phenomenological field to which we are referring and that tends to include all the forms of struggle that surpass the resistance, just as we defined it in the same sentence.

19. Less restrained than Scott's *infrapolitical* definition – below the line, which insists on and exalts the veiled, implicit, disguised, publicly undeclared, hidden character of the resistance. See Scott (2000: 217–37).

20. A consequence of the establishment of conceptual coordinates differentiated and articulated in the direction of a tripartite focus is the *tendency/temptation* to establish *indicators* of subalternity, antagonism and autonomy susceptible of being applied to analyses of concrete cases. Even though it is a delicate theme that surpasses the objectives of this work, it is worth saying that above the risks of a similar operation, the establishment of indicators should be done on the basis of an operation of analytical decomposition similar to the ones that led the *movementologists* to establish dimensions such as *identity, discourse, organization*, and so on. Exercises of this nature proliferate with greater or lesser success. The recent work by Tarrow and Tilly, *La politica del conflitto* (2008), is oriented in this direction. The construction and the application of indicators would have to derive from phenomenal reductions and the hypotheses that accompany them. Indicators that allow us to analyse the intersections of subaltern, antagonistic and autonomous aspects in four dimensions/fundamental processes of every process of political subjectivation: *politicization, organization, mobilization, radicalization,* could be elaborated. On another plane of differentiations, another example could be the construction and application to the analysis of the discourse of indicators of subalternity (conservative and resistant common sense elements), of antagonism (references to conflict, characterization of the enemy), and of autonomy (identity-based affirmation and projections, future images).

21. This can produce the optical illusion that underlies the essentialist statements.

Afterword

1. Gramsci clarifies that the idea of passive revolution is, for Marxism, a criterion or canon of interpretation and not a program as it would be for the bourgeoisie (and for its intellectuals, Benedetto Croce *in primis*). Also see Morton (2007: 63–73).

2. The second wording – text C – is the following: 'We must see if Quinet's formula can be approximated to that of Cuoco's passive revolution; both express surely the historical fact of the absence of a popular integrated initiative in the development of Italian history and the other fact that the development has been verified as a reaction of the dominant classes to the sporadic, elemental, inorganic subversivism of the popular masses as "restorations" that have accepted a certain part of the demands from below. Thus, "progressive restorations" or "revolutions-restorations" or even "passive revolutions".'

3. Liguori observes that the hypothesis of fascism as passive revolution is centred in the valorization of the 'rivoluzionario' side of fascism linked to the renovation in the field of the life of the masses and the intervention of the political in the economic, just as in the corporative agreement: a way of doing what the USSR does but with a political orientation. Yet all this remains as a project and in the twenty years of fascism there is no real renewal. Thus this hypothesis is stated provisionally like many others that Gramsci posed in the *Notebooks*.

4. Whether the case of the USSR could be thought of as a passive revolution on behalf of Gramsci is an object of controversy and interpretation that no longer has any textual references to endorse it.

5. Author's own translation from the Gerratana edition since the Spanish translation of this note in the Mexican edition is so poor its meaning is altered.

6. Voza refers from these formulations by Gianny Francioni and Christine Buci-Glucksmann.

7. On this point, Fabio Frosini (2011) points out we should not maintain the balance between the two points so as to avoid falling in a 'moralistic' reading of the adjective 'passive'. He observes that passivity and passivation are not the same, being that the latter appears post-1968 when people started thinking in terms of new subjectivities, social movements, etc.

8. The differentiation will be finer and more complex once Gramsci introduces the 'qualitative' and 'quantitative' criteria, assuming that in some cases like Napoleon I, one takes a 'step from one type of state to another type, one step in which the innovations were such that they represented a complete transformation', while in cases like Napoleon III one only observes an 'evolution of the same type, according to an uninterrupted line' (ibid., Vol. 5, No. 13: 67).

9. Each one has nuances and differences within it. For example, the autonomist, Marxist-Leninist or environmentalist critiques converge and differ and the oppositions of the right can be more liberal or more conservative on different topics, like the economy, culture or society. In the same manner, there exist several significant variations – particularly interesting and poorly analysed and studied – of critical support within the social and party coalitions that uphold these governments.

10. Carlos Nelson Coutinho (2007), in an attempt to understand neoliberalism, suggested that rather than a *passive revolution*, one should speak of *counterreform* to the extent that the fundamental element of reception of part of the demands from below did not take place. Not only

do I share this opinion regarding neoliberalism but I would add that this element is present in actuality and complements the set that allows us to state that, where progressive political forces govern in Latin America there is a process of passive revolution. Coutinho (1999) himself fruitfully applied the concept of passive revolution to Brazilian history. Also see Morton (2011) on his analysis of passive revolution and its affinity with uneven and combined development in Mexico.

11. Since the process of deterioration of the domination by political parties did not express itself in a rupture but in a cycle of fissures that began with the *Caracazo*, passed through the attempted coup and ended up in the surprising electoral victory of Chávez in 1998.

12. In this temporal sequence the scope of the different interpretations is at play as some consider that the governments are legitimized as an expression of the popular movements and are guided to evaluate them only in regards to the concrete, social and economic transformations promoted as answers to the demands formulated in the anti-neoliberal protests. On the contrary, in the passage from one to the other a betrayal or a substantial modification of the process is produced that leads to failure or a perversion given that, in addition to the limited or null changes in the anti-neoliberal sense, the balance of the new progressive governments is considered negative and reactionary to the extent that it encourages a demobilization that weakens and disarticulates the popular organizations that had been created or strengthened in the cycle of ascension of the social struggles.

13. Comparing one era to the other, we find an interesting similarity in the sequential cycle of popular mobilization and instalment of progressive governments in the 1930s and 1940s, which operated as a solution of compromise, as a way to temper and disable the conflict, inaugurating an age of passive revolution that turned out very successfully until another cycle of mobilization and conflict appeared that began between the end of the 1940s and the mid 1950s and ended in the 1970s, with the militaristic wave that did away with the diverse expressions – national-popular and revolutionary socialist – of popular movements built and strengthened throughout half a century of history at least. The hypothesis of a similarity in the composition of these two historical cycles deserves to be explored by means of a more thorough and systematic treatment.

14. Possibly due to the fact that an ever greater number of actors and popular organizations retreat from the progressive governments and assume that the struggle for vindication has to occur by means of pressure and protest.

15. Ramírez (personal communication) made these comments in a first draft of this essay.

16. See articles by A. Antillano, M. Harnecker and Y. Reyes, in Lang and Santillana (2010).

17. In this regard, Franklyn Ramírez suggests that 'the sociological bases of passivation' be considered, phenomena that go beyond the social movements but cross them and condition the politics of the progressive governments in the meantime: 'Not only do they not promote popular mobilization as they should (although if they did they could also be

criticized for reducing the autonomy of the social) but even if they did the effects would be limited, most probably, to the sphere of the "already" mobilized. That already happened in a certain form in the 90s with the antagonistic exercise of the social movements and their impossibility of political irradiation beyond certain circuits (the thesis of the massiveness of the previous cycle of mobilization can also be taken with a grain of salt). There lies a structural limit for the revolution, and there lies the *quid* of the matter in actuality.' For Ramírez, the central problem is not the passivation of the always active but 'the immobility of those who have always (or for a long time) been passive and subalternized by forms of social coordination and compression that eliminate the centrality of politics/of the national public action/ of collective action and subordinate it to the ethos of the market, the family, religion, sociability/pre and anti-political subjectivity'.

Bibliography

AA. VV. (1965) 'Uso socialista de la encuesta obrera' ['Socialist Use of the Workers' Survey'], *Quaderni rossi*, Vol. 5, April, pp. 67–269.

—— (1977) 'Consejos obreros y democracia socialista' ['Workers' Councils and Socialist Democracy'], *Cuadernos de Pasado y Presente*, Vol. 33.

—— (2003) 'Changer le monde sans prendre le pouvoir? Nouveaux libertaires, nouveaux communists' ['Change the World without Taking Power? New Libertarians, New Communists'], *Contretemps*, Vol. 6, February.

—— (2007) *Reflexiones sobre poder popular* [*Reflections on Popular Power*] (Buenos Aires: El Colectivo).

Agosti, Aldo (2000) *Enciclopedia della sinistra europea nel XX secolo* [*Encyclopaedia of the European Left in the Twentieth Century*] (Rome: Editori Riuniti).

Albertani, Claudio (2003) 'Antonio Negri, Imperio y la extraña parábola del obrerismo italiano' ['Antonio Negri, Empire and the Strange Parable of Italian Workerism'], *Bajo el Volcán*, Vol. 6, No. 1.

—— (ed.) (2004) *Imperio y movimientos sociales en la edad global* [*Empire and Social Movements in the Global Age*] (Mexico: UCM).

——, Rovira, G., and Modonesi, M. (eds) (2009) *La autonomía posible. Emancipación y reinvención de la política* [*The Possible Autonomy. Emancipation and the Reinvention of Politics*] (Mexico: UACM).

Altamira, César (2006) *Los marxismos del nuevo siglo* [*The Marxisms of the New Century*] (Buenos Aires: Biblos).

Anderson, Perry (1981) *Las antinomias de Antonio Gramsci* [*The Antinomies of Antonio Gramsci*] (Barcelona: Fontamara).

—— (1985) *Teoría, política e historia. Un debate con E.P. Thompson* [*Theory, Politics and History. A Debate with E.P. Thompson*] (Madrid: Siglo XXI).

—— (2009) 'Italy: An Invertebrate Left', *London Review of Books*, Vol. 31, No. 5, March, pp. 12–18.

Aricó, José (1988) *La cola del diablo. Itinerario de Gramsci en América Latina* [*The Devil's Tail. Gramsci's Itinerary in Latin America*] (Caracas: Nueva Sociedad).

—— *Nueve lecciones sobre economía y política en el marxismo* [*Nine Lessons on Economy and Politics in Marxism*] (Mexico: El Colegio de México).Bianchi, Alvaro (2005) 'O pretérito do futuro' ['The Past of the Future'], *Crítica Marxista*, Vol. 25 (Campinas: Centro de Estudios Marxistas-Universidade de Campinas).

—— (2011) *Nueve lecciones sobre economía y política en el marxismo* [*Nine Lessons on Economy and Politics in Marxism*] (Mexico: El Colegio de México).

Artiéres, Philippe, and Zancarini-Fournel, Michelle (2008) *68. Une histoire collective (1962–1981)* [*68. A Collective History (1962–1981)*] (Paris: La Découverte).

Artous, Antoine, et al. (2008) *La France des années 68* [*The France of 68*] (Paris: Sylepse).

Balestrini, Nanni, and Moroni, Primo (1997) *L'orda d'oro 1968–1977* [*The Golden Horde 1968–1977*] (Milan: Feltrinelli).

Baratta, Giorgio (2007) *Antonio Gramsci in contrappunto* [*Antonio Gramsci in Counterpoint*] (Rome: Carocci).

Basso, Lelio (1977) *Rosa Luxemburgo* (Mexico: Nuestro Tiempo).

Bensaid, Daniel (2002) *Les trotskysmes* [*Trotskyisms*] (Paris: PUF).

—— (2007) 'Políticas de Castoriadis' ['The Politics of Castoriadis'], *Memoria*, Vol. 222.

Berardi, Franco (Bifo) (2007) 'Genesi e significato del termine autonomía' ['Genesis and Meaning of Autonomy'], in Bianchi, S., and Caminiti, L. (eds) *Gli autonomi. Le storie, le lotte, le teorie* [*The Autonomous. The Stories, the Struggles, the Theories*], Vol. II (Rome: DeriveApprodi).

Béroud, Sophie, et al. (2003) 'Eléments pour l'étude du courant pabliste. Discours et pratiques autogestionnaires' ['Elements for the Study of Pabloism. Self-Management Discourse and Practices'], in Georgi, F. (ed.) *Autogestion. La dernière utopie?* [*Self-management. The Last Utopia?*] (Paris: La Sorbonne).

Beverley, John (2004) 'El subalterno y los límites del saber académico' ['The Subaltern and the Limits of Academic Knowledge'], *Actuel Marx*, Vol. 2.

Bianchi, Alvaro (2005) 'O pretérito do futuro' ['The Past of the Future'], *Crítica Marxista*, Vol. 25 (Campinas: Centro de Estudios Marxistas-Universidade de Campinas).

Bianchi, Sergio, and Caminiti, Lanfranco (eds) (2007) *Gli autonomi. Le stori, le lotte, le teorie* [*The Autonomous. The Stories, the Struggles, the Theories*], Vol. II (Rome: DeriveApprodi).

Blanchard, Daniel (2009) 'La autonomía en SoB' ['Autonomy in SoB'], in Albertani, C., Rovira, G., and Modonesi, M. (eds) *La autonomía posible. Emancipación y reinvención de la política* [*The Possible Autonomy. Emancipation and the Reinvention of Politics*] (Mexico: UACM).

Bonefeld, Werner (2008) 'Marxismo: la auto-emancipación de trabajadoras y trabajadores como proceso abierto' ['Marxism: Self-emancipation in Female and Male Workers as Open Process'], *Herramienta*, Vol. 39.

Borio, Guido (2007) 'Operai contro la metrópoli' ['Workers Against the Metropolis'], in Bianchi, S., and Caminiti, L. (eds) *Gli autonomi. Le storie, le lotte, le teorie* [*The Autonomous. The Stories, the Struggles, the Theories*], Vol. II (Rome: DeriveApprodi).

——, Pozzi, Francesca, and Roggero, Gigi (2002) *Futuro anteriore. Dai 'Quaderni rossi' ai movimenti globali: ricchezze e limiti dell'operaismo italiano* [*Previous Future. From the 'Red Notebooks' to Global Movements: Wealth and Limits of Italian Workerism*] (Rome: DeriveApprodi).

Bourdet, Yvon (1977) 'Karl Marx y la autogestión' ['Karl Marx and Self-Management'], *Cuadernos de Pasado y Presente*, Vol. 33.

Bourdieu, Pierre; Chamboredon, Jean-Claude, and Passeron, Jean-Claude (1998) *El oficio del sociólogo* [*The Craft of Sociology*] (Mexico: Siglo XXI).

Bourdieu, Pierre, and Wacquant, Loic (2005) *Una invitación a la sociología Reflexiva* [*An Invitation to Reflexive Sociology*] (Buenos Aires: Siglo XXI).

Bowman, Paul (2007) *Post-Marxism versus Cultural Studies* (Edinburgh: Edinburgh University Press).

Brehier, Emeric (2003) 'Le CERES et l'autogestion a travers de ses revues: fondement identitaire et posture interne' ['CERES and Self-Management through Its Magazines: Identity Foundation and Internal Position'], in Georgi, F. (ed.) *Autogestion. La dernière utopie? [Self-management. The Last Utopia?]* (Paris: La Sorbonne).

Bricianer, Serge (1975) *Anton Pannekoek y los consejos obreros [Anton Pannekoek and the Workers' Councils]* (Buenos Aires: Schapire).

Burgio, Alberto (2007) *Per Gramsci. Crisi e potenza del moderno [For Gramsci. Crisis and Potency of the Modern]* (Rome: DeriveApprodi).

Buttigieg, Joseph A. (1999) 'I subalterni nel pensiero di Gramsci' ['The Subaltern in Gramsci's Thought'], in Burgio, A., and Santucci, A. (eds) *Gramsci e la rivoluzione in occidente [Gramsci and the Western Revolution]* (Rome: Editori Riuniti).

Cardan, Paul (Cornelius Castoriadis) (1959a) 'Prolétariat et organisation I' ['Proletariat and Organization I'], *Socialisme ou Barbarie* Vol. 27, April–May.

—— (1959b) 'Prolétariat et organisation II' ['Proletariat and Organization II'], *Socialisme ou Barbarie*, Vol. 28, July–August.

Castoriadis, Cornelius (1975) *L'institution imaginaire de la société [The Imaginary Institution of Society]* (Paris: Éditions du Seuil).

—— (1986) *Domaine de l'homme [Domains of Man]* (Paris: Seuil).

—— (1990) *Le monde morcelé [World in Fragments]* (Paris: Seuil).

—— (1997) *Fait et á faire [Done and to be Done]* (Paris: Seuil).

Caumières, Philippe (2007) *Castoriadis. Le projet d'autonomie [Castoriadis. The Project of Autonomy]* (Paris: Michalon).

Chatterjee, Partha (1997a) 'El Estado Nacional' ['The National State'], in Rivera Cusicanqui, S., and Barragán, R. (eds) *Debates Post-Coloniales: una introducción a los Estudios de la Subalternidad [Postcolonial Debates: An Introduction to Subaltern Studies]* (La Paz: Historias-Aruwiyiri-SEPHIS).

—— (1997b) 'La Nación y sus campesinos' ['The Nation and its Peasants'], in Rivera Cusicanqui, S., and Barragán, R. (eds) *Debates Post-Coloniales: una introducción a los Estudios de la Subalternidad [Postcolonial Debates: An Introduction to Subaltern Studies]* (La Paz: Historias-Aruwiyiri-SEPHIS).

—— (2006a) 'Controverses en Inde autour de l'histoire coloniale' ['Controversies in India Surrounding the Colonial History'], *Le Monde Diplomatique*, February.

—— (2006b) *Oltre la cittadinanza [Beyond Citizenship]* (Rome: Maltemi).

—— (2008) *La nación en tiempo heterogéneo y otros estudios subalternos [The Nation in Heterogeneous Time and Other Subaltern Studies]* (Buenos Aires: Siglo XXI-CLACSO).

Chaulieu, Pierre (Cornélius Castoriadis) (1946) 'Sur le régime et contre la défense de l'URSS' ['On the Regime and Against the Defence of the USSR'], *Bulletin intérieur du PCI*, Vol. 31, August.

—— (1947) 'Sur la question de l'URSS et du stalinisme mundial' ['On the Question of the USSR and World Stalinism'], *Bulletin intérieur du PCI*, Vol. 41, August.

—— (1949) 'Les rapports de production en Russie' ['The Relations of Production in Russia'], *Socialisme ou Barbarie*, Vol. 2, May–June.

—— (1957) 'Sur le contenu du socialisme' ['On the Content of Socialism'], *Socialisme ou Barbarie*, Vol. 22, July–September.

Chaulieu-Montal (1949) 'Lettre ouverte aux militants du PCI et de la IV Internationale' ['Open Letter to the PCI Militants and the Fourth International'], *Socialisme ou Barbarie*, Vol. 1, March.

—— (1988) 'La URSS et le stalinisme mundial' ['The USSR and World Stalinism'], in *Les congrés de la IV Internationale*, Vol. III (Paris: La Brèche).

Cleaver, Harry (2009) 'Trayectorias de autonomía' ['Trajectories of Autonomy'], in Albertani, C., Rovira, G., and Modonesi, M. (eds) *La autonomía posible. Reinvención de la política y emancipación [The Possible Autonomy. Emancipation and the Reinvention of Politics]* (Mexico: UACM).

Colectivo Situaciones (2003) *Piqueteros. La rivolta argentina contra il neoliberalismo [Piqueteros. The Argentinian Rebellion Against Neoliberalism]* (Rome: Derive Approdi).

Coutinho, Carlos Nelson (1999) *Gramsci. Un estudo sobre seu pensamento politico [Gramsci. A Study of his Political Thought]* (Rio de Janeiro: Civilizacao brasileira).

—— (2007) 'L'epoca neoliberale: rivoluzione passiva o controriforma?' ['The Neoliberal Age: Passive Revolution or Counter-Reform?'], *Critica Marxista*, Vol. 2.

Corradi, Cristina (2005) *Storia del marxismo in Italia [History of Marxism in Italy]* (Rome: Manifestolibri).

Cuane, Jean (2003) 'La création collective au théâtre: une modalité autogérée de la production artistique' ['Collective Creation in the Theater: A Self-Managed Modality of Artistic Production'], in Georgi, F. (ed.) *Autogestion. La dernière utopie? [Self-management. The Last Utopia?]* (Paris: La Sorbonne).

Cuénot, Alain (2003) 'Pierre Naville et l'autogestion face aux structures du capitalisme et du socialisme d'état' ['Pierre Naville and Self-Management before the Structures of Capitalism and State Socialism'], in Georgi, F. (ed.) *Autogestion. La dernière utopie? [Self-management. The Last Utopia?]* (Paris: La Sorbonne).

Dandé, Serge (2003) 'Le PCF et l'autogestion. Histoire d'un ralliement, 1968–1979' ['The PCF and Self-Management. History of an alignment'], in Georgi, F. (ed.) *Autogestion. La dernière utopie? [Self-management. The Last Utopia?]* (Paris: La Sorbonne).

De Felice, Franco (1988) 'Revolución pasiva, fascismo, americanismo en Gramsci' ['Passive Revolution, Fascism, Americanism in Gramsci'], in Kanoussi, D. and Mena, J. (eds) *Filosofía y política en el pensamiento de Gramsci [Philosophy and Politics in Gramsci's Thought]* (Mexico: Ediciones de Cultura Popular: México).

Dezés, Marie-Genevieve (2003) 'L'utopie realisée: les modéles étrangers mythiques des autogestionnaires francais' ['Utopia Realized: The Mythical foreign Models of the French Self-Managers'], in Georgi, F. (ed.) *Autogestion. La dernière utopie? [Self-management. The Last Utopia?]* (Paris: La Sorbonne).

Dreyfus, Michel (1990) *PCF. Crises et dissidences [PCF. Crisis and Dissent]* (Paris: Complexe).

Dube, Saurabh (2001) *Sujetos subalternos [Subaltern Subjects]* (Mexico: El Colegio de México).

Dussel, Enrique (2006) *20 tesis de política* [*20 Political Theses*] (Mexico: Siglo XXI).

Engels, Friedrich (1873a) 'De la autoridad' ['On Authority'], in *Almanacco Repubblicanoper l'anno 1874* [*Republican Almanac for 1874*] [Electronic], Available: www.marxists.org [August 2009].

—— (1873b) 'I bakuninisti a lavoro. Note sull'insurrezione in Spagna dell'estate 1873' ['Bakuninists at Work. Notes on the Spanish Insurrection in the Summer of 1873'], Available: www.marxists.org [August 2009].

Epstein, Barbara (2001) 'Anarchism and the Anti-Globalization Movement', *Monthly Review*, Vol. 53, No. 4, September.

Frosini, Fabio (2011) 'Hacia una teoría de la hegemonía' ['Towards a Theory of Hegemony'], unpublished.

Galli, Giorgio (2004) *Piombo rosso. Storia completa della lotta armata inItalia dal 1970 ad oggi* [*Red Lead. The Complete History of the Armed Struggle in Italy from 1970 until Today*] (Milan: Baldini Castoldi Dalai).

Georgi, Frank (ed.) (2003a) *Autogestion. La dernière utopie?* [*Self-management. The Last Utopia?*] (Paris: La Sorbonne).

—— (2003b) 'Les rocardiens: pour une culture politique autogestionnaire' ['The Rocardians: For a Self-Managing Political Culture'], in Georgi, F. (ed.) *Autogestion. La dernière utopie?* [*Self-management. The Last Utopia?*] (Paris: La Sorbonne).

Geras, Norman (1980) *Actualidad del pensamiento de Rosa Luxemburgo* [*The Legacy of Rosa Luxemburg*] (Mexico: ERA).

Gorz, André (1980) *Adieux au prolétariat* [*Farewell to the Proletariat*] (Paris: Galilée).

Gottraux, Philippe (1997) *Socialisme ou Barbarie. Un engagement politique et intellectuel dans la France de l'après-guerre* [*Socialism or Barbarism. A Political and Intellectual Commitment in Postwar France*] (Lausanne: Payot).

Gramsci, Antonio (1920) 'Il consiglio di fabbrica' ['The Factory Council'], *L'Ordine Nuovo*, Vol. II, No. 4, 5 June.

—— (1921) 'Due rivoluzioni' ['Two Revolutions'], *L'Ordine Nuovo*, Vol. II, No. 8, 3 July.

—— (1926) 'Cinque anni di vita del partito' ['Five Years of Party Life'], *L'Unità*, 24 February.

—— (1973) 'Democracia obrera y socialismo' ['Workers' Democracy and Socialism'], *Pasado y Presente*, Vol. 1, April–June.

—— (1975) *Quaderni dal Carcere* [*The Prison Notebooks*], Critical Edition by Instituto Gramsci, Valentino Gerratana (Rome: Einaudi).

—— (1981–99) *Cuadernos de la Cárcel* [*Prison Notebooks*], 6 vols (Mexico: Ediciones ERA).

—— (2000) *Cuadernos de la Cárcel* [*The Prison Notebooks*] (Mexico: ERA).

—— (2003) *La generazione degli anni perduti. Storie di Potere Operaio* [*The Generation of the Lost Years. Stories of Workers' Power*] (Turin: Einaudi).

Green, Marcus E. (2007) 'Sul concetto gramsciano di subalterno' ['On the Gramscian concept of the Subaltern'], in Vacca, G., and Schirru, G. (eds) *Studi gramsciani nel mondo (2000–2005)* [*Gramscian Studies in the World (2000–2005)*] (Bologna: Il Mulino).

Guérin, Daniel (n.d.) *Rosa Luxemburgo y la espontaneidad revolucionaria* [*Rosa Luxemburg and Revolutionary Spontaneity*] (Buenos Aires: Anarres).

Guha, Ranajit (1997a) 'Aspectos elementales de la insurgencia campesina en la india colonial' ['Elementary Aspects of Peasant Insurgency in Colonial India'], in Rivera Cusicanqui, S., and Barragán, R. (eds) *Debates Post-Coloniales: una introducción a los Estudios de la Subalternidad* [*Postcolonial Debates: An Introduction to Subaltern Studies*] (La Paz: Historias-Aruwiyiri-SEPHIS).

—— (1997b) (1981) 'Prefacio a los Estudios de la Subalternidad. Escritos sobre la Historia y la Sociedad Surasiática' ['Preface to the Studies of Subalternity. Writings on South Asian History and Society'], in Rivera Cusicanqui, S., and Barragán, R. (eds) *Debates Post-Coloniales: una introducción a los Estudios de la Subalternidad* [*Postcolonial Debates: An Introduction to Subaltern Studies*] (La Paz: Historias-Aruwiyiri-SEPHIS).

—— (1997c) 'Sobre algunos aspectos de la historiografía colonial de la India' ['On Some Aspects of the Historiography of Colonial India'], in Rivera Cusicanqui, S. and Barragán, R. (eds) *Debates Post-Coloniales: una introducción a los Estudios de la Subalternidad* [*Postcolonial Debates: An Introduction to Subaltern Studies*] (La Paz: Historias-Aruwiyiri-SEPHIS).

—— (2002) *Las voces de la historia y otros estudios subalternos* [*The Small Voice of History: Collected Essays*] (Barcelona: Crítica).

—— and Spivak, Gayatri Chakravorty (2002) *Subaltern Studies* (Verona: Ombre Corte).

Habermas, Jurgen (2001) *Teoría de la acción comunicativa II* [*The Theory of Communicative Action II*] (Madrid: Taurus).

Halimi, Serge (2000) *Quand la gauche essayait* [*When the Left Tried*] (Paris: Arlea).

Hall, Stuart (2008) *Identités et cultures. Politiques des Cultural Studies* [*Identities and Cultures. The Politics of Cultural Studies*] (Paris: Éditions Amsterdam).

Hardt, Michael y Negri, Antonio (2000) *Imperio* [*Empire*] (Barcelona: Paidós).

—— (2003) *El trabajo de Dionisos* [*Labor of Dionysus: A Critique of the State-Form*] (Madrid: Akal).

—— (2004) *Multitud. Guerra y democracia en la era del Imperio* [*Multitude: War and Democracy in the Age of Empire*] (Barcelona: Debate).

Hatzfeld, Hélène (2003) 'L'autogestion dans la recomposition d'un champ politique de gauche' ['Self-Management in the Recomposition of a Leftist Political Field'], in Georgi, F. (ed.) *Autogestion. La dernière utopie?* [*Self-management. The Last Utopia?*] (Paris: La Sorbonne).

Hobsbawm, Eric (1963) 'Para el estudio de las clases subalternas' ['For the Study of Subaltern Classes'], *Pasado y Presente*, Vols 2–3.

—— (1999) *Les bandits* [*Bandits*] (Paris: La Découverte).

—— (2001) *Rebeldes primitivos* [*Primitive Rebels*] (Barcelona: Crítica).

Holloway, John (2002) *Cambiar el mundo sin tomar el poder* [*Change the World Without Taking Power*] (Buenos Aires: Herramienta-BUAP).

—— (2006) *Contra y más allá del capital* [*Against and Beyond Capital*] (Buenos Aires: Herramienta).

—— (2009) 'Autonomismo positivo y negativo' ['Positive and Negative Autonomism'], in Albertani, C., Rovira, G., and Modonesi, M. (eds) *La autonomía posible. Reinvención de la política y emancipación* [*The Possible Autonomy. Emancipation and the Reinvention of Politics*] (Mexico: UACM).

Horkheimer, Max (2000) *Teoría tradicional y teoría crítica* [*Traditional and Critical Theory*] (Barcelona: Paidós).

Katsiaficas, George (n.d.) *La subversión de la política: movimientos sociales autónomos y la descolonización de la vida cotidiana* [*The Subversion of Politics: European Autonomous Social Movements and the Decolonization of Everyday Life*]. Translated by Alejandra Pinto. Mimeo.

Kriegel, Annie (1978) (1968) *Los comunistas franceses* [*The French Communists*] (Madrid: Villamar).

Labica, Georges, and Bensussan, Gérard (1985) *Dictionnaire critique du marxisme* [*Critical Dictionary of Marxism*] (Paris: PUF).

Laclau, Ernesto, and Mouffe, Chantal (2004) *Hegemonía y estrategia socialista* [*Hegemony and Socialist Strategy*] (Buenos Aires: FCE).

Lafargue, Paul (1881) 'L'autonomie' ['Autonomy'], *L'Égalité*, 25 December.

Lander, Edgardo (ed.) (2003) *La colonialidad del saber: eurocentrismo y ciencias sociales* [*The Coloniality of Knowledge: Eurocentrism and Social Sciences*] (Buenos Aires: CLACSO).

Lang, Miriam, and Santillana, Alejandra (eds) (2010) *Democracia, participación, socialismo. Bolivia, Ecuador, Venezuela* [*Democracy, Participation, Socialism. Bolivia, Ecuador, Venezuela*] (Quito: Fundación Rosa Luxemburgo).

Lazzarato, Maurizio, and Negri, Antonio (2001) *Trabajo inmaterial. Formas de vida y producción de subjetividad* [*Immaterial Labor. Ways of Life and the Production of Subjectivity*] (Rio de Janeiro: DP&A editora).

Lefebvre, Henri (1966) *Le marxisme* [*Marxism*] (Paris: PUF).

—— (1968) *Sociologie de Marx* [*Sociology of Marx*] (Paris: PUF).

—— (2000) (1974) *La production de l'espace* [*The Production of Space*] (Paris: Antropos).

Lefort, Claude (1956–57) 'L'insurrection hongroise' ['The Hungarian Insurrection'], *Socialisme ou Barbarie*, Vol. 20, December–January.

—— (1958) 'Organisation et parti' ['Organization and Political Party'], *Socialisme ou Barbarie*, Vol. 26, November–December.

Legois, Jean-Philippe (2003) 'L'autogestion universitaire en mai–juin 1968: portée et limite, discours et pratiques' ['University Self-Management in May–June 1968: Scope, Limits, Discourse and Practices'], in Georgi, F. (ed.) *Autogestion. La dernière utopie?* [*Self-management. The Last Utopia?*] (Paris: La Sorbonne).

Liguori, Guido (1997) *Gramsci conteso* [*Gramsci Sought*] (Rome: Editori Riuniti).

——, and Voza, Pasquale (eds) (2009) *Dizionario Gramsciano (1926–1937)* [*Gramscian Dictionary (1926–1937)*] (Rome: Carocci).

L'Ordine Nuovo (1976) 'Colección completa facsimilar, 1919–1920 y 1924–1925' ['Complete Facsimile Collection, 1919–1920 and 1924–1925] (Milan: Teti Editore).

Luxemburg, Rosa (1915) *La crisis de la socialdemocracia (Juniusbroschure)* [*The Crisis of Social Democracy*], mimeo.

—— (1969) 'Problemas de organización de la socialdemocracia rusa' ['Organizational Problems in Russian Social Democracy'], in AA.VV.,

Teoría marxista del partido político [*Marxist Theory of the Political Party*], Vol. II (Mexico: Cuadernos de Pasado y Presente).

—— (1995) *Il programa di Spartaco* [*On the Spartacus Program*] (Rome: Manifestolibri).

—— (2003) *Huelga de masas, partido y sindicato* [*The Mass Strike, the Political Party and the Trade Union*] (Madrid: Fundación Federico Engels).

Lyotard, Jean-François (1959–60) 'Le contenu social de la lutte argélienne' ['The Social Content of the Algerian Struggle'], *Socialisme ou Barbarie*, Vol. 29, December–February.

—— (1961) 'En Argélie, une nouvelle vague' ['In Algeria, a New Wave'], *Socialisme ou Barbarie*, Vol. 32, April–June.

Mandel, Ernest (ed.) (1973) *Contrôle ouvrier, conseils ouvriers, autogestion* [*Workers' Control, Workers' Councils, Self-Management*] (Paris: Maspero).

—— (1990) 'Auto-organisation et parti d'avant-garde dans la conception de Trotsky' ['Self-Management and Vanguard Party in Trotsky's Thought'], *Quatrième Internationale*, Vol. 36, pp. 35–49.

—— (2003) *La pensée politique de Léon Trotsky* [*The Political Thought of Leon Trotsky*] (Paris: La Découverte).

Marx, Karl (1982) [1859] 'Prólogo a la Contribución a la Crítica de la Economía Política' ['Prologue to A Contribution to the Critique of Political Economy'], in Marx, K., *Introducción general a la Crítica de la Economía Política* [*A Contribution to the Critique of Political Economy*] (Mexico: Siglo XXI).

—— (1985a) 'Crítica al Programa de Gotha' ['Critique of the Gotha Program'], in Marx, K. and Engels, F. *Obras Escogidas* [*Selected Works*], Vol. III (México: Quinto Sol).

—— (1985b) 'La guerra civil en Francia' ['The Civil War in France'], in Marx, K. and Engels, F. *Obras Escogidas* [*Selected Works*] (México: Quinto Sol).

—— (1985c) 'Manifiesto del Partido Comunista' ['The Manifesto of the Communist Party'], in Marx, K. and Engels, F. *Obras Escogidas* [*Selected Works*], Vol. I (Mexico: Quinto Sol).

—— (1999) *El Capital. Crítica de la Economía Política* [*Capital*] (Mexico: FCE).

—— (2003) *El dieciocho brumario de Luis Bonaparte* [*The Eighteenth Brumaire of Louis Bonaparte*] (Madrid: Alianza).

Mattelart, Armand and Neveu, Erick (2008) *Introduction aux Cultural Studies* [*Introduction to Cultural Studies*] (Paris: La Découverte).

Mattick, Paul (1976) 'Anton Pannekoek et la révolution mondiale' ['Anton Pannekoek and the World Revolution'], in *Histoire du marxisme contemporain* [*A History of Contemporary Marxism*], Vol. II (Paris: UGE 10/18).

Meiskins Wood, Ellen (2000) *Democracia contra capitalismo* [*Democracy Against Capitalism*] (Mexico: Siglo XXI).

Mellino, Miguel (2008) *La crítica poscolonial* [*The Post-Colonial Critique*] (Buenos Aires: Paidós).

Melucci, Alberto (1999) *Acción colectiva, vida cotidiana y democracia* [*Collective Action, Daily Life and Democracy*] (Mexico: El Colegio de México).

Mena, Javier (2011) 'Sul concetto di rivoluzione passiva' ['On the Concept of Passive Revolution'], in Kanoussi, D., Schirru, G., and Vacca, G. (eds) *Studi gramsciani nel mondo. Gramsci in America Latina* [*Gramscian Studies in the*

World. Gramsci on Latin America] (Bologna: Il Mulino-Fondazione Instituto Gramsci).

Mier, Raymundo (2009) 'Autonomía y vínculo: la creación de la acción colectiva' ['Autonomy and Bond: The Creation of Collective Action'], in Albertani, C., Rovira, G., and Modonesi, M. (eds) *La autonomía posible. Reinvención de la política y emancipación* [*The Possible Autonomy. Emancipation and the Reinvention of Politics*] (Mexico, UACM).

Milana, Fabio, and Trotta, Giuseppe (2008) *L'operaismo degli anni sessanta. Da Quaderni Rossi a Classe Operaia* [*Workerism in the 60s. From the Red Notebooks to the Working Class*] (Rome: DeriveApprodi).

Mills, Charles Wright (1961) *La imaginación sociológica* [*The Sociological Imagination*] (Mexico: FCE).

Modonesi, Massimo (2010) *Subalternidad, antagonismo, autonomía. Marxismo y subjetivación política* [*Subalternity, Antagonism, Autonomy. Constructing the Political Subject*] (Buenos Aires: Prometeo-CLACSO-UBA).

Montal, Claude (Claude Lefort) (1952) 'Le prolétariat et le problème de la direction révolutionnaire' ['The Proletariat and the Problem of the Revolutionary Direction'], *Socialisme ou Barbarie*, Vol.10, June-August.

Morder, Robi (2003) 'Autogestion et autogestionnaires dans les mouvements étudiants et lycéens après 1968' ['Self-Management and Self-Managers in the Student and Schools Movement After 1968'], in Georgi, F. (ed.) *Autogestion. La dernière utopie?* [*Self-management. The Last Utopia?*] (Paris: La Sorbonne).

Morton, Adam David (2007) *Unravelling Gramsci: Hegemony and Passive Revolution in the Global Political Economy* (London: Pluto Press).

—— (2010) 'The Continuum of Passive Revolution', *Capital & Class*, Vol. 36, No. 3: 115–42.

—— (2011) *Revolution and State in Modern Mexico: The Political Economy of Uneven Development* (Lanham, MD: Rowman and Littlefield).

Mothé, Daniel (1957) 'L'usine et la gestion ouvrière' [The Factory and the Workers' Management'], *Socialisme ou Barbarie*, Vol. 22, July–September.

Negri, Antonio (1964) 'Operai senza alleati' ['Workers Without Allies'], *Classe Operaia*, Vol. 3, March.

—— (1981) *L'anomalia selvaggia: saggio su potere e potenza in Baruch Spinoza* [*The Savage Anomaly: The Power of Spinoza's Metaphysics and Politics*] (Milan: Feltrinelli).

—— (2001) *Marx más allá de Marx. Nueve Lecciones sobre los Grundrisse* [*Marx Beyond Marx. Lessons on the Grundrisse*] (Madrid: Akal).

—— (2002) *Il potere costituente* [*The Constituent Power*] (Rome: Manifestolibri).

—— (2004a) 'Crisis del Estado-plan. Comunismo y organización revolucionaria' ['Crisis of the Planner-State: Communism and Revolutionary Organization'], in Negri, A., *Los libros de la autonomía obrera* [*Books for Burning: Between Civil War and Democracy in 1970s Italy*] (Madrid: Akal). Originally published in *Poder Obrero* [*Worker Power*] 1971(4), 25 September.

—— (2004b) 'De *El izquierdismo, enfermedad infantil del comunismo* al *¿Qué hacer?* Para la crítica de la constitución material: autovalorización obrera e hipótesis de partido' ['Towards a Critique of the Material Constitution'], in

Negri, A., *Los libros de la autonomía obrera* [*Books for Burning: Between Civil War and Democracy in 1970s Italy*] (Madrid: Akal).

—— (2004c) [1977] 'El dominio y el sabotaje. Sobre el método marxista de la transformación social' ['Domination and Sabotage: On the Marxist Method of Social Transformation'], in Negri, A., *Los libros de la autonomía obrera* [*Books for Burning: Between Civil War and Democracy in 1970s Italy*] (Madrid: Akal).

—— (2004d) *La fábrica de la estrategia. 33 lecciones sobre Lenin* [*The Factory of Strategy: 33 Lessons on Lenin*] (Madrid: Akal).

—— (2004e) [1975] 'Proletarios y Estado. Por una discusión sobre autonomía obrera y compromiso histórico' ['Proletarians and the State: Toward a Discussion of Worker's Autonomy and the Historic Compromise'], in Negri, A., *Los libros de la autonomía obrera* [*Books for Burning: Between Civil War and Democracy in 1970s Italy*] (Madrid: Akal).

—— (2006a) *Fabrique de porcelaine. Pour une nouvelle grammaire du politique* [*The Porcelain Workshop: For a New Grammar of Politics*] (Paris: Stock).

—— (2006b) 'Fábricas del sujeto. Apuntes para un dispositivo ontológico' ['Factories of the Subject. Notes for an Ontological Device'], in Negri, A., *Fábricas del sujeto/Ontologías de la subversión Factories of the Subject/Ontologies of Subversion*] *Factories of the Subject/Ontologies of Subversion*] (Madrid: Akal).

—— 2006c 'Máquina tiempo, rompecabezas, liberación, constitución' ['Machine Time, Puzzles, Liberation, Constitution'], in Negri, A., *Fábricas del sujeto/Ontologías de la subversión Factories of the Subject/Ontologies of Subversion*] (Madrid: Akal).

Norman, Emma (2007) *El yo político* [*The Political I*] (México: Ediciones Coyoacán).

Pannekoek, Anton (1938) 'Observaciones generales a la cuestión de la organización' ['General Observations on the Issue of Organization'], *Living Marxism*, Vol. 5, November.

—— (n.d.) *Los consejos obreros* [*The Workers' Councils*] [Online], Available: www.marxists.org/espanol/pannekoek/1940s/consejosobreros/index [September 2009].

Panzieri, Raniero (1961) 'Sull'uso capitalista delle macchine nel neocapitalismo' ['On the Capitalist Use of Machines in Neocapitalism'], *Quaderni rossi*, Vol. 1, pp. 53–72.

—— (1977) *La ripresa del marxismo-leninismo in Italia* [*The Recovery of Marxism-Leninism in Italy*] (Rome: Nuove edizioni operaie).

Proust, Antoine (2003) 'Une utopie pédagogique' ['A Pedagogical Utopia'], in Georgi, F. (ed.) *Autogestion. La dernière utopie?* [*Self-management. The Last Utopia?*] (Paris: La Sorbonne).

Portelli, Hugues (1998) *Le parti socialiste* [*The Socialist Party*] (Paris: Montchrestien).

Pucciarelli, Mimmo (2003) 'L'autogestion au quotidien dans un quartier alternatif: La Croix-Rousse, Lyon, 1975–2001' ['Daily Self-Management in an Alternative Neighborhood: La Croix-Rousse, Lyon, 1975–2001'], in Georgi, F. (ed.) *Autogestion. La dernière utopie?* [*Self-management. The Last Utopia?*] (Paris: La Sorbonne).

Ravenel, Bernard (2003) 'Deux théoriciens de l'autogestion au PSU: Víctor Fay et Víctor Leduc' ['Two Theorists of Self-Management at the PSU: Víctor Fay and Víctor Leduc'], in Georgi, F. (ed.) *Autogestion. La dernière utopie? [Self-management. The Last Utopia?]* (Paris: La Sorbonne).

Real Academia Española (1992) *Diccionario de la lengua española [Dictionary of the Spanish Language]*, 21st edn (Madrid: Espasa Calpe).

Revel, Judith (2008) *Vocabulario de Foucault [Foucault's Vocabulary]* (Buenos Aires: Atuel).

Rebón, Julián (2007) *La fábrica de la autonomía [The Factory of Autonomy]* (Buenos Aires: PICASO).

Rivera Cusicanqui, Silvia, and Barragán, Rossana (1997) 'Presentación' ['Presentation'], in Rivera Cusicanqui, S., and Barragán, R. (eds) *Debates Post-Coloniales: una introducción a los Estudios de la Subalternidad [Postcolonial Debates: An Introduction to Subaltern Studies]* (La Paz: Historias-Aruwiyiri-SEPHIS).

Rodríguez de la Vega, Teresa (2005) 'Presente social y complejidad' ['Social Present and Complexity'], in Berenzon Gora, B., and Calderón, G. (eds) *Coordenadas sociales: más allá del tiempo y el espacio [Social Coordinates: Beyond Time and Space]* (Mexico: UACM).

Romano, Paul (1950) 'L'ouvrier américain' ['The American Worker'], *Socialisme ou Barbarie*, Vol. 5, March–April.

Rosanvallon, Pierre (1976) *L'âge de l'autogestion [The Age of Self-Management]* (Paris: Seuil).

Rossanda, Rossana. (1973) *Il Manifesto. Tesis de una disidencia comunista [Il Manifesto. Thesis on a Communist Dissent]* (Mexico: ERA).

Roux, Rhina (2005) *El príncipe mexicano. Subalternidad, historia y Estado [The Mexican Prince. Subalternity, History and State]* (Mexico: ERA).

Rubel, Maximilien (2000) *Marx critique du marxisme [Marx critiques Marxism]* (Paris: Payot).

Salles, Jean Paul (2005) *La Ligue communiste révolutionnaire (1968–1981) [The Revolutionary Communist League (1968–1981)]* (Rennes: Presses Universitaires de Rennes).

Santarelli, Enzo (1997) *Storia critica della repubblica [A Critical History of the Republic]* (Rome: Feltrinelli).

Scott, James (2000) *Los dominados y el arte de la resistencia [Domination and the Arts of Resistance: Hidden Transcripts]* (Mexico: Era).

Socialisme ou Barbarie (1949a) 'Le parti révolutionnaire, Résolution' ['The Revolutionary Party. Resolution'], *Socialisme ou Barbarie*, Vol. 2, May–June.

—— (1949b) 'Editorial', *Socialisme ou Barbarie*, Vol.1, March–April.

—— (1952) 'Editorial de Claude Lefort, L'expérience prolétarienne' ['Editorial by Claude Lefort. The Proletarian Experience'], *Socialisme ou Barbarie*, Vol. 11, November–December.

—— (1964) 'Editorial, Recommencer la révolution' ['Editorial. Restart the Revolution'], *Socialisme ou Barbarie*, Vol. 35, January.

—— (2007) *Anthologie [Anthology]* (Paris: Acratie).

—— (2009a) 'Correspondencia Pannekoek-Castoriadis' ['Pannekoek-Castoriadis Correspondence'], *Políticas de la Memoria*, Vols 8–9 (Buenos Aires: CEDINCI).

—— (2009b) 'El debate Lefort-Castoriadis' ['The Lefort-Castoriadis Debate'], *Políticas de la Memoria*, Vols 8–9 (Buenos Aires: CEDINCI).

Sorel, Georges (1972) *Réflexions sur la violence* [*Reflections on Violence*] (Paris: Marcel Riviére et Cie).

Spivak, Gayatri Chakravorty (2003) '¿Puede hablar el subalterno?' ['Can the Subaltern Speak?'], *Revista Colombiana de Antropología*, Vol. 39 (Bogota: Instituto Colombiano de Antropología e Historia).

—— (2004) *Critica della ragione postcoloniale* [*A Critique of Postcolonial Reason: Towards a History of the Vanishing Present*] (Roma: Maltemi).

Svampa, Maristella (2005) *La sociedad excluyente. La Argentina bajo el Neoliberalismo* [*Exclusive society: Argentina under Neoliberalism*] (Buenos Aires: Taurus).

—— (2008) *Cambio de época. Movimientos sociales y poder político* [*Change of Season: Social Movements and Political Power*] (Buenos Aires: CLACSO-Siglo XXI).

Tarrow, Sydney, and Tilly, Charles (2008) *La política del conflicto* [*Contentious Politics*] (Rome: Mondadori).

Teodori, Massimo (1978) *Las nuevas izquierdas europeas (1956–1976)* [*The New European Lefts (1956–1976)*] (Barcelona: Blume).

Thomas, Peter D. (2009) *The Gramscian Moment: Philosophy, Hegemony and Marxism* (Leiden: Brill).

Thompson, E.P. (1965) 'The Particularities of the English', *Socialist Register*, Vol. 2 (London).

—— (1981) *Miseria de la teoría* [*The Poverty of Theory and Other Essays*] (Barcelona: Crítica).

—— (1989) *La formación de la clase obrera en Inglaterra* [*The Making of the English Working Class*] (Barcelona: Crítica).

—— (2000) 'Historia y antropología' ['History and Anthropology'], in Thompson, E.P., *Agenda para una historia radical* [*Agenda for Radical History*] (Barcelona: Crítica).

—— (2004) *Temps, discipline du travail et capitalisme industriel* [*Time, Work-Discipline and Industrial Capitalism*] (Paris: La fabrique).

Thwaites Rey, Mabel (2004) *La autonomía como búsqueda, el Estado como contradicción* [*Autonomy as Search, the State as Contradiction*] (Buenos Aires: Prometeo).

Trebisch, Michel (2003) 'Henri Lefebvre et l'autogestion' ['Henri Lefebvre and Self-Management'], in Georgi, F. (ed.) *Autogestion. La dernière utopie?* [*Self-management. The Last Utopia?*] (Paris: La Sorbonne).

Tronti, Mario (1962) 'La fabbrica e la societá' ['Factory and Society'], *Quaderni rossi*, Vol. 2.

—— (1963) 'Il piano del capitale' ['The Plan of Capital'], *Quaderni rossi*, Vol. 3, pp. 44-73.

—— (1964a) 'Clase y partido' ['Class and Party'], *Classe Operaia*, Vol. 10, No. 12, December, pp. 2–6.

—— (1964b) 'Lenin in Inghilterra' ['Lenin in England'], *Classe Operaia*, Vol. 1, February.

—— (1977) *Sull'autonomia del político* [*On the Autonomy of the Political*] (Milan: Feltrinelli).

—— (2001) *Obreros y capital* [*Workers and Capital*] (Madrid: Akal).

—— (2008) 'Noi operaisti' ['Us Workers'], in Milana, F., and Trotta, G., *L'operaismo degli anni sessanta. Da Quaderni Rossi a Classe Operaia* [*Workerism in the 60s. From Quaderni Rossi to Classe Operaia*] (Roma: DeriveApprodi).

Trotsky, León (1921) 'Las lecciones de la Comuna' ['The Lessons of the Commune'], *Zlatoouste*, 4 February.

Turchetto, Maria (2001) 'De l'ouvrier masse á l'entrepreneurialité commune: la trajectoire déconcertante de l'operaisme italien' ['From the Mass Worker to Common Entrepreneurship: the Disconcerting Trajectory of Italian Workerism'], in Bidet, J., and Kouvélakis, E. (eds) *Marx contemporain* (París: PUF).

Veil, Claude (2003) 'La revue Autogestion' ['The Magazine Self-Management'], in Georgi, F. (ed.) *Autogestion. La dernière utopie?* [*Self-management. The Last Utopia?*] (Paris: La Sorbonne).

Vigna, Xavier (2007) *L'insubordination ouvrière dans les années 68* [*The Workers' Insubordination during 68*] (Rennes: Presses Universitaires de Rennes).

Voza, Pasquale (2004) 'Rivoluzione passiva' ['Passive Revolution'], in Frosini, F., and Liguori, G. (eds) *Le parole di Gramsci* [*Gramsci's Words*] (Rome: Carocci).

Weber, Max (2006) *Conceptos sociológicos fundamentales* [*The Fundamental Concepts of Sociology*] (Madrid: Alianza).

Wright, Steve (2007) *L'assaut au ciel. Composition de clase et lutte declasse dans le marxisme autonome italien* [*Storming Heaven: Class Composition and Struggle in Italian Autonomist Marxism*] (Marseilles: Senonevero).

Zavaleta, René (1974) *El poder dual en América latina* [*Dual Power in Latin America*] (Mexico: Siglo XXI).

—— (1988) *Clases sociales y conocimiento* [*Social Classes and Knowledge*] (La Paz: Los amigos del libro).

—— (1989) 'Cuatro conceptos de la democracia' ['Four Concepts of Democracy'], in *El Estado en América Latina* [*The State in Latin America*] (La Paz: Los amigos del libro).

Index